The Public Defender

The Public Defender

The Practice of Law in the Shadows of Repute

Lisa J. McIntyre

The University of Chicago Press

Chicago and London

Lisa J. McIntyre is assistant professor of sociology at Washington
State University.

The University of Chicago Press, Chicago 60637
The University of Chicago Press, Ltd., London

96 95 94 93 92 91 90 89 88 87   54321

Library of Congress Cataloging-in-Publication Data

McIntyre, Lisa J.
  The public defender.

  (Studies in crime and justice)
  Bibliography: p.
  Includes index.
  1. Public defenders—Illinois—Cook County.
2. Criminal justice, Administration of—Illinois—
Cook County. I. Title. II. Series.
KFI1799.C62C725 1987   345.73′01   87-5070
ISBN 0-226-55961-0   347.3051

Contents

List of Illustrations

__ List of Tables _____

__ Foreword _____

How can we come to know an institution? As with the blind men de-
scribing the elephant, one's sense of it depends upon the part that one
touches—and ordinarily each of us touches only a small segment of any
institution in our everyday activities. How then can we come to know
the institution?

Lisa McIntyre shows one way that is especially illuminating. Within the criminal justice system, there are many institutions that link together to make up that institutional complex. McIntyre has selected one,
the public defender's office, which is of special interest because of its
paradoxical relation to the rest of this complex. The paradox lies in the
fact that the task of the office is the defense of those charged with criminal offenses against members of society, whom the state is designed to
protect; yet the office is itself an agent of the state. The paradox is seen
even more vividly by noting the proximity of the state's attorney's office, which presses the state's charges, to the public defender's office,
which is in fixed and permanent opposition to it.

McIntyre studies this institution by viewing it from the many vantage points that are denied to those who occupy a particular position,

whether within the institution or outside it. These vantage points include the historical perspective, as well as the way the institution appears from the perspective of all those with whom it interacts—judges, prosecutors, state's attorneys, lawyers in private practice, and the defenders' clients. The vantage points include the internal structure and functioning of the office itself. This means observing the daily activities of lawyers who work as public defenders as well as understanding, from extensive interviews, how they see their role and function. In short, McIntyre has taken the *sociologist's* perspective, which is to look from each of these vantage points and then to reintegrate the diverse forms and character of information they provide into a coherent picture of the functioning of the system. Along the way, she is able to answer such specific questions as how the "stigma" of the office arises and how lawyers who work as public defenders cope with that stigma. But the specific questions are incidental to her major task, which is to illumine the institution as a whole, as well as "how it works." Because she has chosen this paradoxical institution, which in one sense works against the state of which it is a creature, McIntyre contributes to a broader set of questions about institutions. These are questions about how they manage conflicts that are endemic to the structure. This includes grievance procedures in work organizations, ombudsman roles, systems of justice within monolithic authority systems (such as the military, or a state like the Soviet Union), and tribunals held by the victors following a war (such as the Nuremberg trials).

Most of all, however, she shows us how this institution works.

James S. Coleman

Acknowledgments

A great deal is owed to the dozens of assistant public defenders who helped to teach me about the job of public defending and the people who do it. Serving more as coinvestigators and less as research subjects, these lawyers' patience with my questioning was equaled only by their willingness to make suggestions about how best to investigate the sociological and social psychological underpinnings of public defending and the criminal justice system. I am similarly indebted to the many former public defenders who took time from their busy schedules to speak about their experiences. Because I insisted on promising them anonymity, most of these lawyers must go unnamed. But without breaking faith, some can be publicly acknowledged. Ralph E. Brown was always only a phone call away whenever I needed someone to explain the intricacies of various sorts of legal lore. William P. Murphy provided essential information on the history of the Homicide Task Force.

By inviting me to work with them on a capital case, assistant public defenders John A. Friedman, Todd W. Musburger, Stuart A. Nudleman, and Karen Thompson gave me an invaluable opportunity. Among many other things, this experience taught me not only that public defenders are allowed to vigorously defend their clients but that these lawyers accept with skill and enthusiasm the charge to represent the indigent. Their dignity, courage, and persistence in doing a mostly thankless job was awesome.

A special debt is owed to those who undertook to teach me sociology. Jan T. Dykstra's enthusiasm for the subject matter was highly contagious, as was that of Peter I. Rose, who also provided me with my first research experience. Members of my dissertation committee, James S. Coleman, Edward O. Laumann, and Fred L. Strodtbeck, provided important guidance. I suspect that their faith in my ability to manage and finish this project was sorely tested at times, but they never responded inappropriately to my claim that the end product would be worth the wait. Although it does not seem to do justice to his contribution, I thank Professor Coleman for the fact that he was always there when I needed a word of advice or encouragement. I thank Dean Laumann especially for his careful reading of my work and his insistence that it be well written. Professor Strodtbeck played the role of advisor in his own singularly sublime fashion. His tolerance for letting me "do it my way" developed to a point that I am sure he found painful, but, beyond that, any attempt to describe his effect on me and on this research would only tempt one to unfortunate heights of hyperbole; suffice to say that without his helpful, inspiring, frustrating, and irritating influence this book would not have been.

Pam Chao conducted the interviews of former public defenders for me and did an excellent job. Richard Lipinski graciously assisted me with matters pertaining to the computer.

Organizations, as it is widely acknowledged, often present such an unintelligible array of rules and procedures that they can overwhelm the neophyte. Two who helped me survive in—and, indeed, to exploit the resources of—one of the most complex of organizations, the University of Chicago, deserve special mention and thanks: Billie Crawford and Hana Okamoto were unfailingly nurturing and creative in their guidance. Billie Crawford also typed the manuscript and kept the writer calm during its production.

Many of the ideas and interpretations that found their way into the manuscript first surfaced in discussions with colleagues and friends, especially Jan D. Dunham, Richard Lipinski, Mary Utne O'Brien, Mildred Schwartz, and Judy Stone. Donald N. Levine advised me—and proved by example—that a sociologist's theoretical insights need not be boring. Comments from Douglas Maynard and an anonymous reviewer for the Press helped me refine many parts of my argument.

Finally, I must acknowledge the less critical but nonetheless supportive influence of my parents, David and Jean McIntyre, who tried very hard to keep from insisting that I must hurry up and finish.

Introduction

> The Public Defender, as directed by the court, shall act as attorney, without fee, before any court within any county for all persons who are held in custody or who are charged with the commission of any criminal offense, and who the court finds are unable to employ counsel.
>
> *Illinois Revised Statutes,* chap. 34, sec. 5604

Public defenders are social anomalies. They are paid by the state to befriend those whom the state believes are its enemies and to question—and, whenever possible, to thwart—the prosecution of those whom the state suspects are criminals. This research addresses the sociological conditions under which society creates and nurtures a role such as that played by the public defender, and, using the Cook County Public Defender's Office as a source, it develops a model of how the institution—and the individuals who practice law as public defenders—cope with doing work that is, arguably, antisocial.

Thirty years ago the public defender seemed to be little more than a beneficent (though ultimately benign) gesture, on the part of a few county governments, toward poor people in trouble with the law. There was little appreciation that the public defender could achieve much importance in the overall scheme of legal affairs. But following two decades of Supreme Court decisions broadening the rights of criminal defendants, public defenders today play such a crucial role in the administration of criminal justice that without them the work of our urban criminal courts especially would come to a standstill. The courts have made it very clear that access to legal representation is the fundamental right of all persons accused of crime. In the event that a defendant cannot afford to hire an attorney, the state, which prosecutes, must appoint a lawyer and bear the cost of the defense. In an increasing number of jurisdictions these appointed lawyers are typically members of a public defense organization. It is ironic, but, while the sole mission of these lawyers is to *defend,* without their services the courts would find it nearly impossible to convict indigent defendants.

As the scope of public defending increased, so too did the scrutiny of social scientists. Many scholarly accounts of contemporary criminal justice emphasize the tensions that must adhere to any process in which the state attempts to pursue such apparently incompatible goals, and many scholars have come to believe that the conflicts that emerge as the state endeavors to prosecute and defend criminal defendants are resolved to the detriment of the accused.

It has long been the case that *any* defense lawyer is viewed with suspicion and distrust (Wood 1967) by laypersons and scholars alike. As David Neubauer put it, "the general public, the lawyers' clients, and scholarly studies seem to agree on one point: the defense bar is less than exemplary. The only difference is that the public thinks too many crooks are let loose and the client and the academic studies believe the lawyer does not fight hard enough for his client" (1974, 67). Unlike private lawyers who are retained and paid by their clients, public defense attorneys are hired and paid by the state. However disreputable their colleagues in private practice may be, many people believe that, because they owe their jobs to the state, public defenders do not have the same autonomy as private lawyers, autonomy that is necessary for being "real" legal advocates; and so public defense lawyers are reduced to acting as functionaries in the legal bureaucracy who are intent on efficiently hustling defendants through the courts and into the jails (Sudnow 1965). Although it has been acknowledged that many public defense attorneys begin their jobs with a commitment to defending the rights of their clients, it is believed that they quickly become disillusioned (Platt and Pollock 1974); disillusionment follows from the discovery that the system is just not set up to allow public defense lawyers the time or the resources necessary to engage in vigorous, spirited (and expensive) defense work (Blumberg 1967, 1979; Sudnow 1965). Public defenders are thus "bastard lawyers" because they are not seen as real or legitimate attorneys. Eldridge Cleaver summed up the popular view of the typical public defense lawyer when he explained that "P.D." stands for "penitentiary deliverer" (Cleaver 1968, 169).

In the two decades that have passed since Blumberg and Sudnow first published their critiques of public defending, some dents have been made in at least the social scientists' negative view of public defending. As I will discuss in chapter 3, numerous empirical studies have failed to find any evidence that clients of public defenders fare worse (at least in terms of case outcomes) than defendants who are represented by private lawyers. Others have noted that, indeed, even when it *appears* that public defenders are acting as mere functionaries (i.e., by casually plea bargaining their cases), they may be working as effective advocates for their clients.

Yet, notwithstanding evidence of their relative potency as defense attorneys, the image of public defense lawyers has not been fully rehabilitated; their status as real lawyers has not been legitimated. The image of public defending first fostered by Sudnow and Blumberg has proved compelling, for (as I show in chapter 3) it continues to find its ways into contemporary accounts of the criminal justice process.

In this research a new model was sought, a model of public defending that would explain, first, how public defenders manage to do about as well for their clients as private lawyers do for theirs and, second, why public defenders—regardless of the actual quality of their work—continue to be plagued by what one Cook County assistant public defense attorney has labeled the "stigma of ineptitude" (Spencer 1984).

The model of public defending sought in this research was one that would also help to illuminate the motives and rationales of lawyers who do this sort of work. In other words, an answer was sought to the question that most people pose to public defenders, and that is, How can you defend those people? Even though many public defenders refer to this as "that cocktail party question," it cannot—and should not—be dismissed lightly. Having an answer to it means having a way to justify and make sense of the job of public defending, and this is not an easy task. The real difficulty that lawyers have in finding answers to this question is shown in ex–public defense lawyer James S. Kunen's *How Can You Defend Those People?* (1983). Kunen's account of two and a half years spent as a public defender in Washington, D.C., teaches the reader that having an answer is important but that finding a persuasive one is difficult. As Kunen observes at one point, "I'm thinking what a way to spend my energy, my substance, my life . . . on this deadbeat who's guilty anyway, all for some principle that he should be getting the ultimate of my ability in service to him. That would be fine if I were fighting for welfare rights, or tenants' rights, or any important cause that you could apply your legal talents to; but for some deadbeat—what the hell is the point of that?" (1983, 153).

Readers should perhaps be warned that although this is a study of public defending and of the lawyers who do public defense work, it is *not* a study of plea bargaining. This, I expect, will come as a surprise to many readers; and for some, the lack of emphasis on plea bargaining may be seen as a serious deficiency in the work. The lack of attention paid here to plea bargaining is partly due to the fact that plea bargaining has already been the focus of a great deal of very fine research, research to which readers will be referred in the text. But the reason is not only that plea bargaining has been done—and done well—for it is my belief that there has been an *over*emphasis on plea bargaining in the criminal justice literature. As Kenneth Mann recently asserted, "The predominance of plea bargaining in the research agendas of the academy has had a profound influence on more general theorizing about the operation of the criminal justice system. Findings from empirical research have emphasized the dynamics in the criminal justice process that move counter to due process, emphasizing the move to cooperation, bureaucratization, and other values that counter true adversary procedures" (1985, 271–272). While there can be no doubt that bureaucratization and cooperation are the primary fuels on which our criminal justice system operates, it should also be recognized that there are limits to these. The predominance of plea bargaining research, I would argue, has helped to make obscure the forces in our criminal justice system that work *against* cooperation and bureaucratization and, especially, has helped to mask the public (and private) defense attorneys' role in keeping these forces viable. It is the nature of these forces that will be examined most closely in this research; for understanding them is the best way (or so I shall argue) to make sense of the job of public defending and to gain an understanding of how and why lawyers do the job.

In the narrowest sense the research described here is a case study of the Cook County Public Defender's Office and its incumbents. The emphasis owes much to sociologists who have worked in what Perrow calls the "institutional" school of sociology, inasmuch as one goal of the research was to look "beneath the obvious surface" of the organization and gain a deep understanding of the processes and structures that constitute and empower public defending (1979, 177).

But, more important, because the public defender is paid by the state to thwart the efforts of other state agencies, it provides a unique opportunity to explore what is perhaps a more sociologically interesting concern; more broadly conceived, this is a study of how social actors (corporate and individual) attempt to resolve—or, failing that, to manage—problems that emerge when important but apparently conflicting goals must be pursued in the same social arena.

Is Cook County Typical?

Sociologist Howard S. Becker warns researchers of the dangers of assuming that the particular institutions that they study can be held up as generic examples of all others that fall into the same "conventionally defined social category: some elementary schools may resemble prisons, others country clubs, while still others do indeed look like ordinary schools" (1977, 40). The question is, then, How typical of public defense organizations is the Cook County Public Defender's Office?

That is a difficult question to answer; a completely satisfying response would need results from comparable studies, which, at this point, have not been done. Although a great deal is known about some aspects of public defending (e.g., plea-bargaining techniques and strategies), little is known about many others. As Eliot Friedson remarked not too long ago, "Little is known about the conduct of work in law firms that are owned and managed by professionals, even less is known about those public organizations that employ a substantial number of lawyers—public prosecutor or district attorney systems on the one hand . . . and public defender or legal services systems on the other. . . . (1986, 163). Throughout this book mention will be made of the fact whenever arrangements in Cook County resemble or differ from what is known to exist in other jurisdictions. While listing these similarities and differences here, I think, would be an intrusion, a few preliminary points of comparison may be helpful.

The reader will find that in some respects the Cook County Public Defender's Office is quite unlike most other public defense organizations. It is, for example, one of the oldest and certainly one of the largest public defender organizations in this country. According to a recent national survey, the average public defender office is staffed by less than fifty attorneys; indeed, about 75 percent of all counties served by public defenders employ fewer than five full-time lawyers (U.S. Department of Justice 1984). Cook County currently employs more than 300 public defense lawyers. Moreover, there can be little doubt that the contemporary structure of the office has been influenced by the structure and content of Cook County's rather unique political environment. During the mid-1970s, for example, when other jurisdictions were scrambling for Law Enforcement Assistance Administration (LEAA) monies to either start up or augment public defender services, Cook County point-blank refused them. Why? Because accepting federal monies meant accepting federal evaluation—and, it was believed, thereby accepting federal interference in how these monies might be spent. Allowing federal interference was something Cook County judges and politicians were loathe to do.

It can also be noted that Cook County is somewhat atypical in that its chief public defender is appointed by and "serves at the pleasure of" members of the judiciary. In many other jurisdictions, public defenders are appointed by county or independent boards. In addition, the Cook

County office may well be unique in that every lawyer ultimately appointed as an assistant public defender must first be interviewed and then approved by the judges' Committee on Help. In terms of the relationship between defender and the judges, then, the case of Cook County may not only be atypical but could well represent a worst-case scenario for public defense lawyers who might wish to achieve autonomy vis-à-vis judges. It is this, however, that makes Cook County such a good site for the present study. For if we are to understand the mechanisms by which public defenders are able to maintain autonomy and the resources that they can draw on in order to preserve integrity as defense attorneys, what better place to carry out research than in an environment in which such mechanisms and resources must be brought into play?

Notwithstanding these differences, it is important to realize that all public defender services face the similar problem of trying to survive while defending "criminals"—usually an unpopular cause. Similarly, all public defenders (at least in this country) have in common an important resource—laws requiring that even "those people" be defended. It seems not unreasonable, then, to assume that the solutions to problems that have been articulated in Cook County are likely shared by other defender services.

Overview of the Research and Methods

Analysis begins in part 1 with an examination of the relationship between the Public Defender's Office and its environment; knowledge of the social and historical location of the office provides important clues to the nature of what constrains the activities of the public defender. More important, knowledge of the environment is the key to understanding the scope of resources available to the public defender. The latter emphasis is particularly important, for it is the *resources* of the public defender and the public defender's office that are so often ignored or overlooked by many social scientific observers. This section begins, in chapter 1, with a historical account of the rise of the right to counsel in American state trial courts and continues, in chapter 2, with a look back to the origins of public defending in Cook County, Illinois. It will be shown that, although the timing differed, the issues raised at the national and local levels were similar. From an examination of these issues, a model of the public defender's role in criminal justice is developed in chapter 3, where the idea of public defenders as "bureaucratic functionaries" is examined and found wanting. In chapter 4, the conflicts that are inherent in the public defender's role are examined and the public defender's response to the problem of managing these is discussed.

A variety of sources was drawn on to support the discussion in part

1, including Supreme Court rulings and legal histories. Because the Cook County Public Defender's Office (for reasons that will be explicated in the text) does not publish accounts of its activities, in order to construct its history and role in contemporary society, information was taken from Cook County records and local historical and media accounts dating back to the 1920s.

In part 2 the perspective shifts to an examination of the relationship between the Cook County Public Defender's Office and the lawyers who work there. Chapter 5 describes the public defense lawyers, their attributes and their expectations. Particular attention is paid in chapters 6 and 7 to the impact that the office's management of its external relationships has had on its organizational form—and on how this, in turn, has affected relationships within the office. Finally, the impact of the lawyers' needs on the office is discussed.

Developing a perspective on the relationship between lawyers and between the lawyers and their organization involved using a combination of techniques. For three months I observed (and to a lesser extent, participated with) a team of four assistant public defense attorneys in the sentencing hearing phase of a capital (death penalty) case. Many other field days were spent observing and speaking with assistants engaged in more routine cases. Time in the field took me into Cook County criminal, municipal, and juvenile courts; judges' chambers; lock-ups; state's attorneys' offices; and, of course, the offices of public defense lawyers.

In order to augment information gotten from observations, formal interviews were conducted (one and three-quarters to three hours in length) with twenty assistant public defenders who worked in various courts and were of varying levels of seniority. Interview subjects were not randomly selected but instead were chosen to help ensure that my sample included lawyers with opinions that represented the major points of view that exist in the office. Public defenders proved to be willing and extremely helpful informants. Each lawyer whom I asked for an interview cooperated, even when this meant (as it often did) staying after hours or getting to work earlier than usual. After accepting my promise of anonymity, each lawyer allowed me to tape the interview session. Following the interview, many of the lawyers took me around the office and introduced me to others with whom they believed I might find it interesting to speak. Other public defenders—not necessarily on my list of interviewees—graciously allowed me to follow them around in the courts and lock-ups so that I might get a firsthand view, as one attorney put it, "of what it's really like being a PD." In most cases, my guides introduced me to courtroom personnel (including state's attorneys, clerks, and judges) by name only. When I asked one lawyer why this was done, he explained his theory that if I was not known to be a researcher I would get a more accurate picture of what went on in the courts. He presumed that most people would assume that I was a new lawyer or law clerk. Before talking to anyone, however, I identified myself and my affiliation.

In the text, quotes from taped interviews are followed by subject numbers in italics. Quotes from other public defenders are included without subject numbers. Although these remarks were not taped, I am confident that the intent—if not the exact wording—of the lawyer was captured accurately. In a few cases, in order to protect the identity of the speaker, certain parts of quotes are deleted; for the same reason, all references to respondents use masculine gender references. I regret the latter (as many acknowledge, some of the better lawyers in the office are women); but because there are relatively few women lawyers in the office, in many cases anyone familiar with the organization could identify the source of remarks made by women working in particular job slots.

In part because I wished to determine whether the attributes and views of lawyers who serve as public defenders has changed over time, shorter interviews (30–90 minutes in length) were conducted with sixty former public defenders. Each of these lawyers had served as an assistant in the office (for varying amounts of time) between 1960 and 1979 and had subsequently left for private or judicial practice. These respondents were randomly selected from a list of 263 attorneys who had been in the office during the relevant time frame. They too proved a cooperative group—87 percent of the lawyers contacted agreed to be interviewed. After being promised anonymity, about half agreed that the interview could be taped.[1] Interestingly, few differences were found when different cohorts of public defense lawyers were compared.

Data from the interviews with both current and former public defenders constitute the major source of information used in part 3, where in chapter 8 ("But How Can You Sleep Nights?") the individual public defense attorney's relationship to the world outside the office is discussed. Here the central concern is how the lawyers motivate themselves (and each other) and how they manage to justify what they do in the fce of a disapproving public.

In the Concluding section of the book, the survival potential of the public defender is discussed.

1. Interviews with former public defenders were conducted during the summer of 1984; they had been scheduled to take place six months earlier but were postponed owing to fears that the investigation into Cook County court corruption (Greylord) might adversely affect response rates. As it was, in spite of a high response rate, many of the lawyers (especially some of those who refused) voiced their suspicions that the survey was somehow related to Greylord.

A Note on Methods

During the course of this research a tremendous amount of interview and observational data was gathered. How was this information handled? At the end of each day in the field, notes were dictated into a tape recorder and then transcribed and placed into notebooks in chronological order. Similarly, all tapes from interviews with current public defenders and tapes or notes from interviews with former defenders were transcribed and placed into notebooks according to the respondent's identifying number. Information about lawyers' demographic characteristics was entered directly into a computer for analysis. By the end of the research, transcriptions totaled more than 2,000 single-spaced typed pages.

Transcribed interviews and field notes were searched for references to various topics (e.g., lawyers' views on their public image, on clients, on the organization of the office, on defending guilty vs. innocent clients, on what is a "fun case," etc.). The search process was conducted many times, as topics that seemed important to the lawyers were discovered in interviews and during observation of the lawyers at work. Other topics were suggested by the literature.

Excerpts from interviews and notes were labeled with the speakers' respective numbers and filed by topic. Because I wished to keep the original transcriptions intact and because many remarks had to be cross-referenced, the filing-by-topic process was greatly facilitated by frequent use of a photocopy machine.

Once topic files were assembled, they could then be analyzed in order to determine the lawyers' views on various issues. Having all references to a specific topic in one file helped to ensure accurate representations of the lawyers' opinions. Where there was substantial agreement, I selected what I thought was the best expression of that; where there was a diversity of opinions, I selected quotes to show that as well. In all cases where I have quoted what seemed to be a minority viewpoint, I have identified it as such.

One

The Public Defender's Office and Its Environment

The American Tradition: Right to Counsel in State Trial Courts 1

Underlying the concept of right to counsel is a peculiarly American assumption about the relation of the state to its citizens. The English subjects who settled this continent in the seventeenth century had left behind what many viewed as an "archaic, inefficient, and capricious judicial system attempting unsuccessfully to stem a tide of vice and crime" (Chapin 1983, 3). As one historian has noted, colonists "shared the common knowledge that criminal law in England was infamous" (*ibid.*). While not entirely jettisoning the legal baggage they carried, colonists sought reform. Their legislators eschewed the burdensome form of English law with its "loquacity and prolixity," "noise and strife," and replaced the "intricate mass" of statutes written in Latin and Law French with laws written in brief and in English (Chapin 1983, 24). Moreover, spurred perhaps by memories of English courts where "judges spread the hangman's noose wide and wrote wholesale lessons in retribution" (Chapin 1983, 4), colonial lawmakers reduced the list of crimes that called for the death penalty and, for the most part, abandoned the use of this particular form of punishment as a response to any form of theft. An important precept in these new societies was that life was more precious than property.[1]

What colonists did not immediately abandon were the views held by English courts on the right of the accused to have legal representation. Although *The Statute of Henry VII* (1495) provided that justices "shall assign to the same poor person or persons counsel learned by their discretion, which shall give their counsel, nothing taking for the same," the role of any defense lawyer—retained or appointed—was restricted by law and tradition in English criminal courts.

When defense counsel did appear in English trial courts, they were confronted with something called the "facts-law distinction": the defendant was required to present the facts of the case and a plea. Once the facts were before the court, "if the court supposed it would bear discussion, it assigned counsel to argue it" (Beany 1955, 8–9). Lord High Steward Finch, in Lord Conwallis's trial in 1678, explained why defense counsel were allowed to have no say in any "matter of fact or in anything but matter of law": "There is no other good reason can be given why the law refuseth to allow prisoner at the bar counsel in matter of fact . . . but only this, because the evidence by which he is condemned ought to be so very evident and so plain that all the counsel in the world should not be able to answer upon it" (Marke 1977, 225). In theory, in the absence of "evident and so plain" incriminating facts, the judge would acquit the defendant. There was no need for a defense lawyer to speak about the quality of the facts, for the judge would weigh them fairly and be sure to save the defendant from an unjust conviction.

More significant was the fact that regardless of the trial court's judgment about what would not bear discussion by defense counsel, English courts, except for cases of treason, allowed defense counsel to participate only in misdemeanor cases. In other words, at the time of the American Revolution, persons accused of serious crimes in England—regardless of wealth or standing—had no right to counsel except in cases of treason.[2]

The logic behind these rules seems odd to us because a defendant facing a serious charge would seem to be more in need of counsel than would a defendant facing a minor charge. William Blackstone, who was elected to the first chair in English law at Oxford in 1758, found the logic unsettling too: "A rule, which (however it shall be palliated under cover

1. Early Massachusetts statutes did provide that repeat offenders could be hanged for theft. The colony of Virginia limited hangings for theft to those offenders convicted of stealing tobacco from warehouses (Brown 1938, chap. 1).
2. Both the "facts-law" distinction and the rule forbidding counsel from being present in felony courts remained in effect in England until 1836.

of that noble declaration of the law, when rightly understood, that the judge shall be counsel for the prisoner; that is, shall see that the proceedings against him are legal and strictly regular) seems to be not at all of a piece with the rest of the humane treatment of prisoners by English law. For upon what face of reason can that assistance be denied to save the life of a man, which yet is allowed him in prosecutions for every petty trespass?" (4 *Comm.* 349 [cited in Posner 1981, 30]).

Modern legal scholars have argued that this rule was premised on the simple assumption that protecting the interests of society is more important than protecting the interests of individuals accused of crimes:[3] "Misdemeanors did not disrupt the King's peace nearly so much as felonies. . . . It was very important that those who committed felonies should be punished . . . it was considerably less important that those who committed misdemeanors be punished (Moore 1973, 71).

If defense lawyers were welcomed only in misdemeanor courts in England, they found even less favor in colonial courts. Still, given the nature of colonial statutes, which—relative to English law—placed greater emphasis on protecting individual rights (Chapin 1983), the colonial attitude toward lawyers probably ought to be read as simply another sign of the colonists' general distaste for making things complicated. Indeed, so strong was the colonists' aversion to legal complexities that the colonial lawyer was rarely encouraged and sometimes forbidden to practice his craft at all. *The Massachusetts Bay Body of Liberties* (1641) forbade pleading for hire; Thomas Merton, who has been called the first Massachusetts lawyer, was jailed and later expelled for "scandalous behavior." The writers of *The Fundamental Constitutions of the Carolinas* (1669), declared to all prospective attorneys that it was a "base and vile thing to plead for money or reward" (Friedman 1973, 81). One of the settlers in William Penn's community enthusiastically proclaimed its rejection of both doctors and lawyers and remarked his relief at the fact that his settlement had no need for either the "pestiferous drugs of the one or the tiresome loquacity of the other" (Beck 1930, 97).

Yet, as time passed, men of the law gained more than a precarious

---

3. If, as might be inferred, defense counsel were allowed to participate only in those cases in which they might cause the least amount of trouble (and thus in misdemeanor—but not felony—trials), why were they allowed to represent clients accused of treason? Legal historian Charles Rembar provides one answer to this contradiction: "As to treason, a statute changed the common law in 1695. The people who fomented the Revolution of 1688 were, of course, traitors—unless and until they succeeded. Having succeeded, they must have had a vivid memory of what it was like to be on the other side, and [been] keenly aware of what would have happened had they failed in their endeavor. This probably accounted for the new Parliament's decision to allow one accused of treason to get himself a lawyer" (1980, 383).

foothold in the new social order. As Deitrich Reuschemeyer argues, such men were needed: "Expanding transportation and communication facilities make more far-flung operations possible for rulers and merchants alike. With these arises the necessity of making binding commitments and acquiring rights in many places at the same time where traditionally acceptable representatives were [*sic*] unavailable" (1973, 7). But, as Reuschemeyer also suggests, it was not merely a matter of increasing *geographical* distance that promoted lawyers; equally important were increases in *social* distance. In time, even within limited geographical areas, communities came to incorporate a variety of peoples from differing backgrounds. As social diversity increased, lawyers were needed to help define a common ground: "Questions concerning business contracts, business paper, land rights, wills and political liberties grew to be so vital that they required the attention of skilled lawyers" (Brown 1938, 14).

The colonies that banned lawyers were each made up of individuals united by strong consensus about values and expectations (Nelson 1975). The contract did not replace the handshake just because of distance in miles but because of distance in interests. As consensus decreased, lawyers were needed to help define rights and obligations. Evolution from conjoint communities in which people willingly surrendered authority to leaders on the assumption that those leaders had their subjects' best interests at heart to the more disjointed aggregations of later years meant the loss of unquestioning faith in authority. In fact, many believe the Constitution of the United States itself would never have been ratified had it not been for the promise of the Bill of Rights (Friedman 1973, 102).

The first eight amendments to the Constitution were intended to protect individual citizens from the power of the federal—not state or local—government.[4] Prominent among the concerns responded to in the Bill of Rights was the citizens' felt need for protection from the distant government in the event it accused them of criminal wrongdoing. As Lawrence Friedman observed in his historical survey of American law, "the basic rights of man turned out, in large part, to be rights to a fair trial" (Friedman 1973, 133). These rights, as they have come to be accepted in the law of the land, can be expressed in shorthand: no matter how serious the accusation, no matter who voices it, the accused is en-

---

4. In 1930, Roscoe Pound made a similar point when he suggested that it was a lack of trust in "distant" judges by colonists that ultimately led to the "extravagant reliance" on juries in nineteenth-century America: "Colonists were putting their trust in the local jury as against royal [i.e., distant] judges. Thus trial by jury, with great powers confided to the jury, came to be held the first item among our inherited liberties ([1930] 1975, 115).

titled to be presumed to be innocent until proved guilty beyond a reasonable doubt (*Coffin v. United States* 156 U.S. 432 [1895]; *Davis v. United States* 160 U.S. 469 [1895]; *In re Winship* 397 U.S. 358 [1970]).[5] This degree of protection for the accused, as historians have noted, involves standards that would have astonished seventeenth-century judges as "Crown-defying nonsense" (Rembar 1980, 413). Indeed, the Bill of Rights was intended to guard "against tyranny of autocrats and kings" (Friedman 1973, 133). While the citizens of new states seemed confident of their own judgment—and, presumably (as is suggested below), that of their *immediate* neighbors—they remained skeptical of authority and the use of power on the part of a distant government.

Although the Sixth Amendment to the Constitution (1791) provided for assistance of defense counsel in federal courts, similar rights for criminal defendants in most state courts would not be articulated for many years. Some legal historians have puzzled over this apparent discrepancy (see, e.g., Beany 1955, 8–9). Why would citizens not demand from states the same rights that they had demanded from their federal government? The answer may be simply that citizens did not feel that they needed such protection in their own courts.

The Role of Due Process

When they ratified the Fourteenth Amendment (1868), states unquestionably agreed, inter alia, that "no state shall . . . deprive any person of life, liberty or property, without due process of law." As many have noted, the due process clause took on a spirited life of its own over the next 100 years, culminating in the so-called Due Process Revolution of the 1960s and 1970s.[6] The animus of this clause is, in part, due to its indeterminate nature. "Delphic language" characterizes much of our Constitution (Kurland 1970, xvi), but, in this instance at least, one can

5. For the uninitiated, case citations are decoded as, for example: *Coffin v. United States*—involved a plaintiff named Coffin and the United States as defendant; 156 U.S. 432 (1895)—the Supreme Court decided the case in 1895 and the opinion begins at page 432 of volume 156 of the *United States Reports* (the official record of the Supreme Court's decisions).

6. An earlier due process "revolution" had occurred, one that had very little to do with the rights of individuals. In the late nineteenth century, laws intended to regulate businesses and other corporate persons were struck down as unconstitutional because they denied those persons their right to due process. In one case, for example, the Supreme Court ruled that laws fixing freight rates and allowing railroads no relief through judicial review denied the railroads' Fourteenth Amendment rights to due process (*Chicago Milwaukee & St. Paul Railroad Company v. Minnesota* 134 U.S. 418 [1890]). See also Thurman Arnold, *Folklore of Capitalism* (1937).

imagine our ancestors thinking: "We don't need to define words like 'person,' 'life,' 'liberty,' 'property,' or 'due process,' because everyone knows what those words mean." Yet "what everyone knows," as the framers of the amendment may well have anticipated, is not something that remains constant (Berger and Luckmann 1967). As Justice Felix Frankfurter would later remark, it was especially in the very nature of this idea of due process to foment change. Due process, Frankfurter said, is simply a "profound attitude of fairness between man and man, and more particularly between individual and government. . . . Due process is not a mechanical instrument. It is not a yardstick. It is a delicate process of adjustment inescapably involving the exercise of judgment by those whom the constitution entrusted with the unfolding of the process" (*Joint Anti-Fascist Refugee Committee v. McGrath* 341 U.S. 123 [1951]). Stated most baldly, in criminal law, procedural due process is not "justice" but is instead that which it is believed necessary to do in order to achieve justice. In other words, due process procedures are those intended to guarantee that the defendant receives a fair trial—and hence justice. In this country, the right to procedural due process or to a fair trial includes the rights to notice of charges and proceedings and to a hearing and an opportunity to conduct a defense before an impartial tribunal in an atmosphere of fairness. Although historically most have agreed that "we shall have procedural justice" or due process (Thibaut and Walker 1975, 2), the matter of exactly how these rights should be operationalized has been the focus of much controversy. One major bone of contention has been the role of the defense lawyer in the state trial court.

While there is little—if any—evidence to suggest that any defendant who obtained private counsel was ever denied the services of that lawyer (at least in the trial courtroom), whether the right to conduct a defense includes the right to an attorney (which, in turn, suggests the duty of the state to provide counsel if the defendant cannot afford one) is a different question, one that has only recently been voiced. Until the middle of the twentieth century, the situation of poor defendants recalled that of defendants in English trial courts during the days of the facts-law distinction: in theory, it was part of the job of both the prosecutor and judge to ensure that each defendant received a fair trial. It would be going too far to argue that there was any widespread belief that the judge (or the prosecutor) would fulfill all the functions of a defense attorney; but it was believed that if the judge thought you needed a lawyer to ensure that you got what was coming to you, the judge would appoint you one. The remarks of a former minister of justice of fascist Italy are helpful for discovering the basic rationale underlying how state trial courts could justify the fact that not all defendants had lawyers. When asked why defense counsel were not allowed to participate in criminal preliminary proceedings at that time in his country, he said: "The presence of the lawyer is [only] demanded by those who mistrust the judge. This is the general attitude in a liberal and democratic state where authority always inspires mistrust, but one which cannot be admitted in a fascist state because it is in contradiction with the fundamental principles of the regime" (Rogge 1959, 201). As long as we trust our judges, lawyers are superfluous. Such was the logic that governed the role of the defense attorney in our trial courts for most of our history. Of course, defense counsel were allowed in American criminal proceedings, but many people apparently believed them to be unnecessary luxuries—that even if one could not afford to hire a lawyer one could still get a fair trial. It is not until 1932, in the Supreme Court's review of what became known as the "Scottsboro Boys" case, that a strong suggestion can be found that the traditional safeguards of due process (judicial and prosecutorial fair-mindedness) might not always be adequate.

The Seeds of Revolution

In 1931, nine young black men were accused and convicted of raping two white women. Eight of the men were sentenced to die by the trial court in Scottsboro, Alabama. The Alabama Supreme Court upheld the conviction and set an execution date. A few months later, the Supreme Court of the United States reversed that decision, saying that the defendants' constitutional rights to due process under the Fourteenth Amendment had been violated because they had not been adequately represented at their trial. In fact, the youths did have a lawyer, but as one of them remembers it,

> A group of black preachers in Chattanooga raised fifty dollars to hire us a lawyer. He came to see us about half an hour before the trial. He was a white man named Stephen Roddy. He looked us over and asked which ones did the raping. He said, "Now if you boys will tell the truth, I might be able to save some of your lives." I didn't know what a lawyer was supposed to be but I knew that this one was no good for us. He had liquor on his breath and he was as scared as we were. When we got into the courtroom and the judge asked him if he was our lawyer, our man said, "Not exactly" (Norris and Washington 1979, 22).

In its review of the case, the Court held that "given the circumstances"—a capital offense, the hostile environment, the status of the defendants as "young, ignorant and illiterate"—and a crime "regarded with especial horror in the community where they were to be tried," the right to be heard would be "of little avail if it did not comprehend the right to be heard by counsel. . . . The failure of the trial court to make an effective appointment of counsel was a denial of due process within the meaning of the Fourteenth Amendment (*Powell v. Alabama* 287 U.S. 45 [1932]).

The Court's ruling was portentous not merely because of its assertion of the right to counsel but because it found that accepted due process safeguards had been proved—at least in this case—to be inadequate. As it turned out, however, the *Powell*/Scottsboro decision was more limited than it had at first seemed. Ten years later, in 1942, when the Court was again asked to rule on the right to counsel issue, it stepped back from affirming that "being heard necessarily comprehended the right to be heard by counsel."

In *Betts v. Brady,* the Court essentially ruled that Smith Betts (indicted and convicted for robbery in a Maryland state court) had not been denied due process when the trial judge refused to appoint him a lawyer. This case, said the Supreme Court, was different from *Powell* and "asserted denial [of due process] is to be tested by an appraisal of the totality of facts in a given case. That which may, in one setting, constitute a denial of fundamental fairness, shocking to the universal sense of justice, may, in other circumstances, and in light of other considerations, fall short of such denial" (*Betts v. Brady* 316 U.S. 455 [1942]).

In *Powell,* the Court reminded us, "special circumstances" had been involved; such special circumstances were missing from *Betts* and therefore the defendant had not been denied his rights. Still, *Powell* had opened a door and a reading of subsequent decisions suggests that the methods of police, prosecutors, and state court trial judges kept that door open: During the next two decades, the Court found a number of cases that demonstrated—to its satisfaction, at least—the inadequacy of existing due process safeguards. In fact, after 1950 the Court never affirmed a state criminal conviction in a felony case in which the defendant claimed that the court had denied him due process because it had failed to appoint defense counsel.[7] As one observer noted in 1960, "the absence of counsel is in itself the most frequently found constitutional defect in state prosecutions" (Reitz 1960, 465). More and more, it became clear to the Court that, if he was to receive due process, the defendant needed the "guiding hand" of a friend in court.

7. The last Supreme Court decision rejecting a defendant's claim for counsel as a denial of due process in a state criminal proceeding was *Quicksal v. Michigan* (339 U.S. 660 [1950]). Between 1950 and 1963, the Supreme Court decided the dozen right-to-counsel cases that came to it from state courts in favor of the petitioners. Six years after the *Powell*/Scottsboro case, the Court ruled that indigent defendants charged with a felony in federal courts had a Sixth Amendment right to appointed counsel (*Johnson v. Zerbst* 304 U.S. 458 [1938]).

The Due Process Revolution

The 1960s and early 1970s was the era of the Due Process Revolution. A clear indication of what was to come was seen in 1961, when in *Mapp v. Ohio* the Court ruled that Fourth Amendment protection against unreasonable searches and seizures applied to state criminal cases (367 U.S. 643). The application of the infamous "exclusionary rule" to state criminal proceedings brought the Court more public attention than any ruling since *Brown v. The Board of Education* (1954). Yet *Mapp* was only the beginning of the revolution. In a series of cases decided after *Mapp,* the Court ruled that under the guarantees of the Fourteenth Amendment, the Sixth Amendment right to counsel must also be honored by state trial courts.

In 1963, the Court reviewed the case of Clarence Earl Gideon, a white man who had been tried and convicted in a Florida state court. Gideon's case involved no "special circumstances": The crime was not one regarded with especial horror—it was the felony of breaking and entering (a poolroom) with the intent to commit misdemeanor theft. Furthermore, the defendant was not young, or particularly ignorant. Gideon had requested an attorney for his trial, but the judge refused, saying that he could not assign one because Gideon had not been charged with a capital offense. In this the judge misspoke himself, since to appoint counsel was within his power in all kinds of cases, although in Florida it was mandatory only in capital cases.

As Justice Black would later remark, Gideon's case was "strikingly like" the case of Smith Betts. But this time the outcome was different. Though in reviewing Gideon's trial transcripts the justices found that Gideon had conducted his defense "about as well as could be expected from a layman," the Court ruled that this quality of defense was inadequate: the right to legal representation must be granted to all indigent defendants in all felonies. Harking back to its reasoning in *Powell,* in *Gideon* the Court found it an "obvious truth" that a person brought into court "cannot be assured of a fair trial unless counsel is provided for him."

> Lawyers to prosecute are everywhere deemed essential to protect the public's interest in an orderly society. Similarly, there are few defendants charged with crime, few indeed, who fail to hire the best lawyers they can get to prepare and present their defenses. That government hires lawyers to prosecute and defendants who have the money hire lawyers to defend are the strongest indications of the widespread belief that lawyers in criminal courts are necessities, not luxuries. The right of one charged with crime to counsel may not be deemed fundamental and essential in some countries, but it is in ours. (*Gideon v. Wainwright* 372 U.S. 335 [1963])

21

On the same day that the Court ruled in *Gideon,* it also ruled that states were required to appoint counsel for defendants—if requested—on first appeal following conviction (*Douglas v. California* 372 U.S. 353 [1963]). In 1972, on a misdemeanant's petition, the Court ruled that (absent a knowing and intelligent waiver on the part of the defendant) no person may be imprisoned for any offense—even a misdemeanor—unless represented by counsel (*Argersinger v. Hamilin* 407 U.S. 25).[8]

Although (given the Court's then recent history of deciding right to counsel cases) the *Gideon* decision was no surprise to most, it was remarkable inasmuch as it seemed directly to contradict principles firmly laid down in *Betts.* Speaking perhaps for that part of the Court that is loathe to reverse itself, Justice Harlan explained in a separate opinion that the "Court had come to recognize . . . that the mere existence of a serious criminal charge constituted in itself special circumstances requiring the services of counsel at trial." But, he added, this "appears not to have been fully recognized by many state courts, in this instance charged with front-line responsibility for the enforcement of constitutional rights."

Relegitimizing the System: Individuals Versus States

The Court's rulings in *Gideon, Douglas, Argersinger,* and the other cases that made up the Due Process Revolution have meant different things to different observers. On the one hand, many have argued that in making these rulings the Court meddled where it had no right to do so—that the Court's decisions in these cases constituted nothing less than direct attacks on the sovereignty of states, sovereignty legitimated by the princi-

---

8. The Court also broadened the defendant's right to counsel in other stages of criminal proceedings. In the case of *Escobedo v. Illinois* (378 U.S. 478 [1964]), Danny Escobedo had been denied access to his attorney while in police custody. Overturning his conviction, the Court asserted that a suspect had a right to consult with an attorney when the "investigation is no longer a general inquiry into an unsolved crime, and has begun to focus on a particular suspect." This was made more explicit in *Miranda v. Arizona* (384 U.S. 436 [1966]). Speaking for a divided Court, Chief Justice Warren ruled that on arrest an individual had a right to be "warned prior to questioning that he had a right to remain silent, that any statement he does make may be used as evidence against him, and that he had a right to the presence of an attorney, either retained or appointed." In *Miranda,* Warren cited the long history of dubious "third-degree techniques" used by police and said that the state is required to prove guilt by its "own independent labors," without assistance from the defendant. In 1967, the Court held that a postindictment police line-up is a "critical stage" requiring the presence of counsel (*United States v. Wade* 388 U.S. 218 [1967]). In 1970, the Court ruled that the preliminary hearing (where probable cause or the presence of sufficient evidence to warrant prosecuting the case is determined) is another "critical stage" in which due process requires that the defendant be represented by counsel (*Coleman v. Alabama* 399 U.S. 1).

ples of federalism. In other words, it was argued that regardless of whether a state was treating its "subjects" fairly when it denied legal counsel to indigent defendants, the Supreme Court had no legitimate right to interfere (see, e.g., Morgan 1984; Perry 1982, chap. 1; but cf. Dworkin 1977).

Certainly a strong case can be made for the argument that during the Due Process Revolution the Supreme Court went well beyond what strict constructionists view as appropriate interpretation both of the Court's role and of the Constitution itself. The Fourteenth Amendment was part of a package deal intended to help establish and secure the rights of former slaves in post–Civil War America. While it is difficult to assess whether they ultimately would have approved, there is no gainsaying the fact that neither the framers of the Bill of Rights nor the authors of the Fourteenth Amendment could have foreseen the uses to which these amendments have been put during the past thirty years. The specific outcomes of such cases as *Gideon* no doubt do go beyond the intentions of the framers.

On the other hand, if we search for the sociological rule, the issues are different. Since it was ratified in 1868, the due process guarantee of the Fourteenth Amendment has been treated as if it were a principle of natural law—constitutive and nearly sacred. As Max Weber observed, this particular clause in the Constitution is taken as if it owes its legitimacy not to its origins from legitimate lawgivers but to its "immanent" and "teleological quality" (1978, 867, 869). This rule of due process then has primary and not derivative legitimacy; it provides a standard against which derivative laws and institutions are measured. Without stretching a sociological interpretation too far, one could argue that the definition that the Fourteenth Amendment gave to the relationship between citizens and their respective state governments was parallel to that which already existed between citizens and the federal government under the Bill of Rights and that at this metalevel the Court's decision in no way contradicted the intentions of the framers.

Underlying this country's idea of democracy is the basic assumption that individuals have certain rights—and that, notwithstanding the will of a contrary majority, these rights ought not to be infringed. It is on this assumption that the Bill of Rights is based. Seventy-seven years after the Bill of Rights was ratified, the Congress of the United States made it clear that state governments ought not to think that they could play fast and loose with the rights of their citizens: the Fourteenth Amendment was written to help ensure that the majority will of franchised white citizens in southern states did not keep Blacks from claiming the rights due them. What is suggested here is that the Due Process Revolution was merely an extension of that tradition by the members of the Supreme

Court who judged that the interests of the duly elected prosecutorial and judicial elements in some states had become distant or disjointed from the interests of citizens *accused* but not yet *convicted* of crimes and that these citizens were being denied their basic rights.

It was, in fact (at least implicitly), this sort of sociological rule that the Court drew on during the Due Process Revolution. In *Gideon* the judges found that for the states not to ensure that each person accused of crimes had a lawyer in order to protect his or her rights was "fundamentally unfair," that the individual's right to due process took precedence over and was prior to the rule of federalism. As Walter F. Mondale, attorney general of one of the twenty-two states that submitted amici curiae briefs to the Court in support of Gideon's cause, noted,

> I believe in federalism and states' rights too. . . . But I also believe in the Bill of Rights. . . . Nobody knows better than an attorney general or a prosecuting attorney that in this day and age furnishng an attorney to those felony defendants who can't afford to hire one is "fair and feasible." Nobody knows better than we do that the rules of criminal law and procedure which baffle trained professionals can only overwhelm the uninitiated. . . . As chief law enforcement officer of one of the thirty-five states which provide for the appointment of counsel for indigents in *all* felony cases, I am convinced that it is cheap—very cheap—at the price. (cited in Lewis 1964, 145)

Social Response to the Due Process Revolution

Most of the legal controversy generated by the Court's rulings during the Due Process Revolution seemed to focus on whether the Court had a right to interfere in state criminal proceedings. But, as Philip Kurland (1970) pointed out, "the outcry on behalf of federalism . . . seems to hide more than it reveals." Though the "more rabid critics" deplored the fact that "the rules were made by the national government," they deplored too "the rules themselves." Kurland observed that most of the public and press "never knew that the Bill of Rights was not always applicable to the conduct of state government as well as national." It seems, therefore, that it was not the Court's "attack" on federalism that fired controversy in the broader social arena. Instead, it was the perception that the Court was "coddling criminals." It was not a politically appropriate time to attempt to ease the burden of a defendant trying to avoid conviction in criminal court. Ours was a country caught up in a "war on crime," and "the fact that the rise in the crime rate is coincidental with the Court's development of higher standards of criminal procedure is read to suggest that the one is the cause of the other" (Kurland 1970, 82).

Professor Kurland suggests that it was the mentality engendered by this war on crime that led to popular disapproval of the Court's actions during the Due Process Revolution. The irony is that much of the Court's activity during this revolution itself can be traced to the war-on-crime mentality. Ten years before he met Clarence Gideon, Justice Frankfurter apparently saw the revolution coming:

> Loose talk about war against crime too easily infuses the administration of justice with the psychology and morals of war. It is hardly conducive to the soundest employment of the judicial process. Nor are the needs of an effective penal code seen in the truest perspective by talk about a criminal prosecution's not being a game in which the Government loses because its officers have not played according to rule. Of course criminal prosecution is more than a game. But in any event it should not be deemed a dirty game in which "the dirty business" of criminals is outwitted by "the dirty business" of law officers. The contrast between morality professed by society and immorality practiced on its behalf makes for contempt of law. (quoted in Kurland 1970, 83)

The popular complaint voiced against the Supreme Court during the Due Process Revolution was that the Court had effectively "handcuffed" the police and prosecutors (Kamisar 1965). Such rulings, it was charged, could only have been forged out of the Court's ignorance of conditions in the real world, of what was needed to get the job done on the streets and in the trial courts. Others observed, to the contrary, that the members of the Supreme Court had substantial knowledge of the real world and that the Due Process Revolution was a direct result of that knowledge. As one federal judge explained things: "It is not accidental that the United States Supreme Court started its dramatic crusade against what had to be appalling conditions under the leadership of Earl Warren, who had been a prosecuting attorney in California. He knew what the institution of criminal law enforcement was like on the ground, and while he may have abused the process himself when he was young, when he put on his black robe and was thereby translated to sainthood, he set about cleaning up the system" (Neely 1981, 153).

The activities of the American criminal justice system are in great part justified by the principles of due process. Due process can be, as for many years it was, assumed to be taken care of simply because the goodwill of those in charge of the justice system is taken for granted. Before the Due Process Revolution, the Court had ruled that there was no exact relationship between the Bill of Rights and the due process required by the Fourteenth Amendment. Instead, Fourteenth Amendment due process was viewed simply as incorporating all the principles "implicit in the concept of ordered liberty" (*Palko v. Connecticut* 302 U.S. 319 [1937]).

More specifically, as far as criminal procedures were concerned, the Court's stance was simply that the states must provide defendants with "that fundamental fairness essential to the very concept of justice" (*Lisenba v. California* 314 U.S. 219 [1941]). In other words, until the 1960s the higher courts showed a great deal of faith in the general goodwill and sense of fairness of local trial judges. It was not until the 1960s that the Court made explicit any real concern that some state courts were not consistently acting in a legitimate fashion—and, hence, that reliance on their goodwill was no longer enough to keep the courts acting as if they respected the basic principle of due process.

From Goodwill to Proceduralism

Although my special concern here is the increasing articulation of the right to counsel, the pattern revealed by the Court's actions on this issue during the past few decades was replicated in other areas of due process concerns. Traditionally, the Court had decided cases based on the assumption that the police, judges, and prosecutors would (as lawyers sometimes put it) "do the right thing." Doing the right thing meant not only granting an attorney to those who needed one but preventing misuse of police and prosecutorial powers.

It can be noted that, even before *Mapp* touched off the Due Process Revolution, it was illegal for police to conduct unreasonable searches and seizures. Yet, although the Court found that the "security of one's privacy" that was "at the core of the Fourth Amendment" was indeed something that was also invoked by Fourteenth Amendment guarantees of due process, the Court did not require that evidence obtained in violation of these strictures be excluded from state criminal proceedings (*Wolf v. Colorado* 338 U.S. 25 [1949]), even though it had long required exclusion of such evidence from federal trials (*Weeks v. United States* 232 U.S. 383 [1914]). When the Court did find exceptions to this rule of nonexclusion, they were—like the right-to-counsel exception found in *Powell*—held out as special cases. In *Rochin v. California,* for example, the Court found that improperly obtained evidence must be excluded when the violation of rights to privacy guaranteed by the Fourteenth Amendment was such that it shocked "the conscience" of "civilized society" (342 U.S. 165 [1952]).[9] In *Mapp,* however, the Court said that it had had enough of being shocked and ruled that any evidence obtained improperly must be excluded from state proceedings. Just as in *Miranda,*

---

9. Justice Black would later refer to this standard as "the old-shock-the-conscience test" (*In re Winship* 397 U.S. 358 [dissent] [1970]).

where the Court would justify the rule that suspects must be warned of their rights before being interrogated by police, in *Mapp* the Court ruled that extending the exclusionary rule to state criminal proceedings was "the only effectively available way . . . to compel respect for the constitutional guarantee." "Nothing," said the Court, "can destroy a government more quickly than its failure to observe its own laws" (367 U.S. 643 [1961]). New York's Deputy Policy Commissioner Reisman, in an interview with the *New York Times* four years after the *Mapp* decision, remembered: "The Mapp case was a shock to us. . . . Before this nobody bothered to take out search warrants. Although the U.S. Constitution requires warrants in most cases, the U.S. Supreme Court had ruled that evidence obtained without a warrant—illegally, if you will—was admissable in State Courts. So the feeling was, why bother?" (*New York Times,* 18 April 1965).

The Court's loss of faith in state justice apparatus erupted with much more speed and drama when it came to mandating reform in juvenile courts. The Court's findings *In re Gault* (1967), in fact, reflect in microcosm the nature of the growth of procedural due process. Juvenile courts (following a model established by Cook County in 1899), were organized in terms of an explicit doctrine of parens patriae. In other words, in juvenile courts (in much the same way as in postcolonial state trial courts) the fairness of judges and prosecutors was taken for granted, and informality, flexibility, and a caring attitude were assumed to be all that was necessary to protect the interests of the child/defendant—unfettered by procedural constraints, the juvenile courts could do the right thing for the child. In the 1960s, however, many began to question the juvenile court system, arguing that informality and the wide latitude allowed judges was leading, in many cases, to abuse (Platt 1969).

Gerald Gault, whose case was to upset the entire juvenile justice system, was a fifteen-year-old boy who, with a friend, was arrested by police following a neighbor's complaint that they had made lewd and indecent remarks to her over the phone. Gault's parents were never notified by police of the charges against their son, nor were they informed of his arrest. The neighbor, Mrs. Cook, never appeared to testify at Gault's hearing, and Gault was never told of his right to remain silent. No one was sworn at the hearing, and no record of the proceedings was ever made. But we do know that the judge who heard the case ruled Gault delinquent and sentenced him to a state industrial school for a maximum of six years—until Gault reached the age of twenty-one. Gault's parents filed a writ of habeas corpus with the United States Supreme Court, claiming that Arizona's juvenile code was unconstitutional in that it failed to provide sufficient due process safeguards. Already a superior court in Arizona had dismissed a similar petition from Gault, a ruling that had been upheld by the Arizona Supreme Court: Under Arizona's juvenile code, no appeal was possible for juveniles found delinquent. The Court was shocked and took the Arizona courts to task, declaring that "under our Constitution the condition of being a boy does not justify a Kangaroo Court." The Court said Arizona had been unfair in its treatment of Gault and noted that had he been found guilty of the same offense as an adult the maximum punishment for which he would have been liable would have been only a fine of $5–$50 or imprisonment for not more than two months. After reviewing the Gault case, the Court extended many of the procedural safeguards of due process to juveniles, including the right to an attorney (*In re Gault* 387 U.S. 1 [1967]).

Concluding Remarks: The Public Defender's Place

The American legal system owes much to its English heritage, but the elaboration of the defense attorney's role was a distinctly American innovation. Although defense lawyers may make it more difficult to convict defendants, in this country their role is justified by the idea that protecting the rights of innocent people is as important as punishing the guilty.

However remarkable the American courts' sufferance of defense attorneys, until recently the right to counsel was not unqualified. Practically speaking, it meant the right to counsel if you can afford it or if the judge thinks you need it. Defense attorneys, though tolerated, were considered superfluous in all but special cases; prosecutors and judges would work to ensure that the rights of defendants were protected.

During the Due Process Revolution, the view that defense attorneys were unnecessary luxuries was steadily eroded. By 1972, the Supreme Court of the United States had extended the duty of the states to provide counsel to include any defendant, charged in any court, who was in jeopardy of spending time in jail or prison on conviction.

Significantly, although the Courts have diluted some of the protections extended to defendants during the heyday of this revolution, there has been as yet no serious encroachment on the right to counsel;[10] the right to have the guiding hand of a friend in court—to protect against an overzealous state—continues to be the "most pervasive right," since it

10. Recently, in fact, the Court has extended the right to a guiding hand in court to include, in cases where the defendant plans to use an insanity defense, help from a psychiatrist. Justice Marshall, writing the majority opinion, said that the Court has recognized for a long time that "when a state brings its judicial power to bear on a indigent defendant in a criminal proceeding, it must take steps to assure that the defendant has a fair opportunity to present his defense" (*Ake v. Oklahoma* 105 S. Ct. 1087, 84 L. Ed. 2d 53 [1985]).

affects the defendant's ability "to assert any other rights he may have" (Schaefer 1956, 8).

Traditionally the defense of indigents had been provided by members of local bar associations who would take turns receiving appointments (from judges) to represent defendants, often on a pro bono basis; however, this "assigned counsel" system often proved inadequate, especially in urban areas, once more than the occasional defendant needed representation. There are many communities that still rely solely on assigned counsel systems, and these continue to outnumber communities that have defender systems. Yet the problem of providing counsel to indigents increasingly has come to be solved by creating or beefing up public defender organizations. In 1951 a national survey counted only seven public defender organizations; by 1964 (a year after *Gideon*) the total had risen to 136; and by 1973 (a year after *Argersinger*) 573 defender organizations (including sixteen that operated statewide) were representing indigent defendants. Although assigned counsel systems continue to be the primary form of representation for indigent defendants in this country, public defender systems do predominate in larger urban areas. A recent national survey found, for example, that forty-three of the fifty largest counties rely mostly on public defenders and that overall by 1982 68 percent of the population of the United States was being served by public defenders (U.S. Department of Justice 1984).

In the most immediate sense, the function of the public defender is merely to represent indigent defendants; but more important, I suggest, these lawyers have helped to preserve the legitimacy of the courts. Inasmuch as the legitimacy of the criminal justice system hinges on the degree to which it is perceived to both protect individual rights and enforce the law, by adding procedures to safeguard individual rights the Court was, in effect, calling into question the legitimacy of "local" justice. Even if these rulings were not the result of a real legitimacy crisis (between the local courts and popular opinion), they seemed to create one: it is difficult to maintain the appearance that the laws are being enforced when the courts cannot convict wrongdoers; by 1972, it had become almost impossible to sustain a conviction against an unrepresented defendant.

The view that public defenders help to legitimize the courts is crucial to this analysis of public defending; why that is so is a matter that will be taken up again in chapters 3 and 4. But first, in chapter 2, I will discuss how, some thirty years before *Gideon,* the Cook County Public Defender's Office was established to help resolve another crisis of legitimacy in criminal justice. This crisis was homegrown in Chicago.

The Origins of Public Defending in Cook County, Illinois   *2*

The history of the public defender in Cook County begins with a puzzle: although the reform movements spurred by humanitarian zeal during the Progressive Era—1900–1920 (Weibe 1967)—gave rise to the idea, it was clamor for crime control that gave birth to the public defender institution in Cook County. During the years reaching from the early 1920s to the mid-1930s, crime and especially fear of crime increased. Concomitantly, crime control gained salience as a political issue: "The progressive commitment to rehabilitation gave way to a 'get tough' attitude toward crime and criminals. The crises of 1919 [race riots in urban centers], the gangland violence associated with prohibition in the early 1920s, and a number of sensational crimes in the early 1930s all reinforced the concept of a 'crime wave'" (Walker 1980, 161).

Why would Chicago, a city subject to the worst of racial tensions and riots in the late teens (Spear 1967) and terrorized by the exploits of such gangsters as Alphonse "Scarface" Capone and his compatriots, number among its "get tough" responses the creation of a public defender's office?

It might be thought that the public defender in Chicago was a direct result of Progressive Era humanitarian reforms and that the interval be-tween idea and institution was but another instance of cultural lag. If one wished to make such an argument, support could be drawn from the fact that the first American public defender office *was* established in Los An-geles at the peak of the Progressive Era in 1913. Surely Chicago was just a little slow in picking up the idea, was it not? Yet, the Cook County Public Defender's Office, established in 1930, was not really a direct de-scendant of the Los Angeles office. An important fact overlooked in overviews of the history of public defending (see e.g., Albert-Goldberg and Hartman 1983; Herman, Singel, and Boston 1977) is that those early public defender offices (Los Angeles, Portland, Oreg., etc.) were estab-lished with much broader mandates—ones more in keeping with the progressive ideals of social reform. Encouraged by fledgling labor unions, the Los Angeles public defender was appointed to act for clients in all kinds of cases (except divorce), especially compensation cases: in 1915, for example, about one-third of the Los Angeles County public de-fender's clients were people seeking help just in getting past-due wages (Smith 1915, 94). Similar problems and reform impulses existed else-where—including Chicago. During the beginning of the Progressive Era, in 1905, the Chicago Legal Aid Society was created.[1] But the mis-sion and spirit of Legal Aid was different than that of public defending as it was instituted in Cook County: Legal Aid was to be a charitable enter-prise, and its founders were careful to dissociate themselves from the "unworthy poor." To an extent, the Progressive-Era Los Angeles public defender shared this concern: although this office did handle criminal cases, and although it was conceded that work in the criminal courts might have been more "spectacular," it was stressed that civil cases actu-ally took a "greater part of the public defender's time and form[ed] the most broadly useful branch of his work" (Smith 1915, 94). Chicago Legal Aid did not do criminal work, but, unlike the Los Angeles public defender, it would do the occasional divorce. But clients could only get help with divorce under special circumstances. Chicago Legal Aid had a "policy or theory that the fact that a client is too poor to pay an attorney and that he has legal ground for a divorce do not in themselves entitle said client to free legal service" (Hunter 1939, 139). As the senior at-

---

1. Legal aid for the poor had existed in Chicago in one form or another since 1886, when the Protective Agency for Women and Children was formed for the "purpose of protecting young girls from seduction under the guise of proffered employment" (Brown 1939, 5). In 1888, the Bureau of Justice, sponsored by the Society for Ethical Culture, was established to serve the (noncriminal) legal needs of all poor, regardless of nationality, race, or sex. In 1905, these two agencies joined, forming the Chicago Legal Aid Society, which in 1919 became affiliated with the United Charities of Chicago (Gariepy 1939).

torney in charge of the Legal Aid Bureau in Chicago explained, the rare divorce was done, but only when the Legal Aid staff identified some "social necessity" (Gariepy 1939).

By the end of the Progressive Era, Chicago citizens who lacked the means to hire a lawyer had, for certain types of noncriminal cases, an alternative to Legal Aid. In 1915, the municipal court in Chicago helped to pioneer a new branch called the Court of Small Claims—a court where no lawyers were allowed—in order to give members of the working classes access to legal remedies (Speek 1916).[2]

Unlike the Los Angeles and Portland, Oregon, offices, the Cook County public defender was never intended—and indeed was not allowed—to represent clients in other than criminal matters. Although it would be silly to deny that the public defender constituted a humanitarian gesture on the part of the county government, it was not created for charitable purposes. In order to understand the origins of the office, one needs to look at the state of the criminal justice system in Cook County in the 1920s.

The Loss of Criminal Justice Legitimacy

Throughout the 1920s, members of Chicago society showed increasing signs of their lack of confidence in local justice, a lack of trust in both the abilities and inclinations of officials within the criminal justice system. It was, in fact, the *inclinations* of officials that were especially suspect. By the late teens, Republican William "Big Bill the Builder" Thompson (first elected mayor in 1915) had succeeded in his systematic removal of troublesome honest police officers from positions of responsibility. Thompson thereby helped to inaugurate "an era of almost unprecedented cooperation between politicians and criminals" (Haller 1970, 632). In 1921, Kickham Scanlan, chief justice of the criminal court, publicly proclaimed that Chicago "was beyond doubt one of the most lawless communities in the entire country" (Kogan 1974, 145). Although history leaves some doubt as to whether Scanlan's comment was one of dismay or braggadocio (Scanlan was a pal of some rather noted gangsters [see Landesco (1929) 1979]), many of his contemporaries agreed with its substance. One of them, Alderman Charles E. Merriam, a leading reformer and professor of political science at the University of Chicago,

2. Although Chicago is sometimes credited as being *the* pioneer of small claims courts (Smith 1915), in 1914, a year earlier than in Chicago, a small claims branch of the district court opened in Portland, Oregon, as a result of an act of the Oregon state legislature. Chicago courts did, however, show "commendable initiative" by not waiting for their state legislature to act (Bear 1939, 58).

heralded Chicago as "unique": "It is the only completely corrupt city in America" (quoted in Kobler 1971, 158). In 1921, in a front page article in the Chicago Bar Association's *Record,* editor Frederic Ulman decried increases in "such crimes as street robberies, burglaries, and mayhem and the recent escape of Terrible Tommy O'Connor from the county jail on the eve of his scheduled hanging for a murder of . . . a policeman [Patrick O'Neill]" (Kogan 1974, 145).[3]

Besides noting a failure to prosecute, convict, and punish the guilty, Chicago Bar Association (CBA) members charged that law enforcement officials showed misplaced zeal in going after poor and relatively innocent defendants. "Is it the function of the State," they asked, "once the indigent has been charged with a crime to set all its vast machinery in motion against this individual with a view to finding him guilty of committing the crime whether he did actually commit the offense or not?" (Mishkin 1933, 496).

Apparently, in the view of many CBA members, this was exactly how the state defined its role. The typical defendant, it was strongly suggested, would not receive a fair shake from the court. As a CBA member later recalled in a *Journal of Criminal Law and Criminology* editorial, "the prosecutor often forgot that he was not a persecutor—that he should not attempt to convict the innocent" (Baker 1934; Mishkin 1933).

The election of respected jurist William E. Dever resulted in attempts to clean up the city, but these were rather short-lived. Though Dever was partly responsible for crime boss Johnny Torrio's decision to leave the city for an extended vacation in Italy, Torrio's absence left a void soon filled by his right-hand man Al Capone (née Caponi), who set up headquarters in nearby Cicero. Dever lost his reelection bid in 1927— and Chicago-style infamy won out. The gangsters were aided in their cause by reinstalled Mayor Thompson, by the apparent reluctance of the Democrat-controlled finance committee of the county board to appropriate sufficient funds for crime fighting, and (some evidence suggests) by "anticrime" State's Attorney Robert E. Crowe's collusion with anti-anticrime forces (Kobler 1971; Kogan 1974). (Crowe is now best remembered for his prosecution of the Leopold-Loeb case.)

If the police and courts obviously lacked the inclinations to control

---

3. Terrible Tommy escaped from jail on December 11, 1921. One indication of the depth of O'Neill's brother officers' lust for revenge is the fact that, although Illinois switched to death by the electric chair in the 1930s, a set of gallows was kept for fifty-five years in anticipation of catching Terrible Tommy alive in order to hang him. Supposedly, in 1977, the gallows were removed from the basement of the criminal courts building at 26th and California where they had been stored. Rumor has it, however, that this apparatus is still being stored in the old courthouse at Hubbard and Dearborn (*Chicago Tribune,* 20 May 1984, Sec. 3).

crime and promote justice, many Chicago citizens did not. In 1919, after a particularly spectacular daylight bank robbery, Chicago business leaders established the Chicago Crime Commission. Over the next decade this group would become an increasingly nagging thorn in the side of police, prosecutors, and judges and would actually take over many of the functions of those criminal justice agencies that members of the commission believed were failing the public trust. In order to gain information about what the courts were doing, the commission placed observers throughout the system—including one in every felony courtroom in the city. These observers kept systematic and detailed records on "the work performed by the individual judges; on the number of cases each judge disposed, on the felony waivers approved by him, on the number of defendants he convicts, and on the hours he spends on the bench" (Lepawsky 1932, 212). That members of the commission became increasingly impatient with the lack of "social responsibility" shown by members of the judiciary is suggested by the fact that in 1928 the commission went a step beyond their usual tactics of intimidation by observation and actually brought legal action against a group of judges whom they charged were "paltering with crime" (*ibid.*).

As a result of such efforts, members of the Chicago Crime Commission succeeded in proving themselves more trustworthy than the system. In a report based on a study funded by the University of Chicago's Social Science Research Committee, Albert Lepawsky noted that "many specific complaints by victims and witnesses are made in the first instance to the Commission rather than to the state's attorney. . . . Even where the case is instituted through official channels the detailed daily reports on the progress of all felony cases serve as a basis for advisement and recommendation" (Lepawsky 1932, 211–212). As Ernest Burgess of the University of Chicago observed (perhaps wryly), "The Crime Commission . . . has done a splendid service in . . . stimulating public officials in the performance of their duties" (Burgess [1929] 1979, 282).

Members of the CBA also attempted to effect court reform in Chicago. A reading of its materials from the late 1920s almost persuades one that the CBA's primary motivation was a deep and abiding concern for the rights of indigents accused of crimes. While I cannot argue that CBA members had no such concern, evidence suggests that, in the beginning at least, their concern for the poor was coupled with a concern that their own claims to respectability—and to being considered legitimate professionals—were in jeopardy. As organized crime and Prohibition got rolling in Chicago, the legal community received a large measure of the blame for the shambles that was created in the criminal justice system. In some respects, as noted in the previous chapter, lawyers had always been suspect, but during the 1920s public criticism of the profession took on a new tenor: when the public and press began to speak of lawyer and gangster in the same breath, CBA president Roger Sherman called for remedial action—including the disbarment of dishonest lawyers. But, Sherman cautioned, the public ought not to think—and the media ought to stop implying—that there was anything inherently wrong with doing criminal defense work: defending a criminal does not make a lawyer into a criminal. "The Association owes it to itself and to the profession to see that lawyers generally are not charged with offenses of which they are not guilty. To satisfy public demand, the press too frequently lays the blame for many things at the door of lawyers, when in fact the lawyers are not in the least to blame" (Kogan 1974, 146).

Exhortations to be fair were not enough to cleanse the image of the Chicago lawyer, and in time members of the CBA themselves began to issue increasingly vitriolic attacks against their colleagues who practiced at the criminal bar. The typical criminal lawyer, the association would charge in the mid 1920s, was "legal vermin."[4] He was either too "young and inexperienced" to know what he was doing or guilty of "conniving with defendants," "chicanery," and other vile and unethical practices (Mishkin 1933, 494, 505). The criminal lawyer, as seen by members of the legitimate bar, had only one object in mind: to "Get the Jack." The tactics of criminal defense lawyers, the CBA claimed, resulted in "almost unbelievable stories of human depravity" (CBA 1924, 96–99).

This distancing of itself from the criminal bar was a new twist for the CBA. Years before, in 1912, in the spirit of progressivism, it had created the Committee on Defense of Indigent Prisoners Accused of Crimes. The committee presented to judges of the criminal courts a list of "competent and public-spirited attorneys willing to represent prisoners" (Mishkin 1933, 493). Although support of this sort from the organized bar continues to this day, by the mid-1920s it had already become clear that the committee was not doing the job that needed doing. In the first place, reputable lawyers became more and more reluctant to taint their practices by taking criminal cases. Increasingly the committee's annual call for volunteers went unanswered.[5] More impor-

4. During this era members of the criminal defense bar were called by an amazing assortment of nicknames. Besides the still familiar term "shyster," these included "jail runners," "vampires," "snitch lawyers," "winkle advocates," and so forth.
5. This was in spite of the fact that, beginning in 1926, a $200,000 trust (donated by Mrs. Anna Louise Raymond) was used to hire a "managing attorney" for the committee. This attorney organized a cadre of volunteer law students who were available to assist appointed lawyers in "gathering facts and law" (CBA *Record* 1926, 96). Perhaps to make volunteering less distasteful to the more squeamish, lawyers who volunteered were allowed to stipulate their willingness (or lack thereof) to "defend colored persons" (CBA *Record* 1924, 3).

tant, as time passed, the lack of volunteers did not seem to matter: judges whose role it was to appoint counsel for indigents tended to ignore the lawyers from the CBA who did volunteer. Research conducted by the CBA in the late 1920s found that in one ten-month period "counsel were appointed by respective judges to represent indigent defendants in 1225 non-capital cases, and in [only] 126 of these cases were appointments made of attorneys on the Chicago Bar Association list. Of non-association lawyers appointed, nineteen received 15 appointments each" (Mishkin 1933, 493). The inference drawn by the CBA was that the judges had corrupted the process; judges were handing appointments to their favorites and ignoring lawyers with better reputations.

Crisis in the Courts

It seems likely that the lives of Chicago judges in the 1920s were uncomfortable. For more than a decade they endured the "constant aggravation" of having their every move scrutinized and reported by members of the Chicago Crime Commission, who regularly charged them with corruption and leniency towards gangsters (Lepawsky 1932). At the same time, members of the CBA were charging the judiciary with being in league with corrupt lawyers out to abuse the rights and steal the money of poor persons.

During the 1920s scandals and reform crusades regularly erupted in Chicago, but these never seemed to result in lasting change. Sociologist Ernest Burgess of the University of Chicago would remark at the close of this troubled decade: "All intelligent readers of newspapers in Chicago know that for years there had been a succession of exposés of crime, vice, of gambling, of bootlegging and of graft, and likewise a series of crusades against these evils with little or no permanent effect (Burgess [1929] 1979, 227).

But the citizens of Chicago were becoming increasingly dissatisfied with their justice system. The ultimate push for reform can be traced to a specific event that took place on the 27th of April in 1926. At 8:40 P.M., in a saloon at 5613 West Roosevelt Road, 26-year-old Assistant State's Attorney William H. McSwiggin and his two companions were machine-gunned to death by unknown persons. Upright Chicagoans who had heretofore dismissed gangland violence ("they are only killing each other"), lost much of their complacency: McSwiggin (they believed) was one of their own. What was most remarkable—and confusing—about this event was that no one knew (or was willing to say) why the murders had occurred. Who was the intended victim? Complicating the issue was the fact that while McSwiggin was a noted and successful prosecutor of gang murderers, his companions were of less exemplary repute: one was a known gangster named James J. Doherty; the other was a known gangster's minion who went by the name of "Red" (Tom) Duffy. Were the gangsters killed in the murder of McSwiggin? Or was McSwiggin killed accidentally in the murder of the gangsters (whose beer distribution business in Cicero made them direct competitors of Capone)? Over the next several months, a series of six grand juries would be convened to investigate these killings. The members of the first of these were initiated into their task by being taken to the home of each victim and made to swear over the bodies of the dead men that the truth would be uncovered. The truth, however, proved elusive—in part because witnesses died or mysteriously disappeared after being approached to testify.

The theory proposed by the *Chicago Daily Tribune* was that the gangsters were the main target—because they were known to have helped State's Attorney Crowe's machine in a recent primary election. In other words, other gangsters killed Doherty and Duffy out of jealousy over their share of the election spoils. Amid accusation and counteraccusation though, the grand juries' investigations came to naught. They did, however, manage to uncover evidence of a great deal of previously unsuspected corruption—including the existence of a "company" that sold paroles from prison. Even some hardened Chicago observers called the disclosures "amazing" (Burgess [1929] 1979, 277).

As did many others, G-man Eliot Ness took it for granted that Capone was behind these murders (Ness 1969, 30). Not surprisingly, Capone denied the charge, and his denial ultimately proved embarrassing to State's Attorney Crowe. Said Capone: "I'm no squawker, but I'll tell what I know about this case. All I ask is a chance to prove that I had nothing to do with the killing of my friend, Bill McSwiggin. Just ten days before he was killed I talked with him. There were friends of mine with me. If we had wanted to kill him, we could have done it then. But we didn't want to. We never wanted to. I liked him. He was a fine young fellow." Capone also informed reporters that he really had no reason to kill the young and apparently honest prosecutor: "I paid McSwiggin. . . . I paid him plenty and I got what I was paying for" (Kobler 1971, 172).

In spite of their failure to find and indict McSwiggin's murderers (or anyone else for that matter), the dirt uncovered by the grand juries reinforced the importance of the mission being undertaken by the newly formed Illinois Association for Criminal Justice. This group of lawyers and business leaders came to publish, in 1929, the "Illinois Crime Survey." The survey, to hardly anyone's surprise, found that the Cook County courts were a failure. The courts were not punishing criminals, especially those of the organized-crime persuasion.

It has been argued that the survey "had almost no public impact"

(Haller 1979, ix), but the report did add significant weight to the arsenal already in the hands of influential citizens pushing for court reform. Other studies had shown similar findings; what gave this one more credibility was its use of "scientific technique" and the fact that much of the research had been conducted by "objective" social scientists (e.g., Raymond Moley of Columbia, Clifford Shaw and Henry McKay of the Institute for Juvenile Research, Ernest Burgess of the University of Chicago, etc.). These scientists made recommendations that warmed the hearts of Chicago Crime Commission members who had long been trying to rationalize the system, to get it out of the hands of politicians. Burgess, for example, stated that "what is needed is a program that will deal with the crime problem in detail and consecutively, that is by analyzing the crime situation into its elements, by taking up each crime situation separately, and one by one working out a constructive solution. This is only the application of business methods and scientific procedure to the study and solution of the crime situation" ([1929] 1979, 6).

In introducing the commission's report, Chicago attorney and reform activist Andrew A. Bruce summed up the situation this way: "As long as crime is organized and efficient, and the administration of justice is unorganized and inefficient, so long will crime be a problem in the Community" ([1929] 1979, 6).

The System's Response

Shortly after the report was published in 1929, the Cook County Board of Commissioners established and funded the Judicial Advisory Council. The council, made up of three judges and two lawyers, was formed to supervise and bring innovation to the criminal courts, to guide them to efficiency. Three years later, Lepawsky was able to report that the council "had shown special vigor and influence in securing important modifications of judicial practices" (1932, 207). One of the first recommendations of the council was that a public defender's office be established in Cook County.[6]

In September of 1930, a call went out for an "outstanding attorney" to take on this office. Within a few days, the Judiciary Advisory

6. According to Lepawsky, though some of its innovations met opposition, the council was not easily deterred: "Some of the changes that the council failed to secure through legislative or administrative action it obtained through means of test cases, most of which originated in the courtroom of one of the members of the council and culminated in opinions written by another member of the council who was the supreme court justice from the Chicago district. Under these supreme court decisions it is now permissible to try felony cases without a jury and to conduct jury trials in which the jury no longer acts as judge of the law" (Lepawsky 1932, 208).

Council had found their man: on the 25th of September, Benjamin C. Bachrach was appointed public defender for Cook County. The fifty-six-year-old, South Side–Chicago resident was chosen because of his stature among criminal lawyers.[7] Bachrach, it was reported, accepted the position because of "his sense of public duty and at a financial sacrifice." Furthermore, said Judge Sullivan in announcing Bachrach's appointment, "selection was made entirely on merit and no suggestions were received from politicians" (*Chicago Daily Tribune,* 26 September 1930).

On September 29, 1930, Bachrach established his office on the sixth floor of the newly completed—and still unpopular (owing to its distance from the city's legal district)—Criminal Courts Building at 26th and California. To vanquish doubts that Bachrach might not be given his due, it was reported that he spent the first week getting settled into his "suite of rooms consisting of a vacant courtroom and accompanying rooms forming such suites as are occupied by judges of the Criminal Courts." The first week Bachrach also busied himself with the task of hiring assistants (five attorneys and a stenographer),[8] and gathering up

7. Bachrach had practiced in Chicago since 1896. Prior to his appointment as public defender, Bachrach had enjoyed a rather spectacular career. According to the biography given in *Who's Who of Chicago* (1936), he had

> appeared in defense of Alderman Thomas O'Malley, acquitted of murder; Baron Von Biedenfeld, acquitted of murder; Charles W. Spaulding, banker, acquitted of embezzlement; police officer Baginski, acquitted of murder; John Kiebel, acquitted of murder; Edward R. Hibbard, convicted in U.S. Court of using mails to defraud, cases afterward reversed; David Rosenbaum, acquitted of murder; counsel for Ullman & Keller, Supreme Court of the United States, white slave law declared unconstitutional; attorney for "Mike de Pike," acquitted of conspiracy; for Jack Johnson, former champion heavyweight pugilist, convicted of violating Mann Act, case reversed by U.S. Circuit Court of Appeals; for Joseph Fish, fire insurance adjuster for the assured, indicted for eighteen cases of arson, trials in two cases ending in acquittals . . . (Marquis 1936, 49).

Bachrach's chief claim to fame, however, was participating (with his brother Walter) as cocounsel with Clarence Darrow in the defense of Nathan Leopold and Richard Loeb for the murder of 14-year-old Bobby Franks in 1924. The Bachrach brothers were related to the Loebs, a prominent Chicago family.

8. Three of the assistants chosen by Bachrach—Wilbert F. Crowley, Wendall E. Green, and John Alden Ryan—had practiced law for ten years or more prior to their appointments as assistant public defenders. Two assistants—Dennis E. Sullivan, Jr., (whose father was a judge) and Lester N. Grossman—had only recently been admitted to practice. The stenographer's name, lest she be lost to history, was Ella E. Spradling.

Four years later, of the original group of assistants, only Grossman remained. By 1934, Crowley had become first assistant state's attorney and Sullivan had become a master of chancery. By 1937, Crowley, Green, and Ryan had all settled into private practice in Chicago (*Gunthrop's Legal Directory 1934; Sullivan's Chicago Law Directory 1937*).

necessary law office accoutrements: "In due time dockets, filing enve-
lopes, typewriter and other necessary supplies for maintaining the docket
were received," and from that point on, said Bachrach, "appointments
came thick and fast" (Bachrach 1930, 10).

After three months in office, Bachrach reported the results of his
efforts to the Judicial Advisory Council of Cook County. This report
was reprinted in the CBA's *Record*. During its first quarter, the public
defender's office had represented a total of 582 defendants. In keeping
with the goal of helping to effect efficient justice, Bachrach noted, his
office had disposed of nearly two-thirds of the cases that had been assigned to it. In slightly more than a third of these, defendants had pleaded
guilty. In another third, the state had declined to prosecute. Only twenty-
five cases had been heard before a jury, and of these the public defender had won twelve (eleven findings of not guilty and one finding of
insanity). Of the cases that had been heard by a judge and no jury, the
public defender had won 34 percent.[9]

Besides statistics, Bachrach reported to the council his happy conclusion that

> It is the sincere belief of the undersigned that the disposition of cases . . .
> has been entirely satisfctory to the State's Attorney's Office, to the Judges
> of the Criminal Court, to the Public Defender and his assistants, and, not
> least, to the unfortunates who received sentences. It is also the sincere belief
> of the undersigned, that the dispositions of such cases wherein sentences
> had to be pronounced, was of such character that the defendants receiving
> such sentences necessarily felt that they were justly treated by law, and
> instead of feeling hatred toward the law, now have respect for the law.
> (Bachrach 1930, 11)

Response to the Public Defender

Proponents had an almost utopian vision of the public defender's role in
criminal court, one that in many respects anticipated the *Gideon* debates.
Public defending was seen as a positive response to concerns about both
court efficiency and court justice—concerns that, by the end of the 1920s
seemed to have become inextricable. Public defending was not, they argued, an expression of undue sympathy for or of coddling of criminals
but was rather a way that participants in the system got what they—by

---

9. It is clear that Bachrach was not much of a statistician. He said that he and his
assistants had disposed of 177 cases; the list of outcomes, however, totals only 152.
Having observed this fact, Newman Baker of Northwestern University later said,
"doubtless the discrepancy could be explained" (Baker 1934).

law—deserved. It was, moreover, a way to ensure that participants learned "respect for the law" (Mishkin 1933, 505). Innocent clients would be taught respect because "if the defendant has a good case, he is given an adequate defense—not a perfunctory one—thereby truly safeguarding his interests." Guilty defendants, on the other hand, would be "honestly advised to plead guilty." Professional criminals would not turn to the public defender, for "experience has shown what should be obvious to anyone giving thought to the matter, that it is not the gangster or habitual criminal who would rely on the services of the public defender—he would not trust him, as the public defender would not be party to a possibly dishonest defense. It is only the casual defender, poor and often innocent, accidently enmeshed in the law and not knowing his rights, who is the usual client of the public defender" (Mishkin 1933, 503).

The desire for efficiency, proponents argued, would be well served by the public defender. He would in general try cases more "expertly." He would, whenever it was appropriate, waive jury trials or plead his client guilty, thereby "avoiding unnecessary trials." All in all, it was argued, the time of the court, jury, and others would not be "wasted by needlessly protracted" litigation (Mishkin 1933, 503; see also Baker 1934, 5–9).

The public defender did not disappoint its supporters; the office was judged a success in Cook County. For many observers, the increase in efficiency was proved by the economy that the office brought to the courts: Judge Philip J. Finnegan, Chief Judge of the Criminal Court of Cook County, credited the office with saving the County $400,000 during its first few years in existence (1936, 718).[10] The editor of a local law journal agreed, estimating that within its first three years, given its annual budget of approximately $26,000, the office had likely paid for itself "five times over" (Baker 1934, 8). The CBA seemed satisfied with Bachrach's handling of things, though it seemed to lose interest in its progeny after it was firmly entrenched in the system and had received legislative sanction in 1933. Bachrach's first reports were the only ones ever reprinted in the CBA *Record*.

The public defender's local success was not unqualified. Despite Bachrach's pride in the accomplishments of his office and the approval of judges, state's attorneys, and officials of the CBA, there were those who were not pleased with the public defender's performance. William Scott

---

10. The high degree of Judge Finnegan's enthusiasm for Bachrach's work is perhaps indicated by the fact that most of Finnegan's 1936 article about public defending in the *Journal of Law and Criminology* was directly lifted (i.e., plagiarized) from Bachrach's first report to the Cook County Judicial Advisory Council.

Stewart, an assistant state's attorney who had retired to practice as a private defense lawyer, wrote a lengthy and passionate indictment of the public defender, which was published in 1936 in the *John Marshall Law Quarterly*. Stewart, himself a member of the CBA, claimed that the concept of public defending was fundamentally wrong and that all Bachrach had managed to do was to prove this. The public defender, Stewart argued, "is the agent of the judges and through him they are enabled to dictate and to control the defense" (1936, 246). Stewart agreed that the public defender did indeed make the system more "efficient" but said that this efficiency cost the client justice. Stewart charged that the efficiency of the new system was entirely due to the fact that "the Public Defender makes a virtue of giving up to the prosecution without a struggle and pleasing the judge in every such case." This could not happen with private defense attorneys, Stewart said, for even "the lowliest 'shyster' . . . would never have had the nerve to [so] brazenly throw away all the rights of the defendant. If he did as the public defender does today, he could not have faced his brother lawyers and could never have hoped to secure employment no matter how small. His ignominy would have proceeded him if he ever had the audacity to talk to any other defendant about his undertaking his defense" (1936, 258).

Bachrach claimed that the system—in the eyes of defendants—had rewon legitimacy because of the public defender, that even the unfortunate clients who ended up in prison seemed to be satisfied and to have learned respect for the law. Stewart argued that this legitimacy was an illusion, as much a fraud he said as the justice dished out in the new system. Yes, said Stewart, public defender clients do not complain—but only because they cannot complain! "No one can hurt the Public Defender with his clients. . . . Under the present system his victims are hustled out of the jail to the penitentiary or the electric chair before they have an opportunity to tell of his infamy" (1936, 258).

As public defender offices were established elsewhere in the country, similar criticisms were heard. When a reporter asked defense attorney Samuel S. Leibowitz (famed for his involvement in the *Powell/Scottsboro* case) his opinion of public defenders, he compared their offices to public health clinics and implied that quality was lacking in both.[11] Edward J. Reilly, former counsel to Bruno Richard Hauptmann (charged in the Lindbergh kidnapping case) said he too was opposed to the idea of public defending. It could not work, said Reilly, for "there

11. On the other hand, some years later (in 1947), when *Judge* Samuel Leibowitz visited the Los Angeles County Public Defender's Office, he announced: "I'm now convinced that the public defender is the best answer to the old problem of getting justice for all, regardless of means" (Bloom 1950, 26).

could be no fair trial for a criminal whose case was entrusted to a legal agent of the state. . . . I have seen the public defender system in operation. The lawyers are politically minded, inexperienced, and incompetent. Working for the state, they have no personal interest in the person they are defending" (*Literary Digest* 1935, 26).

No doubt many people discounted criticisms of the public defender inasmuch as they were heard mostly from private defense attorneys—a group whose interest in justice had long been suspect.[12] Stewart's criticisms, for example, were less compelling given that his most passionate complaint was that his clients were being stolen by the public defender. Many defendants represented by the public defender, Stewart said, were not *really* indigent. Many of the public defender's clients could, with time, manage to borrow enough money to pay a private lawyer. Stewart reminisced that under the old system, the time between indictment and arraignment was such that defendants could spend weeks in jail. Spending weeks in jail, Stewart pointed out, gave defendants the time *and* incentive to borrow money from family and friends in order to hire their own lawyers. The efficiency of the new system and the speed with which cases were dispatched, Stewart complained, were hurting the private defense lawyer. Similarly, Stewart complained that the image of private defense attorneys was suffering by comparison with the public defender: "the propaganda to the effect that the Public Defender is a capable, skillful, experienced, high-minded and high-grade lawyer hurts the lawyer in private practice" (Stewart 1936, 267–268).

The early Cook County Public Defender's Office chose not to respond to these attacks, and there was apparently little need for it to do so. To a large extent, the reputation of the public defender's office was protected by the high esteem in which many held public defender Bachrach (Arado 1935). In fact, some saw the criticisms as proof of Bachrach's success. As Chicago attorney Henry P. Chandler noted in an address before the Association of American Law Schools in 1933, "today we have a Public Defender whose ability is so generally acknowledged that lawyers who have specialized in criminal practice complain that he is hurting their business, and that even clients who can afford to pay for

---

12. Unlike many defense lawyers of this time, Clarence Darrow was apparently a proponent of the public defender idea. In fact, he once espoused this concept in a talk before a group of prisoners at the Cook County jail: "If the courts were organized to promote justice the people would elect somebody to defend all these criminals, somebody as smart as the prosecutor—and give him as many detectives and as many assistants to help, and pay as much money to defend you as to prosecute you."

"Too radical" was the comment of one prisoner when a guard asked him what he thought of the idea (Weinberg 1957, 12, 15).

counsel much prefer to have the Public Defender if they can" (Chandler 1933, 1020).

Concluding Remarks: The Public Defender's Place in Local Society

During the 1920s, decades prior to the *Gideon* case, the legitimacy of the Cook County courts was attacked on two fronts. Judges, prosecutors, and police were charged with closing their eyes to the activities of gangsters—and thus with failing to effectively enforce the laws and prevent crime. At the same time, many charged that judges, prosecutors, and private defense attorneys were indifferent to the rights of the poor: relatively innocent folk who found themselves in trouble with the law were apt summarily to receive more punishment than they in fact deserved.

Although the Cook County public defender was hired to represent indigents, it is clear from historical accounts that the office was created more to serve the needs of the courts than to serve those of defendants. The courts accepted the public defender as a way to make the system seem more efficient, more fair. The implications of this will be examined more closely in the following chapters of part 1.

Owing to Bachrach's stellar reputation as a defense attorney, the office weathered the initial round of criticism. But, even among supporters, questions remained. Can the state fairly defend as well as accuse? John Wigmore of Northwestern University Law School was hopeful but skeptical: "What of the future? Can the Public Defender's Office resist the pressure of corrupt influence . . . ? The institution has been founded with the most sincere and careful determination to organize competent personnel, unhampered by any partisan consideration. But can it last, with that independence and trustworthiness? Can the public defender hope to remain immune to . . . temptations?" (1931, 689). As I will show in the next two chapters, such questions are still awaiting answers.

The Autonomy — 3
of the Public Defender

The public defender helped Cook County courts silence both critics who charged that the system was inefficiently handling its caseload and critics who accused the courts of unfairly treating indigent defendants; but doubts remained. Although the office weathered the first storm of criticism owing to the good reputation of Bachrach (and the poor reputation of the private defense bar), questions about the propriety of the state's assumption of both roles—prosecutor and defender—have never been resolved. Because they are paid by the state, public defense lawyers are often suspect—and not just in Chicago.

More than a quarter-century after the creation of the Cook County office, Edward J. Dimock, a judge of the U.S. District Court for the Southern District of New York, attacked the proposal that the government hire defenders for the federal court system. In an article for the *American Bar Association Journal,* Dimock charged that creating a federal defender system would be the "first step toward a police state" (1956, 219). Public defenders, he said, cannot zealously defend the interests of their clients because ultimately, in order to survive, they would have to "consider every move in light of [their] relations with the judge or judges." Judges would not, Dimock said, allow public defense lawyers as much latitude as they allowed private attorneys (220).

A decade later, Dan H. McCullough, past president of the National Association of Defense Lawyers, echoed Dimock's concern: "I just cannot bring myself to believe that the tough, hard job of the defense of one charged with crime can be done by a bureaucrat. . . . Often the lawyer is required to fly in the face of public opinion. I just can't see the public defender defending the little individual. He is more likely in company with his opposite bureaucratic number, the prosecutor, to sweep another mistake under the rug" (Downie 1971, 181).

Many social scientists have shared this view. Although it is often emphasized that public defenders tend to be legal neophytes who come to the job for training, stay a year or two, and then leave for greener pastures (Oaks and Lehman 1968), and although it is sometimes suggested that those who stay longer do so probably only because they cannot make a living elsewhere (Spencer 1984), social scientists have put more stress on the nature of the criminal justice system—and, in particular, on the public defender's place within the system—than on the talents or inclinations of the lawyers themselves. David Sudnow, in his widely reprinted paper, "Normal Crimes: Sociological Features of the Penal Code in a Public Defender Office" (1965), can be said to have set the tenor for many studies of these organizations. Sudnow argued that the job of the public defender is *not* to "defend" but to sort through defendants, categorize them according to the nature of the charges against them, and help the courts dispose of these criminals in a "businesslike" fashion. The public defender's activity, said Sudnow, "is seldom geared to securing acquittals for clients" (260). Instead, the public defender's version of "defense" (Sudnow always brackets this word with quotation marks when talking about public defenders) is perfunctory and geared to "with a minimum of strain, properly place the defendant behind bars" (273).

Of other social scientists who followed Sudnow, Abraham Blumberg, whose work is still cited as "path-breaking" (Jacob 1983), argued that the criminal justice system is geared to "economy" and "consists of strategies and evasions calculated to induce pleas of guilty" (Blumberg 1967, 4). Pressures toward cooperation were acknowledged to affect private defense lawyers as well, but because public defense lawyers owe their jobs to the state, they were suspected of being more susceptible to coercion or persuasion from judges and prosecutors. As Blumberg noted in 1979, "public defenders *as* defenders are still viewed with skepticism by accused persons, other lawyers and social science observers" (234).

Today, some twenty years after they first published their critiques, it might be argued that the views of Sudnow and Blumberg have been

discredited. There is some evidence that this is so. Shortly after Sudnow's paper appeared, sociologist Jerome Skolnick's own study of a
public defender's office led him to conclude that "critics of the public
defender have tended to underestimate the quality of defense provided by
the public defender" (1967, 67). After Skolnick's came numerous empirical studies that failed to find any evidence that clients represented in
court by public defenders fared worse (at least in terms of case outcomes)
than defendants who had private lawyers (see, e.g., Arthur Young &
Company 1975; Casper 1978; Herman, Singel, and Boston, 1977; Levin
1977; Wheeler and Wheeler 1980).

Other scholarly accounts of the criminal justice process and the
public defender's role in that process have offered persuasive evidence
that Sudnow's and Blumberg's portrayals are simply inadequate charac-
terizations of what actually takes place in criminal courts (see, e.g., Alschuler 1975; Casper 1978; Galanter 1974, 1975; Lydon 1973; Maynard
1984; Utz 1978). Malcolm Feeley, for example, reported the interesting
finding that in the jurisdictions he studied, public defenders, far from
pushing assembly line–quick justice, often had to rein in impatient
clients:

> Defendants whose applications for a PD have just been approved often
> approach a PD asking for and expecting an instant opinion, something that
> the PDs are loathe to express. Invariably the PDs firmly and politely tell
> them to make an appointment so that they can review the case in detail.
> While most defendants accede to these suggestions, many of them continue
> to press the PD, emphasizing that they want to get their case "over with
> today," and become irritated when the PDs refuse. This results in tension
> between PDs and many of their clients, a tension that contradicts popular
> opinion. For it is the defendant, anxious to get his case over with, who
> wants the quick advice, and it is the PD, anxious to preserve a sense of
> professionalism, who wants to extend the case and review it more care-
> fully. (1979, 222)

Thus, a great deal of evidence suggests that the views of Sudnow
and Blumberg on public defending *ought* to have been discredited by
now—and that, at least among some scholars, they *have* been discredited. In light of all of this evidence, what is surprising is that the issue
of the public defender's alleged lack of autonomy continues to surface in
scholarly accounts. Martin Levin, for example, in his book *Urban Politics
and the Criminal Courts,* argues that the public defense lawyer's "pre-
dominant desire is to satisfy the judges in his court" (1977, 79). In support of this assertion, Levin notes that in one of the two cities that he
studied "the board of judges directly appoints the chief public defender
and makes budget recommendations for the staff to the county govern-

ment"; in the other city "the judges are quite influential and politically close to the county officials who make these decisions" (292n). Similarly, Charles E. Silberman, in his well-known treatise *Criminal Violence, Criminal Justice* (1978), argues: "Unfortunately, many defender services seem to feel as much of a responsibility to the court as to the individual defendant, consciously or unconsciously, they see themselves as production workers whose job it is to move cases along the assembly line as rapidly as possible. In some cities, where judges hire and fire defenders, that *is* their job" (305). For political scientist Paul Wice, the issue of the integrity of the public defender's role in the courts has certainly not been resolved in the public defender's favor. As recently as 1983 Wice wrote: "It is rather frightening to realize that the very same institution that is attempting to convict the defendant is also paying the salaries of men who are theoretically doing their utmost to refute these charges and win an acquittal. The obvious question in the minds of many disillusioned individuals convicted of crimes after being defended by a public defender is how far his lawyer was willing to go in pushing his client's case if such an aggressive posture jeopardizes his future employment by angering other criminal justice actors" (1983, 4). Similarly, the author of a recent textbook in criminal justice has suggested that judicial interference may keep the public defender from providing quality representation to clients even in jurisdictions where judges do not participate directly in the hiring and firing of these lawyers: "Even where defenders are not indebted to the courts for their jobs, judicial threats to remove 'uncooperative' public defenders may result in the same questionable quality of defense services. 'Uncooperative' defenders may be those who delay prompt and permanent disposition of cases by entering frequent not guilty pleas, filing regular pretrial motions, demanding jury trials, and appealing convictions" (Robin 1984, 262).

Perhaps one reason why public defenders *as* defenders are still viewed with skepticism is that studies showing that public defenders do about as well as private attorneys—and even studies showing public defenders taking adversarial and combative stances in the courtroom—have failed to explain how this can be so given the public defenders' status as court/judicial employees. In other words, social science has failed to show how a public defender can manage to avoid being only " 'an expert on tap, not on top,' subject to the judges' ultimate direction" (Blumberg 1979, 215). Showing the public defenders as adversarial or combative—or even showing them to be competent advocates for their clients—is not, I think, enough. The spectre raised by Sudnow and Blumberg will not be laid to rest until it is understood *how* public defenders are able to act as real lawyers—even in jurisdictions where they owe their jobs to the courts.

Using the Cook County Public Defender's Office as an example, in this chapter I will begin to unravel, from its beginnings, the essential nature of the public defender's relationship to the judiciary—and, at the same time will delineate the nature and origins of the resources that public defenders can draw on in order to escape being mere bureaucratic functionaries.

The Cook County Experience Reconsidered

Members of the *University of Chicago Law Review* conducted a detailed study of the Chicago courts' activities during the 1968 "disorders" (the riots and attending mass arrests that followed the assassination of Dr. Martin Luther King, Jr.). This study's view of the public defender's office was straightforwardly in the Sudnow tradition:

> The Cook County Public Defender's Office was not created and is not maintained for the primary purpose of providing effective representation for indigent criminal defendants. From its beginning the public defender movement in the United States was based as much on the needs of Judicial economy as on humanitarian considerations. . . . The Cook County Board of Commissioners continually stresses the fiscal economies of the public defender system in its Annual Reports; the present Public Defender of Cook County has reaffirmed the view that his office has remedied "a chaotic situation in the administration and disposition of cases."
>
> The effectiveness of the Public Defender then, is more likely to be measured, at least among court officials, by his success in efficiently handling heavy caseloads than by his success in representing an indigent defendant. In short, the Cook County Public Defender is forced to serve as a functionary of the Court. (Warren 1969, 607)

Yet, on the same page, in a footnote, the authors of this document reported a contradictory observation: public defense lawyers "did not see themselves as bureaucratic functionaries, and did not act as such" (607n).

No attempt was made to resolve this contradiction,[1] but the source of it seems to be that the information given in the footnote was obtained from a then ongoing study of the public defender's office being conducted by Anthony Platt of the University of Chicago Center for Studies of Justice.[2] The assertion in the text—that the public defender is "forced

---

1. At least one other commentator who has used the Warren report to bolster his argument about the subordination of the public defender resolved this contradiction by ignoring the footnote—and its possible implications (Downie 1971, 181).
2. Unfortunately, Platt never completed his study of the Cook County Public Defender's Office (personal communication to the author, December 14, 1982).

to serve as a functionary"—was, on the other hand, logically deduced from the authors' knowledge of the public defender's environment and history.[3]

Illinois statutes make it quite clear that the public defender of Cook County owes his position and is responsible to members of the judiciary.[4] Assistant public defenders are appointed by judges, not hired by the public defender (*Illinois Revised Statutes,* chap. 34, §5606). Moreover, in Cook County, as in some other jurisdictions (Levin 1977), public defender budgets are subject to judicial review and are presented to the county board by the chief judge, not by the public defender.

Notwithstanding the nature of the public defender's employment situation, could the relationship between the court and the public defender be read differently than it has been read by many observers? Must the public defender, given his ostensibly subordinate position, be viewed as a mere "functionary?" I suggest that Platt's observation that public defenders do not see themselves as and do not act as functionaries is an important hint that the dynamics involved here may be more complex than Warren's logic allows.

Given the history of the office, it is difficult to quarrel with the idea that the public defender's role was created more to serve the needs of the courts than to serve those of indigent defendants. But is it proper to define those needs of the court that the public defender serves as being exclusively—or even primarily—the needs of "judicial economy?"

Historical evidence is persuasive that those who supported the public defender in the 1920s as a way to make the system more efficient did so out of a sincere belief (however misguided one may find this today) that efficiency would bring justice rather than simply cut costs. Roscoe Pound, for one, argued throughout the 1920s that the criminal justice

---

3. The deduction process was, however, assisted by reference to a quote from Public Defender Gerald Getty that was taken out of context. Warren's reading of Getty clearly misrepresented the point: The "chaotic" situation to which Getty referred, resulted (he said) from the shortage of experienced lawyers willing to do criminal defense work for indigent clients. Cases could thus not be disposed of promptly, and "prisoners were not given the speedy trial as guaranteed by the Constitution, thus needlessly lengthening their stay in jail, oftentimes when innocent." Getty went on to emphasize his view that the public defender's office in Cook County has "repeatedly established a precedent of fairness and fair dealing" (Harrington and Getty 1956, 1140, 1142).

4. In this, Cook County is not alone. Most public defenders are appointed, not elected. A national survey of public defense organizations found that most public defenders are appointed by public officials, either by the judiciary (23 percent), the county board (31 percent), or some combination of the two (10 percent). About a quarter (26 percent) are appointed by independent boards, and a few (3 percent) by governors. Only 7 percent are elected. Most public defenders (67 percent) serve at the pleasure of the appointing body (Singer and Lynch 1983, 110).

system must be made more efficient in every respect if it were to be truly just and capable of teaching citizens the right and proper "idea of law and law enforcement" (Pound [1930] 1975, 193). "There should be no intrinsic reason why democratic institutions should be inefficient," Pound argued, for "the people at large suffer most" when justice is unorganized (199). Ideas such as "scientific method," "rationality," and "efficiency" implied *better,* not cheaper. The public defender was touted as a *scientific* response to a difficult problem: "The time is ripe to throw off the shackles of an outworn system. It must be replaced with one adapted to present day needs. . . . There must be a scientific readjustment of the new sphere of social progress. Public defense is as logical as public prosecution. . . . The public defender is a progressive, logical adjunct to modern criminal law administration. . . . Equal justice must come *by law*— not by favor or charity" (Goldman 1939, 22).

This sort of reasoning was not limited to those interested in criminal justice reform but was pervasive throughout society.[5] As one historian observed, "In the 1920's the nation was captivated by scientific developments in electricity, by the new world of radioactivity, even by more mundane matters like calories and vitamins; science, many believed, was a universal balm that would answer every need" (Leuchtenberg 1958, 221). The feeling was that through the use of scientific methods, social arrangements could become more fair: "that the laws of science might serve class interest did not seem to be a possibility" (Haber 1964, 96). Faith in these modern ideas approached the point of being "superstition in another guise" (Leuchtenberg 1958).

The major problem with the narrow economic interpretation is that it obscures both the real basis of the criminal justice system's negotiations of legitimacy with society and the role played in these by the public defender. Bachrach was appointed in 1929 to help make the system more efficient. His job involved not just speedy dispositions but making sure the system was responsive to the rights of poor defendants.

5. For an account of the influence of these ideas on education, see Callahan (1964), *Education and the Cult of Efficiency: A Study of the Social Forces That Have Shaped the Administration of the Public Schools;* for social work, see Lubove (1965), *Professional Altruist: The Emergence of Social Work as a Profession* (esp. 20). The idea that justice and efficiency are inextricable is not, of course, out of fashion: see, for example, Posner (1981), *The Economics of Justice.*

It can be remarked that many behaviors that we routinely define as "corrupt"—for example, bribery or nepotism—only come to be seen as illegitimate when measured against standards that derive from such ideas as "efficiency." Other logics could be used—and indeed have been used in other times and places. For example, in societies in which loyalty owed the state is superceded by loyalty owed one's family (see Scott 1972), showing "favoritism" to family members is hardly illegitimate.

It was therefore Bachrach's job to put the brakes on the so-called disposition derby in the event that a defense was available for the accused. The
public defender's role was created by the courts to strengthen the perception that justice was being done. In other words, the public defender's
role was to make the system more legitimate.

There is no reason to believe that this role has changed, no reason
to believe that the public defender is maintained for reasons other than
the court's desire to maintain legitimacy. The courts have not, I suggest,
allowed the office to grow to its present size owing to concern with
economy. Since the right to counsel has become more and more an unqualified right, the public defender has grown to help the courts stay
legitimate. The public defender's office is maintained—and the number
of its members has increased—because the judiciary *is* concerned about
the rights of defendants—either because it really is concerned or simply
because the higher courts say it must be concerned. One assistant public
defender made this point rather cynically: "Today the courts can't even
convict somebody unless he is represented by a lawyer" (*202*).

Sociological analyses of the relationship between the judge and the
public defender often emphasize the dynamics of the employer-employee
relationship. From this perspective, the public defender's position is
viewed as that of a bureaucratic functionary; and the implication is that
the public defender's role is more like that of a court clerk than that of a

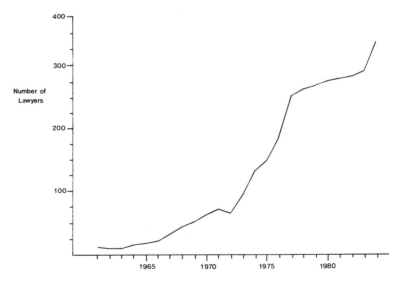

FIGURE 1. Growth of the public defender's office, Cook County, Illinois,
1961–1984. Compiled from *Sullivan's Law Directory for the State of Illinois,* annual eds., 1960–1984.

private attorney. Does conceptualizing the public defender's role as one that serves the needs of judicial *legitimacy* rather than the needs of judicial *economy* change this? In order to answer that question, the nature of legitimacy must be examined.

Legitimacy: Right versus Might

Following Weber (see, e.g., 1978, 212), most writers on the subject have conceived of legitimacy in terms of the probability that superiors would receive willing and uncoerced compliance from subordinates (Dahl 1961, 1964; Lipset 1963). Weber's notion of legitimacy was not restricted to strictly political relations but embraced social relations in general (Weber 1946). Just as legitimacy justifies the leader's command of compliant obedience in a power relationship and hence validates the leader's claims to the right to command, so too, organization theorists argue, does legitimacy justify the organization's right to exist in the eyes of its peer and superordinate system. Legitimacy, then, validates the organization's claim to the right to "import, transform and export energy, material or information" (Maurer 1971, 361).

Many have argued that a great deal of the strength of legitimacy stems from society's ability to inculcate into its members certain values and expectations, including the expectation that they ought to comply with legitimate demands (Dahl 1961; Thibaut and Kelley 1959). In other words, we follow legitimate demands because it is right to do so. Others have found this view of how things work difficult to swallow. It seems likely, as Stinchcombe noted, that what ultimately makes legitimacy work is a recognition (by those involved) that the power to sanction exists in the background of the relationship (1968, 158–163). In other words, we may obey legitimate demands because it is right to do so, but, when push comes to shove, we obey these demands because we know we will get into trouble if we do not. Randall Collins, for one, argues that the power to sanction is more important than being right. In his discussion of why employees will accept employers' orders as "legitimate" and follow them, he argues that, ultimately, people follow orders because they understand what will happen if they do not: "The foreman has [legitimate power] over his employees because he can always call on his superior to fire someone, the superior in turn can call on the police to eject him if he does not leave and the policeman can call on other police and ultimately on the army to reinforce him against resistance" (1975, 291). To put it into the vernacular, Collins's argument is that might makes right. From this perspective, legitimacy is an empty concept. More to the point, from this perspective it is difficult to see how the public defender's status relative to the judge is anything like that of a private attorney—the private attorney is hired by the client, whereas the public defender is hired by the judge. If a client does not like his attorney, the attorney loses the client. By this logic, if public defenders do not bow to the superior power of judges, they may lose their jobs.

Still, one ignores the *social* basis of legitimacy at one's peril, for ignoring it causes one to overlook the essential fact that social embeddedness can transform power resources. While Collins's assessment may ultimately be a valid one, in the present view—given the social circumstances—the more appropriate equation is that right makes might. Collins forgets the fact that, to the extent that legitimacy is sought, an employer's latitude for using power is constrained by social norms (Bierstedt 1976, 141), that workers can be issued only certain kinds of orders, can only be fired for just cause.[6] Even when legitimacy is not sought, issuing certain types of orders can, for example, land an employer in jail. Thus, while it has been said that "covenants without swords, are but words and of no strength" (Hobbes [1651] 1962, 129), words can be used to invoke bigger swords than are personally held by the parties in any particular relationship. In the parlance of social psychological exchange theory, the presence of *n*th parties can transform the values of resources held by actors in any transaction (Blau 1964; Kelley and Thibaut 1978).

Theoretically, then, because it is not in their role as expeditors but as defense attorneys that public defenders serve as resources in the courts' negotiations of legitimacy, public defenders may have unexpected power in their relations with judges: it is likely, for example, that if a judge ordered a public defender *not* to defend a particular client zealously the public defense lawyer could get that judge into a lot of trouble. Do events in Cook County lend any support to this sort of thinking? It is difficult to say for sure, for, as I discuss in greater detail in chapter 4, the specific dynamics of the public defender–judiciary relationship are usually hidden from public view. Fortunately, however, the veil behind which this relationship exists has, at times, been rent. On occasion, crises force the structure of the relationship between public defender and judiciary to be brought into the open. This has occurred, as far as I can determine, only twice in Cook County.

In 1956, the chief judge of the Criminal Court of Cook County, Cornelius J. Harrington, and the public defender of Cook County, Gerald W. Getty, responded to Dimock's criticism that the public defender idea is unsound (see above). Noting that Dimock's article had caused a "deluge of comment and discussion" in Cook County, Har-

---

6. Stinchcombe, on the other hand, makes it clear in his discussion that the authority or legitimate power of the police officer is limited because conditions under which his superiors will back him are limited (1968, 16).

rington and Getty responded emphatically that "the Public Defender is without obligation of any kind to judge, prosecuting officers, or the appropriating authority" (1140), adding that "while cordial friendship is permitted, and required between [the public defender's office] and the court and prosecuting personnel, still there is no fraternizing to the detriment of the client. Thus, there is a distinct cleavage between the court, the prosecuting officials and the Public Defender, *in exactly the same sense and degree that would exist between the same parties and private counsel*" (*ibid.,* emphasis added). Judge Harrington had served on the bench for more than twenty years at that point and was a clear supporter of the public defender's independence. An obvious question is, Must the freedom of the public defender rely on the goodwill and fair-mindedness of the judge? That was tested some years later when crisis brought the relationship of the Cook County public defender and a chief judge into the open.

On February 16, 1972, Chief Judge John Boyle announced that, owing to "serious irregularities" that he had uncovered in a "secret investigation," he had taken over complete administrative control of the public defender's office, the jury commissioner's office, and the adult probation office. Boyle never revealed any details of the alleged defects found in the latter two departments, but his charges against the public defender were disclosed: nepotism, financial mismanagement, and improper use of influence.

First, Boyle revealed his discovery that of more than 170 employees in the public defender's office, as many as three were Getty's relatives: Getty's daughter Marie was working as a secretary (while being paid at the higher rate usually reserved for investigators); Getty's sister-in-law's brother, Vincent Cerri, was working as an assistant public defender; and Getty's stepson, Douglas Kragness, was an investigator for the office.

Next, Boyle claimed that Getty was mismanaging office funds and personnel. First, Boyle said that the public defender had simply asked for too much money when submitting his 1972 budget. The requested $1,750,000 represented a 22-percent increase over the 1971 appropriation of $1,433,000. Boyle claimed that such an increase was unwarranted and said that he, Boyle, had held the increase to only 4 percent (holding the budget to $1,493,000). Second, Boyle—without questioning the quality of their work—said that Getty and his assistants were spending too much money in their efforts to appeal convictions. Third, Boyle insisted that office printing costs were too high. This issue of printing costs seemed to make Boyle especially irate. The year before, a team of county budget experts had suggested that the public defender use photocopying instead of having legal briefs printed. This would result, the experts had said, in savings of $35,000–$45,000 per year. Getty, insisted Boyle, had refused to follow this recommendation. Fourth, Boyle reported that his investigator had uncovered the fact that two assistant public defenders had other jobs. One, Chester P. Majewski, who was being paid more than $21,000 a year by the public defender, was receiving a salary as a paid trustee of the sanitary district. Another lawyer, Shelvin Singer, was teaching law at Chicago Kent College of Law where he held the rank of associate professor.

Finally, Boyle pointed out that Getty's son-in-law, former Evanston fire fighter Leo Ranachowski, held a $15,000-a-year position as chief investigator for the federally funded Illinois Defender Project. By noting that Getty sat on the board of that project, Boyle implied that Getty had improperly used his influence in Ranachowski's favor. Boyle also mentioned that Getty's son, Michael L. Getty, was working as an assistant state's attorney (*Chicago Tribune*, 16 February 1972).

A few days later, Getty responded to Boyle's charges. First, he argued that there was no impropriety inherent in the fact that he employed a few of his relatives—and he supported this by citing the example of John Kennedy's appointment of Robert Kennedy to the post of attorney general. Getty said of his relatives: "They are all competent people and they are earning their money."

Regarding his son's position in the state's attorney's office, Getty said that he had had nothing to do with it, that he "didn't even make a phone call." Yes, admitted Getty, he was a member of the Illinois Defender Project's board, but his son-in-law's appointment as chief investigator to the project predated Getty's appointment to the board. Of Singer, the public defender/law professor, Getty said only that Singer was putting in more than forty hours a week at his job as public defender. Getty made no mention of Chester Majewski—the sanitary distruct trustee had apparently already resigned from the public defender's office.

Finally, in response to Boyle's charges that the office was spending too much money, Getty simply noted that while the current budget of the Cook County public defender was not quite $1.5 million, the public defender office in Los Angeles (which had responsibility for a jurisdiction only slightly larger than Cook County) had a budget of around $8 million (*Chicago Tribune*, 19 February 1972).[7]

7. However one seems to cut it, the Los Angeles public defender was better funded than the Cook County office. Still, the moral implications of the discrepancy are not as glaring as they seem. In part, the difference between the two figures is due simply to the fact that Los Angeles employed 368 attorneys and Cook County only 77; the total appropriation per attorney was then about $21,700 in Los Angeles and $19,500 in Cook. Public defenders in Cook County in 1972 were staffing every available criminal courtroom—one problem was that there were not very many courtrooms. In 1964, there

56

A. Boyle versus Getty: Might, Not Right

What does this episode tell us about the nature of the relationship that existed between the public defender and the judiciary? On the surface these events seem to give weight to the idea that the public defender *is* at the mercy of the judges. Boyle did (he claimed) investigate and then take control of the office, and it does seem as if the points of contention between Boyle and Getty involved the fact that Getty was simply not running things the way that Boyle thought that they ought to be run. Moreover, the public version of the case that Boyle built against Getty suggests that the judge's chief concern was the economy (or lack therof) of the office. Never once did Boyle question the quality of the work that Getty and his staff were doing, only the fiscal costs of their efforts; thus, Boyle's concern with the appeals division was *not* whether it was capable of doing a good job—or even whether the cases pursued were frivolous—but simply that it was spending too much money.

Complicating any analysis of this situation is the fact that the day before Boyle announced his charges and the facts of his takeover of three agencies, Public Defender Getty had made an even more startling announcement: he was the alleged victim of a $50,000 extortion plot. According to the *Chicago Tribune* account, Carolyn Jaffe, the assistant public defender who headed the juvenile division of the office, and Gerald S. Hartsman (a former investigator with the office who had been fired by Getty) had attempted to blackmail the public defender. Initial reports on the exact nature of the extortion threat were vague, the *Tribune* saying only that Jaffe and Hartsman had threatened to expose Getty to "hatred, contempt and ridicule" (*Chicago Tribune,* 16 February 1972). Later it was disclosed that the two had threatened to claim "publically that Getty had sexual relations with Miss Jaffe" (*Chicago Tribune,* 23 March 1972). Boyle claimed that he had become aware of the blackmail attempt only after reading about it in the *Tribune* and that his own revelations of wrongdoing in the office were unrelated to Getty's announcement that he had been the victim of attempted blackmail.

Despite his denials of administrative wrongdoing, on March 23, 1972, five weeks after his alleged ignominy had been made public, Getty

---

were, for example, only eleven felony courtrooms disposing of indictments in the county. By 1982, after a burst of openings during the late 1970s, felony cases were being heard in thirty-nine courtrooms; as I note elsewhere, concomitant with the openings of these courtrooms was the hiring of a great many additional public defense lawyers in Cook County. Recently, authors of a study comparing public defense offices throughout the country noted that Cook County has "one of the more affluent public defender offices" (Albert-Goldberg and Hartman 1983, 97).

announced his resignation from the public defender's office. That same day Getty testified at Jaffe and Hartsman's preliminary hearing. On March 30, 1972, two days before Getty's resignation was to become effective, James J. Doherty, an assistant public defender since 1958, was named acting public defender for Cook County. The judges of the circuit court had unanimously approved Doherty for the job.

I suspect that it was not Boyle's charges but the fact that Getty had somehow gotten himself into trouble with blackmailers that ultimately led to his resignation. In fact, the seriousness of Boyle's charges seemed overblown. Nepotism? Improper use of influence? This was Mayor Daley's territory, and Chicago was a city where clout was king, where "according to some unverified rumors, over one hundred of Daley's relatives held government jobs" (Rakov 1975, 52). Judge Boyle himself was one of Daley's protégés (Royko 1971, 82). Financial mismanagement? The issue of printing costs especially seemed to have been blown out of proportion: the possible economy involved was only 2.8 percent of the office's total budget. Moreover, county budget experts had made the same recommendation about photocopying to the state's attorney's office, where they were also ignored. Even Boyle's claim that *he* had held the office to a small (4-percent) increase in budget is suspect—or is it only coincidence that many agencies in this part of the county budget were held to unusually small increases in that election year? The state's attorney's office, for example, over which Boyle had no fiscal control, was in 1972 limited by the county board to a 1-percent increase over the previous year's budget (see fig. 2). Finally, one wonders why Boyle never disclosed the nature of the alleged irregularities that his investigation had uncovered in the jury commissioner's and adult probation offices.

It was, I think, the fact that Getty had been caught (apparently) in flagrante delicto with one of his assistants that was his undoing.[8] This sort of indiscretion, it has been noted (O'Connor 1975), was perhaps the one mortal sin available to Chicago politicos. It was as if Boyle had simply looked for something to divert attention away from the blackmail, to make it look as if he (Boyle) was on top of things. The scandal, it was perhaps feared, would continue to grow as long as Getty remained securely in office. In fact, once Boyle announced *his* charges, scant mention was made of the extortion plot.

8. My speculation on this point was fueled by the way in which some of Getty's former assistants in the office remember the story. Boyle was never spoken of as a contributing factor in Getty's undoing. Instead, it was remembered that "it was a big sex scandal. It was brought out that Getty was having a sexual liaison with one of the women lawyers in our office and she was trying to blackmail him. Of course, he blew the whistle on her, and of course, he didn't look so good when it came out. So, he was out."

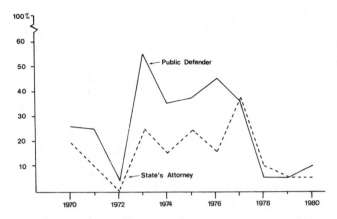

FIGURE 2. Public defender's and state's attorney's appropriations: percent increase over previous budget year, 1970–1980. Compiled from Cook County Annual Appropriations Bills, 1969–1980. The public defender's total appropriation in 1969 was $920,404; in 1980, it was $10,159,157. The state's attorney's total appropriation in 1969 was $4,233,945; in 1980, it was $19,335,910.

At the same time there is some evidence that Boyle and Getty had, in fact, been at loggerheads for years. First, there was tension caused by the fact that it was on Getty's office that the ultimate responsibility lay for the "Summerdale Scandal" in 1960. One of the public defender's clients, Richard Morrison, who became known as the "Babbling Burglar," let it be known that the other members of his burglary gang were "burglars in blue"—full-fledged members of Chicago's finest who for two years had been "carrying the loot away in squad cars while on duty." The gang included "at least eight policemen . . . including the son of a captain and several veterans on the force" (Royko 1971, 116–122). Morrison's information was brought to the attention of Republican State's Attorney Adamowski (by an assistant public defender), who proceeded to make political hay with it. Getty's scrupulous attention to client Morrison certainly could not have endeared him to Mayor Daley—or to Daley's protegé, Judge Boyle.

It is significant, then, that Getty remained in office as long as he did, for he had long balked at Boyle's attempts at control. For example, Getty apparently refused to employ only attorneys hired by the judges' Committee on Help.

B. Judge versus Public Defender: Right, Not Might

What are particularly interesting are the events that followed the revelations of Getty and Boyle. Averting the possible disaster of a sex scandal

59

by forcing Getty to resign following charges of fiscal mismanagement meant that Boyle's alleged takeover—and apparently dramatic cost cutting—had to be made public. Ironically, this, in turn, created a crisis of legitimacy for Boyle and his administration of the courts. Within a week of Boyle's takeover announcement, the American Civil Liberties Union, the Legal Aid Bureau, and the Businessmen for the Public Interest announced that they had joined forces and filed suit in federal court to "wrest control" of the office from Boyle and place it back where they said it belonged—in the hands of a public defender (*Chicago Tribune*, 23 February 1972). Even the *Tribune,* which had earlier editorialized approval of the investigation of Getty's management, conceded "there is a valid question whether a public defender must owe his job and his budget to the same judge before whom he must appear in the course of defending indigent clients" (19 February 1972). Two months later, the Chicago Council of Lawyers called for an independent investigation and evaluation of the office to determine whether charges made by Boyle were true. The council charged that Boyle's takeover of the office was in direct violation of "the American Bar Association's standards that the Office be free from either political influence or judicial interference." Yes, said the council, the office is inefficient—but this may be due to the fact that the public defender, with only seventy-seven lawyers and seven investigators, is "seriously understaffed" and "underfinanced." The council, like Getty, compared the resources of the Cook County office with those of the Los Angeles public defender and found Cook County wanting: Los Angeles, serving a population only "⅕ larger than Cook," employed 368 lawyers and 46 investigators (*Chicago Tribune*, 23 April 1972. See n. 6 above).

The suit against Boyle never came to anything, for Boyle backed down. Administration of the office was returned to the hands of a public defender—James Doherty was eventually selected by the judiciary to take Getty's place. Doherty was one of six candidates for the job, and, before the judges made their choice, all six had been found qualified by the CBA. (Parenthetically, officials of the CBA had wondered at "the small number of applications for the position which paid $28,992 a year" [*Chicago Tribune*, 9 January 1973]). Moreover, as figure 2 shows, Boyle's budget slashing was short-lived: subsequent budgets more than made up for funds lost in 1972.

Concluding Remarks: Keeping the System Honest

Many popular and scholarly assessments of public defenders would have it that these lawyers are little more than bureaucratic functionaries, by virtue of the fact that they are paid by the state. In Cook County, this logic seems ill conceived. The lessons learned from the Getty versus Boyle incident are telling.

First, it is likely that Getty did not lose his job because he refused to "go along" with Judge Boyle (he had apparently been refusing to go along for years) but because he was indiscreet in his personal life. Had Getty not been vulnerable in this way, there is little doubt that he could have survived Boyle's charges. In fact, it seems unlikely that Boyle would have made any attacks were it not for Getty's indiscretion. The second lesson is that even if the public defender does come under fire from the judiciary, there are outsiders who will scrutinize the validity of that attack—and, in the event that the judiciary meddles in an illegitimate fashion, these outsiders can protect the supposedly subordinate public defender.

In retrospect, the most remarkable aspect of this whole controversy is the fact that not once did anyone question the quality of the counsel that Getty and his assistants were providing their clients. If the autonomy of the public defender and the quality of public defending do not depend on the fair-mindedness of the judge, do they then depend on the inclinations of the public defender himself? Who or what keeps the public defender honest?

These questions have been unduly ignored by social scientists, in part perhaps because of the assumptions that the chief public defender has no control over the work of his office, and that because of their subordination to the judges, public defense lawyers cannot function as "real defense counsel." In part 2 and part 3, I will return to the question of what keeps the public defender honest. But first, my examination of the quality of the relationship between the public defender's office and its environment will conclude with a look at the nature of the relationship between the office and the wider social order and at the impact that the public defender's role in the courts has on this relationship.

Institutional Accommodations: ___ 4
The Stigma of Ineptitude ___

In the previous chapter, I suggested that public defenders—at least in terms of their autonomy within the system—have more in common with private attorneys than many commentators acknowledge; that even where the public defender appears to be under the thumb of the judges, there is more to the relationship than meets the eye. In this chapter, a related problem is addressed; given their autonomy, which theoretically does not lag behind that of private attorneys, why does the idea persist that public defenders—relative to private attorneys—are "less effective, less hard working, more interested in 'deals' and less interested in their clients?" (Dahlin 1974, 117).

Now it can be noted that it is not just the public defense lawyer who has problems with "image." As I have shown in previous chapters, the private defense attorney has long been viewed as somewhat disreputable. Those who practice criminal law are accorded low prestige and suspected of "sharp practices that are contrary to the prevailing ethical norms of the professions" even by their colleagues at the bar (Heinz and Laumann 1982, 124; Wood 1967). The question I wish to address in this chapter, however, has to do with why public defenders, relative to private attorneys, are more subject to what Tom Reynolds, Cook County's second assistant public defender, calls "the stigma of ineptitude" (Spencer 1984).

Donald C. Dahlin, director of the Criminal Justice Studies Program at the University of South Dakota, has made an important attempt to answer this question. He began by pointing out that the most obvious explanation for the public defender's image problem would be that public defenders *are* less competent, less effective, and less hard working than private counsel. But in his review of studies that compared the outcomes of cases in which defendants were counseled by public defenders and those of cases in which defendants were counseled by private attorneys, Dahlin, like others, found very little support for the idea that public defenders do less well than private attorneys. But, unlike many other scholars, Dahlin did not stop there. Dahlin, for reasons I will show below, does not consider this an insignificant question.

Explaining the Stigma

Having noted that indeed public defenders do about as well for their clients as private counsel do for theirs, Johnathan D. Casper has suggested that the difference in evaluations of the two types of lawyers is "to a significant extent a product of the fact that private lawyers spend more time in face-to-face contact with their clients. . . . The degree to which public defenders suffer in terms of client evaluation relative to private lawyers is not simply the product of some generalized client mistrust of the public defenders or of their institutional position as employees of the state. Rather, it is related to the amount of time public defenders choose or are able to spend in direct contact with their clients" (Casper 1978, 36).

Casper may well be correct in his observation that public defenders and private lawyers spend different amounts of time with clients (see, e.g., Alschuler 1975). But even for private lawyers, the amount of time spent with a client likely varies a great deal with the client's financial resources and, indeed, with the nature of the case (Mann 1985). In any case, Casper's suggestion does not help us understand why we—as nondefendants—have such a poor image of public defenders; most people have never seen a public defender in action, yet still feel fairly sure that public defenders, relative to private attorneys, are bum lawyers.

It might be argued too that public defenders cannot do as well as private attorneys simply because their caseloads are such that they have no time to do a good job defending their clients—no time, for example, to take to trial cases that ought to be tried instead of plea bargained. Most public defenders with whom I spoke acknowledged that their workloads were heavier than they might wish, but many cautioned me that "the numbers don't tell the whole story":

> You get a guy who was caught red-handed with the proceeds, with the stuff, and he's already confessed. . . . The state's attorney offers a good deal, and my guy's happy with it. As long as my client is happy with it, and especially as long as I can't see how by pushing it we could do better, then I tell him to go ahead and cop, and take the plea. So, essentially the case is over. It maybe only took a half hour; hell, it maybe only took five minutes. But why should I spend any more of my time on it? Sometimes I pick up maybe 15 cases like that in one morning. Sometimes more. (019)

Significantly, I think that the idea that public defenders are bad lawyers simply because of the pressure of caseloads presupposes the fact that because of the exigencies of the situation public defenders—more than private lawyers—are forced to suspend their professional judgments about what really ought to be done in a client's case. This, of course, clearly echoes the notion that public defenders are not good lawyers because they are not *allowed* to be good lawyers and is ultimately tied to the idea of the public defender as a bureaucratic functionary (a conceptualization of public defending with which I dealt in the previous chapter).

It might also be suggested that public defenders are contaminated by their clients, thought less of simply because they work with indigents. This notion, loosely derived from the work of Everett C. Hughes (1971), gains some support from the fact that the wealth of clients is often offered as an important, albeit crude, explanatory variable in sociological accounts of professional prestige (see, e.g., Heinz and Laumann 1982). Yet the strength of the contamination idea is undercut by the fact that some people, far from being degraded for such service, are elevated because of it. Examples that immediately come to mind include that of Mitch Snyder, the Washington, D.C., advocate for the homeless, and Mother Teresa, who was awarded a Nobel Prize for her work with indigents. I suggest that what distinguishes the attorney who is regarded as a heroic defender of poor people from one who is regarded as a bum lawyer is the amount of choice that the lawyer is perceived to have. Lawyers who could be making big bucks by defending wealthy clients but instead choose to help the less fortunate are heroes. On the other hand, lawyers who defend poor people because that is all that they can do are bums. Public defenders, as I discuss in chapter 5, are typically believed to belong to the latter category; they are seen as lawyers who can't make it in the private sector and thus have no choice but to work for the poor.[1]

1. Depending on how one judges the importance of helping poor people in trouble with the law, instead of heroes, public defenders who do such work by choice may be

A related possible explanation of the public defender stigma has to do with the notion that you get what you pay for; in other words, because the services of the public defender are offered for free, those services are not worth much. This seems plausible until someone poses the hypothetical case of an indigent who is offered—gratis—the services of a well-established, well-regarded trial attorney. I suspect that if the average indigent defendant were offered the services of a Clarence Darrow, he or she would be loathe to complain. The point is that we do not, I think, necessarily reject that which is free, but we will reject that which no one else would pay to get; we devalue that which has not proved or legitimated itself in the marketplace (but compare Casper 1978).

That brings us back to what may be the most provocative explanation of the public defender's lack of repute. Dahlin, in his review essay, concludes that, in essence, the public defender's poor reputation is the public defender's own fault. The major failure of the public defenders, says Dahlin, is simply that they have not successfully promoted social recognition of the fact that they are effective lawyers.

Dahlin concludes that, notwithstanding the public defender's real effectiveness, the failure to negotiate the *impression* that it is an effective legal institution is a serious one. For in failing to show themselves as good lawyers, public defenders have failed to promote social recognition of the fact that they have helped the system become more fair in its dealings with poor defendants. He suggests, moreover, that if the public defender could successfully negotiate legitimacy, then the legitimacy of the entire criminal justice system would be strengthened (1974, 118).

Dahlin's suggestion is an interesting one, especially because it would seem to lend itself to empirical verification: in jurisdictions where the public defender's office has achieved a status as a legitimate defense organization, is the legitimacy of the entire criminal justice system (other things being equal) stronger?

There is evidence that actors who work within local justice systems can tell a good public defender organization from a bad one. Silverstein, for example, in his national survey of judges and prosecutors found that "on the whole, these answers indicate that the defender is as able as retained counsel and that he is often more experienced. The replies indicate, however, that in a relatively few counties the defender does not compare well with retained counsel" (1965, 46).

Yet, theoretically, in order to do the job that Dahlin believes needs

---

perceived as crackpots—in the sense that a crackpot is one who makes a sacrifice for ridiculous reasons, as in Joel Feinberg's example of "the dedicated crackpot who nearly freezes to death trying to convert the indifferent Eskimos to Caribbean voodooism" (cited in Fishkin 1982, 14).

doing, it is not insiders who need to be convinced of the public defender's effectiveness but members of the general public—including the public defender's clients. The real difficulty that one encounters when attempting to test Dahlin's hypothesis that a legitimate public defender office would enhance the legitimacy of the criminal justice system is that, as far as can be determined from the literature, there is *no* public defense organization whose lawyers do not suffer from the stigma of ineptitude. As far as the public is concerned, their defenders are everywhere tarred with the same brush of ineptitude.

If Dahlin's hypothesis is correct, then one might think that the public defender—and the courts—might take steps to ensure that the public defender is seen as a legitimate legal organization. To put it in simple terms, if the office does deserve to be seen as legitimate, if it does do a good job, why can it not—or why does it not—communicate this to outsiders?

If it is the public defender's job to make his office be seen as a legitimate legal enterprise, to communicate the effectiveness of its lawyers to outsiders, then one must conclude that the public defender of Cook County has failed. After more than a dozen years in office, Mr. Doherty has not succeeded in becoming a household name; he is not—and has never been—news. Nor is his office. During the Getty scandal, Doherty was approached by a reporter from the *Tribune* and asked for an opinion; all the reporter got was, "You'll get no comment from me on anything, mister, no comment at all" (*Chicago Tribune,* 18 February 1972). Doherty's response to that reporter has indeed been prophetic.

A search of *Tribune* indicia of the first eight years of Doherty's tenure as public defender (1973–1980) revealed few mentions of either Doherty or his office.[2] Not surprisingly, references to the state's attorney were legion. The state's attorney may more aggressively seek publicity because he holds an elected position. But unlike many other county agencies, including the state's attorneys, which are public service oriented, the public defender not only avoids intrusions of the media but

2. Of the thirteen references found, two were leftovers of the Getty scandal. Beyond those, one article profiled a young lawyer who worked in the public defender's juvenile division; one briefly mentioned the fact that an assistant public defender had been arrested and charged with rape. One article reported that Judge Boyle, who, like many Chicago politicians at that time, was loathe to allow the federal government a hand in local arrangements, had refused a grant from LEAA intended to augment the public defender's budget. Four articles discussed the question of whether nonindigent defendants were faking poverty in order to get representation from public defenders; another, an editorial, suggested that clients ought to get counsel earlier in the course of their prosecution. Finally, Doherty (see below) was quoted in one article.

produces no brochures, no pamphlets, no annual reports of its own. Typically, the voice of the public defender is conspicuous only by its absence. Rarely does anyone from the office issue statements; the office has, in fact, no designated spokesperson for making statements of policy.

Even when the lack of a statement from the office leaves an obvious gap, it usually remains unfilled. For example, in the spring of 1982, it was disclosed that the Chicago police, as a matter of routine, were allegedly withholding information (by keeping it out of official files) potentially crucial to defense attorneys. In a *Tribune* report on the implications of the discovery of these "street files," comments from four defense attorneys were published. Although two of these attorneys were in fact assistant Cook County public defenders, in neither case was there any reference to their affiliation with the office (*Chicago Tribune,* 19 April 1982). Six months later, a defendant successfully appealed his murder conviction by claiming that his counsel was incompetent.[3] In an article about this case the question was raised as to how common such appeals were. State's attorneys were quoted as saying that this was just "another method to get the defendant off." Though the article stated that "public defenders and other defense attorneys disagree," no public defender from Cook County was quoted (*Chicago Tribune,* 25 September 1983).

The most glaring example of the silent public defender involved a battle between Criminal Court Judge James M. Bailey and Assistant Public Defender Clair Hillyard. In open court, Bailey called Hillyard's competency into question. Because she had asked for continuances in a case, the judge accused Assistant Public Defender Hillyard of "doing nothing." Bailey then threatened to lock her in the courtroom until she was ready for a trial. Although the incident received prominent attention from the press, no word was heard from anyone in the office except Hillyard herself, who was quoted as saying that she believed that Judge Bailey was being "unfair" (*Chicago Tribune,* 27 April 1982; 8 May 1982).

Contrary to what some apparently believe, lawyers from the office of the public defender do not get into trouble for talking to the press. Lawyers from the office do talk to the press, even to the extent of discussing how the office operates.[4] But they are careful to leave the impression that they speak only for themselves and not for their office.

---

3. Successful appeals of this sort are rare in Illinois. Victory for this appellant came only after his lawyer had been disbarred for actions in another, unrelated case. It should be observed that the lawyer in question was not—and never had been—a public defender.

4. Eisenstein and Jacob, for example, observed in their well-known study *Felony Justice: An Organizational Analysis of Criminal Courts* (1977), that in Cook County, in the public defender's office, and in the courts in general, "individual participants [did not]

Since he assumed the role of public defender in 1973, James Doherty has rarely spoken to (or at least has rarely been quoted in) the local media. I did manage to find two instances in which he did so speak. Although his statements give an indication of how Doherty views his role as a public defender, they are hardly what one might call detailed policy statements:[5]

> In our Judeo-Christian society, the basis of all criminal sanctions should be love and not fear and, if not, then we should take all the crosses and stars of David and make the symbol of our society a statue of a man with a rifle at port arms. (speech before the Illinois Judges Association, reported in the *Chicago Tribune,* 7 December 1974)

> "How can you defend those people? I'll tell you how. Because you don't sit in judgment of them. Canon Five of the Code of Professional Ethics says it's not the duty of the prosecutor to win a case. His job is to see that justice is done. The duty of the defense lawyer is to win by every means legally available. . . .

-----

invite press coverage for themselves, because notoriety was clearly more dangerous for their career than anonymity . . . a public defender featured in a *Newsweek* story about the operation of the office quickly became a private attorney" (131).

Eisenstein and Jacob may have their basic facts correct (an assistant public defender did speak to *Newsweek,* and shortly after that he did leave the office), but their interpretation of these is, I believe, wrong. While it was not documented in their book, I did manage to find what I think is the article in question ("Justice on Trial," *Newsweek,* 8 March 1971). The article featured Constantine Xinos, an assistant public defender who was clearly on his way out of the office anyway. Xinos told the reporter: "The city is dead. . . . The Negroes are going to take over, and when they do . . . they're going to f- - - us over for a while. I don't want to live in a city full of Negroes."

So, said the *Newsweek* reporter of Xinos, "he is thinking of going into private practice with an old pal in Florida" (Goldman and Holt 1971). In fact, Xinos practices in Chicago today.

Although, when responding to my survey, one former public defender did say that his having been on page two of the *Sun Times* did "bring some heat down on my head," other public defenders assured me that they were indeed allowed to speak to the press and that that sort of thing was left to their discretion. I have found several examples of lawyers who had submitted to the press but have found no evidence that notoriety for these lawyers has any negative consequences. For example, one lawyer, Stuart Nudleman, who in 1977 was profiled as a young public defender in the Sunday magazine of the *Sun Times* (Galloway 1977), later rose to a supervisory position in the office and recently has been appointed to the bench.

5. Before he became the public defender, Mr. Doherty was somewhat more forthcoming—at least to the legal community. While serving as chief of the Cook County Public Defender's Office's appeal division, for example, Doherty wrote two articles for the *National Legal Aid and Defender Association Briefcase:* "Bullpen Ethics of a Plea of Guilty," based on remarks made at the 1965 National Legal Aid and Defender Conference (1966), and "Out on the Street" (1971).

You can only serve God through his creatures," says Doherty, the Sunday school teacher and American Legion Chaplain. "The Bible says, 'As you do to the least of these, you do to me. . . . '
Defendants are human beings," he continues, his voice rising in indignation. "It's not my job to say if defendants are guilty or not. My job is to give them the best possible defense. And if I don't, they oughta kick me outta here." (Spencer 1984)

Interestingly, Doherty—like his assistants—speaks as an individual and not as the head of a county agency established to defend the poor. He does not say, "It's *our* job"; he says, "My job is to give them the best possible defense."

Mr. Doherty is not the first public defender to avoid the limelight; indeed, as the *Tribune* noted during the Getty/Boyle controversy, the public defender's office also kept a very low profile during the seventeen years that Getty led the office. The editors of the *Tribune* found that suspicious: "the latest outcroppings of Cook County scandals has occurred in the Office of Public Defender Gerald W. Getty. Judging from the disclosures so far, Mr. Getty and his family and friends have thrived on the relative obscurity in which his Office functions" (19 February 1972).

Admittedly, however diligent the search, it is difficult to prove one's case by showing that there is a lack of information. But the near invisibility of the public defender is consistent with the view that Doherty (and his office) have deliberately kept a low profile—as did Mr. Getty and his office. Given some of Chicago's more dubious political traditions, it is tempting to believe that low visibility implies some sort of political corruption. In fact, there is no evidence to suggest that Doherty is either corrupt and using his office for personal gain or that Doherty is even a machine politician. In fact, even his detractors have admitted to me that corruption is the last thing that one ought to suspect of James Doherty.

I argue that Doherty does not go public because it is not in the public defender's best interest to do so. However nicely the public defender can play its role as a legitimizing resource for the broader criminal justice system, the task of negotiating its own legitimacy while doing so is more complicated, perhaps impossible. The public defender's problem with society—and, to the extent that the courts must reflect society's expectations in order to be legitimate, with the courts—exemplifies what may be the legal profession's oldest and biggest problem: throughout history lawyers have had to endure accusations of both "incompetence and . . . wrongful competence" (Friedman 1973, 84). In other words, members of the legal profession are most vulnerable when they lose cases

69

that ought to have been won or win cases that ought to have been lost. In both situations, lawyers are seen to perpetuate injustice.

Unlike legal scholars, social scientists, and philosophers, the naive observer does not appear to have much trouble deciding what is just and what is unjust—especially when it comes to matters of criminal justice. An important problem for the legal system as it attempts to maintain legitimacy is the potential divergence between social and legal definitions of what is just—as these get to be articulated in terms of outcome. The difference has had, and continues to have, great potential for "disarticulating" the criminal justice system from the wider social system of which it is part (Janowitz 1978). Dahlin's suggestion that the public defender's legitimacy would enhance the legitimacy of the rest of the system is, I will suggest, overly simplistic. The situation is much more complex.

When the Public Defender's Effectiveness Helps

While researching the life of the public defender's organization in Cook County, two cases caught my attention. Both were milestones—each in its own way—in public defender history, and each captured the public defender at his best as a legitimizing asset to the court. The first case was actually the first case—the first defense conducted by a public defense lawyer in Cook County. In 1930, James O'Neill, a 23-year-old father of a small child, was arrested and charged with five burglaries. Although O'Neill pleaded guilty, the state's attorney recommended that the judge give him a very harsh sentence: "1 to life" in prison. Public Defender Bachrach "made an investigation of the case" and found that his crimes had netted this hapless burglar less than five dollars each. "He asked that the sentence be reduced to 1 to 10 years," and this request was granted by the judge (*Chicago Daily Tribune*, 2 October 1930).

The second case involved Richard Speck.[6] Public Defender Gerald Getty, along with assistants James Doherty and James N. Gramenos, conducted the defense. Despite the unpopularity of their cause, accounts of the trial suggest that Getty and his lawyers worked vigorously to secure their client's acquittal. Though Getty, whom *Newsweek* called the "respected Public Defender" from Chicago (17 April 1967), failed to win freedom for Speck, he proved that despite the heinous nature of his crimes, Speck could still receive a fair hearing—all courtesy of the state. Getty summed up what he saw as the essential aspect of the public defender's role in this case: "We tried this case to the best of our abil-

6. Richard Speck was accused of the brutal murder of eight student nurses.

70

ity . . . I feel we tried it in the best traditions of the legal profession" (*Chicago Tribune,* 16 April 1967).

These two cases—O'Neill and Speck—stand out because they exemplify the American justice system's promise to be fair and the public defender's role in operationalizing that promise. Bachrach's winning a reduction for the ineffective and relatively harmless indigent burglar James O'Neill satisfied observers that the little guy need not fear abuse from prosecutors obsessed with overpunishment. Thirty-seven years later, Getty's hard work and forceful defense—coupled with his loss—was no doubt even more satisfying to onlookers: Getty's zealous defense of Speck helped to remove doubts about his guilt. Because everything that could have been done was done in an attempt to find reasonable doubt and Speck was still found guilty, it was fair that he receive the full weight of society's wrath. It is through such cases that effective work by the public defender clearly helps to secure the legitimacy of our courts in the eyes of the general public.

When the Public Defender Hurts the System's Legitimacy

Other sorts of cases are fraught with peril for the public defender in its role as court legitimizer. The problem seems to boil down to differences in social and legal conceptions of the system's responsibility toward those whom it accuses of criminal behavior. The tradition articulated within our legal system is that a defendant is presumed—treated as if—innocent until proved legally guilty of a crime. What is justice in the broader social arena, on the other hand, is typically predicated on a very simple calculus: to the extent that factually guilty people—and only factually guilty people—are punished or negatively sanctioned, the criminal justice system maintains legitimacy. When a discrepancy is perceived to exist, the legal system is seen as compromising social notions of justice—and thus, it loses legitimacy.

As one might expect, because legal standards serve only as what is considered to be a good approximation of whatever justice really is, discrepancies are likely to arise. The public defender, perhaps more than any agency within our system of local justice, is vulnerable on this very point, for it is in the hands of the public defender that such discrepancies are likely to become visible. Unlike prosecutors, who are enjoined by ethics from prosecuting people whom evidence suggests are innocent, the defense attorney is ethically required to zealously defend even the most guilty and abhorrent criminal defendant. In a sense, if the state commits a grievous sin by prosecuting the innocent, the defense attorney wins special grace by defending the guilty. Consider, however, the impact on the system should the successes of the public defender be too frequent or too public. While the occasional defense victory in a trial that ought to have been lost (see, e.g., Hinckley, who attempted to kill President Reagan) may in fact be lauded (as Hinckley's case was by the judge who heard it) as evidence of the essential "integrity of our . . . system" (Parker 1982, 5), arguably the system cannot endure too many victories of this sort without serious threats to its legitimacy.

The precariousness of the public defender's role in the system was highlighted recently for me by a group of (private) lawyers who were discussing the problems that arise because of the public defender's seeming subordination to the judiciary. One of the lawyers suggested that a way around these problems would be to make the public defender's an elected position. After a pause for reflection, the lawyers all laughed as it dawned on them that an aspiring public defender "would have to promise to plead them all guilty to win." The public defender's situation is complicated by the fact that its every legitimate victory potentially undermines the legitimacy of the rest of the system. If the public defender does win fairly, then it can only mean one of two things: (1) the defendant was actually innocent and ought not to have been arrested in the first place and prosecuted in the second or (2) the police and/or prosecutor failed to properly handle the case such that a conviction could be won. From the point of view of everyone, the startling conclusion must be that in a system where everyone is doing his or her job properly, the public defender *does not win* cases.

If the public defender is to help preserve the legitimacy of the rest of the system, he must offer more than a perfunctory defense, however. If all that can be done for a defendant is not done, then this will (as it did during the Due Process Revolution) become obvious to higher courts; convictions will be lost on appeals, and the legitimacy of local justice will be eroded.

The public defender is thus subject to tremendous cross-pressures, and I suggest that, given the complexity of his situation, Doherty has proved himself very effective at impression management: he has managed things in such a way that his office has survived in spite of all of these contradictions. As have his predecessors, Doherty has used obscurity as a tool to manage conflict; he has minimized the strain of cross-pressures by remaining in the shadows. The lack of visibility serves in lieu of legitimacy as protection against threats from outsiders; it can be assessed as a reasoned response to a situation in which the values, expectations, and norms of society as a whole, those of the judiciary, and those of the lawyers within the office often conflict. As a *Sun Times* reporter observed in a masterful understatement in 1977: Doherty does not "trumpet" his record because it would be "impolite": "It's a record that Public Defender Doherty doesn't trumpet. A just society should give equal consideration to both sides in an adversary system, but it's impolite to boast about the accused you get off when you're paid by a public that clamors for convictions and that may not really pay much more than lip service to the principle about being innocent until proven guilty" (Galloway 1977).

Have public defenders in other jurisdictions adopted obscurity as a survival technique? It is difficult to say, since this aspect of public defending has, as yet, been little studied. What little evidence there is, however, suggests that there are other public defense organizations that choose life in the shadows as a way to manage their relationships with outsiders. For example, a public defender from Alameda County, California, reported to Platt and Pollock that

> we feel that the more obscurity we have the more likely it is that we will be permitted to do what we think we ought to do. Basically, I think the public and the Board of Supervisors do not look on us with favor because, to be oversimplified about it, I think they have a kind of gut reaction that we are employed to raise impediments in the way of the conviction of bad people. . . . So we have always felt that we will stay out of the press. We have never called, to my knowledge, in all my years in the office, a press conference. (1974, 9)

Though the office may thrive while in hiding, obscurity is not without costs. An obvious victim is the client. Given the vagaries of the legal system, defense work is more craft than science, and unless the client receives an acquittal, he or she cannot easily judge the quality of the work that the defense lawyer does. Trust is an important part of a successful lawyer/client relationship (Barber 1983, chap. 1). Unless the client trusts the lawyer—and thus can believe it when told "this is the best possible outcome for you"—the client may feel as if he or she has been ripped off and treated unfairly. So, because public defense lawyers are not seen as legitimate professionals, even when they do quality work for their clients, the clients will probably never really know that they got a fair shake in court.

Concluding Remarks: The Lawyers as Victims

In an article written while serving as chief of the Public Defender's Appeals Division in Cook County, James Doherty warned young lawyers to expect no accolades even when they do a terrific job: "Take the case of a defendant who deserves maybe five to ten, who through your efforts receives a two to four on a plea of guilty. You have wrung the prosecutor and the judge out like a dish rag; you squeezed the last bit of sympathy you could out of the case, and you got him a two to four. He is down in the penitentiary about a year when someone asks him what happened. 'Ah hell, I was innocent, but the damn public defender sold me down the river!' " (1966, 130).

Doherty's remark suggests that another victim, more innocent and perhaps less tragic, is the lawyer who works for the public defender's office. In part 1, I have argued that theoretically the public defender has the freedom from judicial interference necessary to do a good job. This freedom, I have argued, is a result of the Supreme Court's elaboration of defendants' rights to an attorney, as well as of the judges' reluctance to get into trouble. In subsequent chapters, it will be suggested that the right of these attorneys to do what must be done for their clients is indeed well established in practice. But, because they are public defenders, these lawyers are denied much that private attorneys are not. How the lawyers compensate—and the hand taken by the office in this process—will be discussed in part 2.

Two

The Public Defender's Office and Its Incumbents

Public Defenders: 5
"We Are the Bastard Children
of Cook County"

Reprinted by permission of Tribune Media Services

What sorts of lawyers join the public defender's office in Cook County? Like most of the lawyers who practice in Cook County, most public defenders are white males. Still, the office is somewhat more differentiated than the local bar: as table 1 shows, there are higher proportions of nonwhites and females in the public defender's office. At least in terms of the proportion of women lawyers, progress toward nonrepresentativeness has gained much in recent years, as I show in figure 3.

Data from a survey of former Cook County public defense lawyers conducted for this research can be used to help flesh out a picture of, if not current public defense lawyers, then at least the characteristics of their immediate predecessors—lawyers who have served in the office over the past twenty-five years.[1] In at least one important respect, the survey findings suggest that public defenders are not as different from the average Chicago lawyer as the image of public defenders might lead

1. In the survey interviews were conducted with sixty former public defenders whose names were randomly selected from a list of 263 lawyers who had served and left the public defender's office some time between 1960 and 1979.

one to expect. The majority (72.8 percent) of lawyers interviewed reported that their fathers had worked at jobs that fell into the higher status
categories of professional, technical, or managerial. Similarly, 73.2 percent of the 545 Chicago lawyers who responded to questions about father's occupation in Heinz and Laumann's 1975 survey (1982, 190) (but
only 58.1 percent of the 535 Chicago lawyers interviewed in Zemans and
Rosenblum's 1975 study [1981, 34]) said that their father's occupation
had been in these categories.

In other respects, public defenders do tend to be different from the
average Chicago lawyer. When it comes to religious preference, for example, former public defenders tend to be less traditional than the lawyers surveyed by Heinz and Laumann. As indicated in table 1, former
public defenders were more apt to indicate "none" or "other" (e.g.,
monotheist, pantheist) when asked about their choice of religion. About

Table 1   Selected Characteristics of the Chicago Bar and Public Defenders

	% Chicago Bar	% Public Defenders
Sex:		
Male	84	78
Female	16	22
Race:		
White	98	96
Black and other	2	4
Religion:		
Catholic	31	32
Jewish	33	27
Protestant	25	15
Other	—	9
None	12	17
National political preference:		
Democrat	37	38
Republican	22	5
Independent	41	53
Other	1	5

Note.—Sex and race statistics for the total bar reflect the percent of each group within the total
number of lawyers registered to practice in Cook County in 1983, cited in "Chicago Lawyer
Alamanac, 1985" (*Chicago Lawyer Magazine*, February 1985). Sex statistic for the public defender's
office is based on names of public defenders as listed in *Sullivan's Law Directory for the State of
Illinois, 1984–85*. Race statistic for the public defender's office is from Monroe Anderson, "How
Institutional Racism Works," (*Chicago Tribune*, November 2, 1984: sec. 1). Religion and political
preference statistics for the local bar are taken from Heinz and Laumann (1982, 13); religion and
political preference statistics for public defenders are from my survey of former public defense
attorneys.

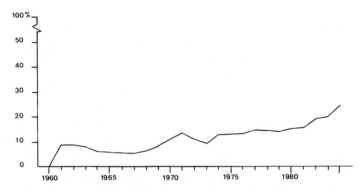

FIGURE 3. Percent of assistant public defenders who are women, 1960–1980. Compiled from *Sullivan's Law Directory for the State of Illinois,* annual eds., 1960–1984.

the same percent said that they were Catholic as did in the larger sample of Chicago lawyers, but fewer former public defenders said that they were Jewish or Protestant.

Heinz and Laumann (1982, 14) noted with some surprise that "a profession that is often thought to be conservative includes so few Republicans and so many . . . independents." Compared to the Chicago bar as a whole, former public defenders appear to be even less conservative and even more independent: only five percent of the sixty former public defenders surveyed would admit to being Republican.

Where the former public defenders are most different from the rest of the bar is in terms of their choice of law school: 65 percent received their law degrees from one of Chicago's four local law schools: DePaul, IIT-Kent, John Marshall, and Loyola. In contrast, only 46 percent of the lawyers responding to Heinz and Laumann's survey (1982, 13) and only 42 percent of those interviewed by Zemans and Rosenblum (1981, 47) said that they had received their degrees from one of these "less prestigious" institutions. Interestingly, the former public defenders' choices for their undergraduate training reflected a great deal of diversity: among the sixty lawyers surveyed were graduates of thirty different colleges or universities, and about half of the lawyers had attended college outside Illinois.

Tenure in the Public Defender's Office

Public defending, like prosecuting, is generally regarded as a short-term job, a "transit station" on the road to a legal career (Heinz and Laumann 1982, 198). For example, the American Bar Association's Committee on

Specialization, Criminal Justice Section, reported in 1976 that "most prosecutors and public defenders Offices are places where neophytes right out of law school go for their training in the courtroom. They usually stay for eighteen months to two years and then move on to private practice" (cited in Kahn and Kahn 1977, 291).

The bulk of public defenders hired each year in Cook County do tend to be young, newly credentialed lawyers with little experience in the practice of law. Among the sixty former public defenders interviewed in this study, for example, 68 percent said that public defending was their first law-related job after passing the bar exam; an additional 15 percent said that although they had held other jobs, they had done so only while waiting for a space in the public defender's office to open up. Similarly, sixteen (80 percent) of the twenty lawyers interviewed who were still serving as assistant public defenders said that it was their first job since being admitted to the Illinois bar (although two of them had taken short-term law jobs while waiting to get into the office).

Not surprisingly, many public defenders said that at the time that they joined the office, they expected to remain no more than a year or two. In fact, several of the current public defenders told me that they had been counseled by law professors *not* to stay more than a year or two: one lawyer remembered that a former public defender had cautioned him that while public defending is an exciting place to begin the practice of law, it is perhaps too exciting; public defending, he was told, is dangerously addicting. But, for the most part, the lawyers remembered thinking when they joined that the major drawback to long-term tenure in the office was that they would be losing out on income from more lucrative forms of practice. In other words, most of the public defenders had joined the office with short-term and pragmatic goals: "A year and a half, *maybe* two years. That's all I wanted to do. To get in, to stay for a short time, learn what I needed to know, get some experience, and then get out" (*004*).

When they are in the middle of a difficult case or having trouble with a client or a judge, it is not uncommon to hear public defenders remind (or perhaps reassure) themselves, "I can't spend my whole life as a public defender; I can't do this forever." The question is, What amount of time falls appropriately short of forever?

In their examination of the patterns of lawyers' careers, Heinz and Laumann suggested that, in the long run, a rapid exit from one's first job is a bad career move, since

> a person's relative chance of survival in his starting job is positively associated with his competitive advantages for subsequent career advancement. At least short-term stability in a starting position, we argue, should facili-

tate the acquisition and consolidation of critical practical learning experiences and the development of useful linkages with colleagues and clients. In contrast, too rapid job turnover is usually disruptive and disorienting to the individual both personally and professionally. Insecurities and uncertainties may be likely to have particularly adverse impacts at the start of careers. On these grounds, we shall regard a high rate of exit in a given status category as reflecting relative vulnerability of persons in that status. (1982, 199)

In terms of its impact on their careers, if public defenders do spend only a short time in the office, then the costs of public defending to the young lawyer may well be greater than simply the sum of foregone income. In addition, in terms of *institutional* needs, if the public defender's office not only hires inexperienced lawyers but also fails to retain them past the point where they have learned the essentials of their craft, then the costs (to both the office and the clients) may well be staggering.

Is public defending, as a first job, as unstable or as short-lived as might be expected? Evidence suggests that, in Cook County at least, it is not. My examination of lists of public defense lawyers published yearly

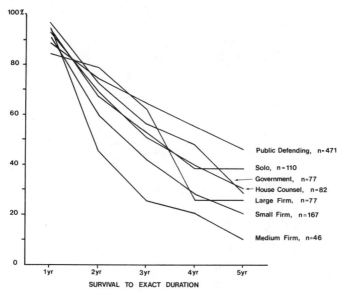

FIGURE 4. Five-year survival functions for first major legal jobs in each practice context. Public defender survival data compiled from *Sullivan's Law Directory for the State of Illinois,* annual eds., 1960–1984, for lawyers hired between 1960 and 1979. Other survival functions from Heinz and Laumann, *Chicago Lawyers* (1982, 200).

in *Sullivan's Law Directory* shows that 65.8 percent of the 471 lawyers hired between 1960 and 1970 were still in the office by the end of what Heinz and Laumann designate as the crucial third year. For the sake of comparison, the "survival function" of these public defenders is plotted with Heinz and Laumann's survival functions for "first major legal jobs in each of five practice contexts" in figure 4. Unexpectedly, the finding is that public defending is one of the most stable practice contexts for new lawyers.

Heinz and Laumann completed their data collection nearly a decade before I assembled the figures for public defenders. Do the differential survival rates say more, for example, about changes in the economic climate for lawyers during the late 1970s and early 1980s than about the public defenders' tenacity or staying power? In other words, has the length of tenure increased owing to a lessening of practice-context alternatives for lawyers? In figure 5 survival functions for four cohort groups of public defenders are plotted. Although the functions seem to indicate that the stability of public defending in the young lawyers' careers has varied over time, it is clear that—relative to other forms of law practice—public defending has been a stable place to start a career in law.

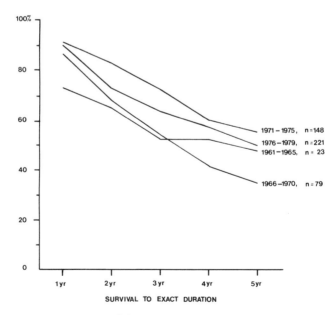

FIGURE 5. Five-year survival functions for assistant public defenders hired 1961–1965, 1966–1970, 1971–1975, 1976–1979. Compiled from *Sullivan's Law Directory for the State of Illinois,* annual eds., 1960–1984.

Whatever the effects that the economic climate outside the office may have had on the lawyers' decisions to stay or leave, it is likely that changes within the office have had an impact. As I discuss below, one of the major attractions of public defense work for the young lawyer is that it provides an almost unparalleled opportunity for courtroom experience. Because the office has increased in size and broadened the scope of its statutory responsibilities in different types of courts, it probably takes lawyers longer to move up to the more coveted trial courts. Thus, the sort of trial experience that the lawyers join to receive has come to occur later in their careers within the office. But more important, I think, the creation of "vertical representation units" (which are discussed in detail in subsequent chapters) has made longer-term defending more attractive. Lawyers in these special units are usually selected from among the more experienced and better lawyers in the office and have more autonomy and often more interesting cases than the average public defender. Finally, one thing that most likely has made longer-term public defending more palatable, if not more attractive, is the fact that salaries for public defenders increased noticeably during the 1970s. (The financial aspect of public defending is attended to later in this chapter.)

However long they stay, it is important to note that most lawyers who choose to do public defending do not spend their entire careers in the office. In figure 6, the ten-year survival rate for public defenders hired between 1960 and 1974 is plotted. Although at five years nearly 45 percent of the lawyers have remained in the office, by the end of the tenth year this figure has dropped to 28 percent.

In the minds of some, the unexpectedly low exit rate from the public defender's office may raise another question: Is the office what Heinz and Laumann would call a "repository" (1982, 198) of lawyers who, as the comic suggests, are jerks who can't make it in the private sector? I asked lawyers who had spent ten years or more in the office, "why haven't you left?"

A lot of people wonder why I'm doing this when I could be making more money at something else. But I'm a cornball, it's my way of redistributing the wealth. I don't have any wealth to distribute, but if I use my skills, it's the same thing. I could see myself staying here until I retire, but our salaries are going down now, by inflation, so I don't know how long I'll be able to afford this. I couldn't afford this if I were married.

I like doing criminal law, but I talk to people all the time who are out on their own, and it just doesn't seem all that appealing. The least appealing aspect of criminal law is trying to get paid, and working out the financial arrangements. Here it is just like a little ivory tower. I get to just be here and deal with the law but not the money end of it. I never dread coming to

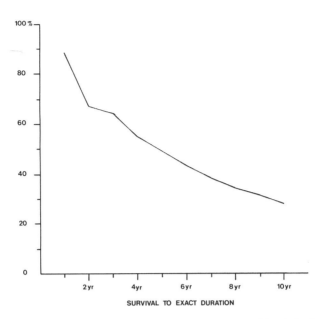

FIGURE 6. Ten-year survival functions for 215 assistant public defenders hired 1960–1974. Compiled from *Sullivan's Law Directory for the State of Illinois,* annual eds., 1960–1984.

work. My work is divided between my desk work, in-court work, in-court trial work, negotiating, interviewing clients, motions, bench trials, jury trials—all of them are different. Plus all the time I spend out on the street, looking for people, looking for information. So, it's not like it is any one job, it's not like it's any one job you could get tired of easily. But unfortunately, the money end of it is pretty low, and I think that the time is coming when I will have to face up to the reality and move on.

I have no way of determining whether the more senior public defenders tend to be lawyers who could not make it on the outside (or even whether not being able to make it on the outside means the lawyer is a bad lawyer).[2] On the basis of the sorts of attributions that their colleagues tend to make about these diehards in the office, I sense that for some it is true; for many others, it is not. But it can be remarked that, if

2. It is difficult to predict, at least on the basis of any demographic characteristic, what sort of lawyer will stay the longest in the office. When, for example, one compares the survival rates of lawyers who attended the less prestigious law schools with the survival rates of those who attended the more prestigious schools, no significant differences are found.

84

there is anything that suggests the fact that the public defender's office is not perceived as a legitimate legal institution, it is how quickly the idea of the office as "repository" follows after the finding that it is not just a short-term job for many of its lawyers. Logically, it need not, of course, be one or the other—unless one presumes that there is something wrong with public defending.

Before leaving the subject of tenure, it is important to note some implications of the fact that public defenders stay on the job longer than expected. Figure 7 shows the proportion of lawyers in the office each year who have stayed longer than the normal eighteen months or two years. The solid line indicates the percent of lawyers who are in their fifth year or more. Clearly, the public defender's clients are more apt to get experienced counsel than one might have expected.[3] In chapter 6 I will explore in more detail how lawyers with different levels of seniority can expect to be assigned to different sorts of clients and cases.

FIGURE 7. Percent of lawyers in the public defender's office in their third year or more and percent of lawyers in their fifth year or more, 1961–1983. Compiled from *Sullivan's Law Directory of the State of Illinois,* annual eds., 1961–1983.

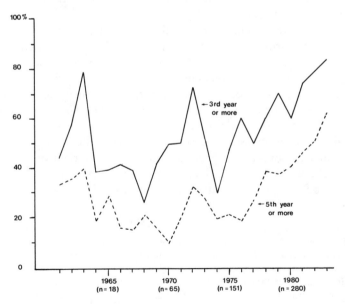

3. It may seem presumptuous to call a lawyer in his or her third year of practice "experienced." Indeed, most of the public defenders with whom I spoke agreed that even after three years a lawyer has a great deal to learn. But, they said, three years of public

Public Defenders' Expectations

> They are a fraternity of the righteous, these low-paid lawyers, dogmatists of
> the criminal justice system, who often find themselves lining up on the side
> of rapists, murderers, child molesters and drug dealers. (Spencer 1984, 1)

When it comes to understanding what public defending is and how it
works, more important, I think, than *who* public defenders are is what
they wish to become. What moves a lawyer to begin his or her career in
the public defender's office? There is a variety of reasons, of course, but
among lawyers who have worked as Cook County public defenders one
reason stands out: all but one of the twenty current public defenders and
72 percent of the sixty former public defenders interviewed in the course
of this research said that they had joined the office because they believed
it to be a good place to gain experience and to practice law as a trial
attorney. Many (fifteen of the twenty current and about half of the former public defenders) also mentioned that they saw public defending as a
way to make a positive contribution to society, but the chief attraction
for most was the opportunity that public defenders have to do trial work.
As one lawyer pointed out, "There were several kinds of public service
things I could have done, but I wanted to be a trial attorney, and so I
became a public defender" (*012*).

There are few other options available to the lawyer who wants immediate gratification of a desire to gain the skills and experience necessary to be a good trial lawyer; one alternative is to be become a
prosecutor, and many public defenders mentioned that they had applied
to the state's attorney's office at the same time that they had applied for a
job with the public defender's office. On the other hand, for most new
lawyers the idea of becoming a solo practitioner (as one of them expressed it) was unthinkable, out of reach because they lacked the necessary financial resources and legal skills to make it on their own right out
of law school. At the same time, no job with a law firm is considered
such a good prospect for gaining litigation experience quickly (Stewart

---

defending provides the courtroom experience of a dozen years in private practice. As one
former public defender put it, "After six years in the office, I probably had the trial
experience of a fifty-year-old" (*061*).

    In fact, in several states (Florida, Minnesota, Nebraska, Nevada), only three years
of practice as a criminal lawyer is sufficient for the lawyer who wishes to qualify as a
specialist in criminal law (there are other requirements, of course, including, in various
states, a certain number of trials, continuing legal education credits, etc.). In other states,
more than three years is required to become certified (Washington state requires four
years; California requires at least five years) (Kahn and Kahn 1977).

1983). In a private law firm a lawyer may wait years before being allowed even to speak in a courtroom. The experience of Martha Solinger, a fourth-year associate in a prominent New York law firm who was profiled in the *American Lawyer's* "Up and Coming" column (December 1983) provides a good example. Although described by a partner in her firm as a "good litigation associate," during her years with the firm Solinger had taken active part in only one trial, where she was allowed to conduct *one* direct examination. Public defenders, as I discuss in greater detail in chapter 6, usually are not made to wait a moment for prominent courtroom roles. While a few lawyers complained they had not moved up in the office quickly enough, every one of them acknowledged that if there is one thing that a public defense lawyer gets, it is courtroom experience. Other expectations the lawyers had, however, were not so happily met.

Surprises

When I asked current public defenders what had surprised them about the job, almost all responded by saying that one of their biggest surprises (and disappointments) had been the lack of respect given public defenders. There is no doubt that new public defenders encounter a lot of surprises, but, for the most part, they do not *remember* anything else. The issue of respect was one that surfaced time and time again whenever I talked with public defenders. Ask, "Who does not respect public defenders?" and the typical response is, "Everyone."

Public defenders are quite certain that people in the community do not appreciate the quality of their work, do not respect them as capable, competent lawyers. Some put this assessment quite succinctly: "We have a reputation as crummy lawyers" (*002*); "Everybody thinks the Public Defender's Office is just dreck" (*010*). "There is a notion," another lawyer said, "that public defenders are an inferior breed compared to real lawyers" (*008*).

According to public defenders, it is not only unknowing outsiders who fail to acknowledge their worth as attorneys; a lack of respect is something that they encounter in the courtroom as well. Although some public defenders believe that many judges are prosecution minded—and thus generally tougher on defense attorneys than on prosecutors—they seem to regard this as inevitable, if not entirely fair. What the lawyers find less easy to accept is that judges often treat them as second-class lawyers. In some courtrooms, I was told, this merely meant that judges are more considerate of private attorneys, calling their cases before calling the public defenders' cases—so that private defense attorneys do not have to "hang around all morning to get through their call" (*013*).

"There is good reason," one public defender allowed, "for calling the public defender's cases last: time is money for the private attorney" (*007*); "But still, the private attorney walks in and gets his cases called and he's out of there. The public defender's cases don't get called sometimes until 11:00 or 11:30. After a while, something as small as that can really gall you. When it starts to gall you is when you know that you are a busy person too" (*001*).

Only one lawyer said that a judge's attitude toward public defenders had ever hurt a client's case. It was not the public defender's freedom to be able to defend clients as well as private lawyers could that seemed to be at issue but the public defender's right to be treated as a "real lawyer":[4] "[Judges] view the public defenders very similar to how they view court clerks. We are the gophers, we run for things. Whenever there's something the judge needs done, if there is not a clerk available, the judge gives it to the public defender and has him do it. They would *never* think of having a state's attorney do it. But public defenders have to do this *silly* stuff" (*007*).

Public defenders seem to learn to put up with a lot, just because they have to. But I was assured that they do have their limits. There are, I was told, some things that a lawyer cannot put up with, some things that a lawyer cannot allow a judge to do. If something is going to hurt a client's case, the lawyers said, they must object. One lawyer told me, for example, of a case in which he had actually pursued his objection to the Illinois Supreme Court, where he sought and received a writ of mandamus—a ruling telling the trial court judge to follow the law properly. Over and over I was told that when a judge refuses to let you argue a motion that is important to your case, you must object; when the judge allows into evidence what you believe to be incompetent or improper material, you must object: "There are times when you have got to say, 'Come on judge, let's take off our coats, and let's get it on.' You have to do that sometimes and *of course* it's scary. Now I have been scared, and I've backed down sometimes when I shouldn't have. But I go back in there the next day and start all over again, because I will have gone home that night and chewed myself out for backing down" (*003*). But when a judge's treatment of a lawyer merely reflects a disregard of the lawyer's dignity, the lawyers feel that to fight back will *hurt* their client: "Everything you do is going to affect your client, you know? If I'm acting like an asshole, if I'm being a jerk, *or if I'm taking myself too seriously*, I've got a client who's going to suffer. As opposed to sometimes if I can shuffle or

4. Fuchs-Epstein heard similar comments from New York Legal Aid attorneys, who complained that judges "would never call you by name, or call you 'counselor': they would just shout 'Legal Aid' as if you weren't a professional person" (1983, 125).

tap-dance a little bit, I get my client to walk out with no criminal record, or time served, or whatever. And it never bothered me to do that [shuffle or tap-dance], never. [Pause] Well, as I'm getting older perhaps it *is* starting to bother me a little bit" (*004*).

So, public defenders learn not to take themselves too seriously, to "laugh a lot at dumb jokes that judges make" (*002*), and they do it, they say, not to promote themselves but to promote their clients' cases.

Ironically, it is the clients—for whom the public defenders swallow their pride—who tend to be among the most dismissive of the lawyers' claims to respect. Two-thirds (66.7 percent) of the former public defenders interviewed agreed with the statement, "My clients often seemed to doubt my ability as a lawyer just because I was a public defender." As many of the current public defenders told it, many of their clients even refused to recognize the public defenders as lawyers: "I was *really* surprised by the way my clients felt about me—the clients' attitude can be summed up by what we heard again today: 'I don't want a PD, I want a real lawyer.' That happens all the time. They just won't believe we are really lawyers" (*005*).

There can be little doubt that public defenders are irked by what they see as the refusal of many judges, most clients, and many others to recognize the validity of their claims to being "real lawyers." As one public defender emphasized to me, "I'm a real lawyer, I went to a real law school, I passed a real bar exam!" (*019*).

Money

A cynical observer might suspect that a more vulgar concern is hidden by the lawyers' indignation about having their claims to real professionalism dismissed so cavalierly by clients, judges, and even people whom they meet in random social encounters. Such cynicism might be encouraged by the fact that when you ask one of these lawyers, "What's the *worst* thing about being a public defender?" they do not say, "The lack of respect"; the unhesitating reply is apt to be, "The money."

What belies the cynical assessment, however, is the fact that no public defender said that he or she had ever expected to make a fortune as a public defender; all of them knew that it was, for a lawyer, a relatively low-paying position. Most of them said that they had joined for something more valuable than money—the chance to gain experience and/or do social service. The telling thing, I think, is the fact that when public defenders complained about money, they did so with respect to the fact that they were being paid less than their counterparts in the state's attorney's office. Within the office there is a widespread belief that public defense attorneys are paid less than assistant state's attorneys.

Officially, this belief is wrong. In the mid-1970s, James Doherty, the public defender, sought and was said to have received parity between the salaries of his assistants and the lawyers who work in the state's attorney's office (see Cook County Annual Appropriations Bill 1979).[5] When reminded of this, most assistant public defenders concede that there is *supposed* to be parity but deny that it actually exists. Why do they refuse to believe the official line? Some just know state's attorneys are paid more because "that's what everyone says." Others cite evidence that they say they have accumulated through personal comparisons; says one who is reputed to be one of the best lawyers in the office: "I know I have been here nine years. I know others who have been in the State's Attorney's Office nine years who are making four or five thousand dollars a year more than I am. So you just know. It doesn't take much to figure it out."

There was a time when lawyers in the Cook County public defender's office clearly were paid very much less than state's attorneys. In 1931, for example, the ceiling on an assistant public defender's salary was $300 a year, while assistant state's attorneys were earning as much as $1,000. The custom of paying public defenders less than state's attorneys was one followed for many years, although eventually the differences became smaller. By 1955, for example, while the highest salary for an assistant state's attorney was $1,200 a month, an assistant public defender might earn only as much as $750.

More recent comparison shows that the discrepancy between public defenders' and state's attorneys' salaries has diminished even more—especially since "parity" was achieved. In table 2, the cumulative proportion of lawyers in each office who are paid at the various levels is shown. Clear progress toward parity has been made over the past decade. Notwithstanding official pronouncements, however, examination of budgetary figures shows that, in 1984, public defense attorneys, on average, were paid $817 a year less than state's attorneys: in 1984, the average assistant public defender was paid $29,863, and the average assistant state's attorney's salary was $30,680.

A few (very senior) assistant public defenders *had* resolved the difference between the office's position that parity has been achieved and the widespread feeling that it has not. These lawyers suggested that salary differences *within* the office account for the perception that public defender salaries are subpar. Some of these lawyers (illicitly) obtained a

5. Historically, such salary differences were rife throughout the country. In 1973, for example, Legal Aid lawyers in New York went on strike to protest their low salaries and poor working conditions. Owing to their efforts, they won parity in salaries with their courtroom adversaries, the assistant district attorneys (Fuchs-Epstein 1983, 127).

Table 2 Budgeted Salary Distributions for Assistant Public Defenders (PD) and Assistant State's Attorneys (SA)

Yearly Rate ($)	1973 %PD	1973 %SA	1977 %PD	1977 %SA	1981 %PD	1981 %SA	1984 %PD	1984 %SA
$51,000+								100.0
48,001–51,000							100.0	98.1
45,001–48,000							98.8	97.1
42,001–45,000						100.0	97.1	93.9
39,001–42,000				100.0	100.0	99.8	92.6	89.6
36,001–39,000			100.0	99.8	98.3	99.0	88.1	82.6
33,001–36,000			97.7	98.2	88.1	98.2	82.7	79.5
30,001–33,000		100.0	95.0	94.8	81.8	82.7	75.3	72.1
27,001–30,000		99.5	89.7	93.1	71.9	82.7	54.5	55.5
24,001–27,000	100.0	99.5	82.1	80.1	55.2	72.1	39.3	36.8
21,001–24,000	98.5	91.3	64.2	66.4	37.7	55.0	20.2	17.5
18,001–21,000	96.1	79.2	35.3	46.0	16.0	37.4		
15,001–18,000	89.7	56.0	12.9	17.5		16.1		
12,001–15,000	61.9	10.6						
9,000–12,000	11.1	2.4						
N	126	207	263	448	286	528	336	555

Source.—Cook County Annual Appropriations Bills (1973, 1977, 1981, 1984).

list of who gets paid what. On two separate occasions lawyers who had seen this list explained their findings to me. As one told it, salaries are closer to parity than had been expected—but until he had seen the list he could not have been expected to understand this, because he did not know the "whole picture."

Q: So, what is the whole picture?
R: See, before we had been looking at state's attorneys who had been lawyers as long as us and knew or had found out that they were getting paid much more than we were. Now we find that the problem is that there are a lot of ghosts in our office.
Q: Ghosts?
R: Yea, ghosts—people you don't see, who get paid a lot of money.
Q: What are they doing? Why don't you see them?
R: [Laugh] They are doing their private practice, and they have enough clout to get by without doing their jobs here.

Table 3 Comparison of Total Appropriations and Selected Budget Categories Per Assistant in the Public Defender's Office and in the State's Attorney's Office, 1984

Budget Category	Public Defender's Office (N)		State's Attorney's Office (N)	
	Total Budgeted Amount ($)	Per Assistant (336)	Total Budgeted Amount ($)	Per Assistant (555)
Transportation	75,000	223	85,000	153
Communication	74,412	221	375,000	675
Postage	15,000	45	90,000	162
Printing and photostat	125,000	372	100,000	180
Professional and technical memberships	0	0	1,000	2
Books, periodicals, and publications	15,000	45	75,000	135
Office supplies	27,000	80	1,175,000	315
Total appropriations (excluding salaries and wages of regular employees)	1,633,113	4,860	5,334,282	9,611
Total appropriations	14,281,182	42,500	28,861,267	52,000

Source.—Cook County Annual Appropriations Bill, 1984.

Q: Are you telling me that there were names on the list, names of people you didn't even know were public defenders?

R: [Laugh] No, no, no. We knew they were public defenders, but we didn't know they were making that much money, and we knew they weren't doing anything for *that* kind of money.

In other words, what I heard from a few attorneys was that there *is* salary parity—or almost parity—between the public defender's office and the state's attorney's office but that the average public defender does not benefit from this parity, since some of the money that would bring parity to the average public defender is being siphoned off by ghosts. (I should add that I did not ever see this list and that I have no knowledge of whether lawyers in the state's attorney's office have made similar discoveries about ghosts on their payroll.)

A further look at budget materials suggests that the public defenders' perception that they are being treated unfairly by those who hand out the money (i.e., the county board) may be fueled as well by the fact that, compared to the state's attorney's office, the public defender organization is underfunded. In 1984, the public defender received a total appropriation of $14.3 million from the Cook County Board of Commissioners. The state's attorney's office received more than twice that, $28.9 million. Because the state's attorney's office is quite a bit larger, the two figures are not directly comparable. One way of comparing their budget totals, however, is to divide by the number of attorneys in each office: in 1984, the state's attorney has budgeted slots for 555 assistants; the public defender has 336. Simple division shows that the county invests $52,000 per lawyer in the state's attorney's office while the public defender receives only 82 percent of that or $42,000 per lawyer. What does this imply about the quality of life within each office? As table 3 shows, the availability of resources that the lawyers might use is much more limited for attorneys in the public defender's office. In terms of supplies, for example, the state's attorney has four times the budget allocation per attorney.[6]

Public defense attorneys feel poor, and they often refer to them-

---

6. I have learned that one must be cautious when making detailed comparisons between budgets of different agencies. Several informed sources have warned me that money budgeted to fund one account may be "robbed" to cover a shortfall in another account. For example, an overage in photocopy costs may be paid out of supplies money.

Similarly, I judged it unwise to compare salaries of public defenders within different units (e.g., the average salary of a public defender to the average salary of a state's attorney, both of whom are assigned to the juvenile divisions of their respective offices) because the salary of a lawyer serving in a particular division may be (and often is) paid out of funds appropriated to pay lawyers in another division.

selves by such phrases as "the bastard children of Cook County," "cousins in the country," "soldiers at the last outpost," etc. Much of their dissatisfaction seems to stem more from a feeling of relative deprivation than from anything else. Public defenders do not seem to feel, in other words, that they should be paid more per se but that they should be paid as much as state's attorneys who are, they think, doing comparable work. In an important sense, the issue of money is one of respect. Being paid less than state's attorneys is taken as yet another sign that their professional status—and the value of their services as lawyers—is being ignored.

Concluding Remarks: The Importance of Respect

As argued in part 1, the failure of judges, clients, and others to acknowledge the validity of the individual public defense lawyer's claims to legitimacy as a lawyer—or, in other words, the failure of judges, clients, and others to perceive public defenders as real lawyers—results from the peculiar relationship that exists between the public defender organization and its environment, from the institution's failure to (or choice not to) negotiate its own legitimacy. In this and in the chapters to follow, the level of analysis shifts to a focus on the organization and its relationship to its incumbents. While what the public defender appears to be to outsiders is strongly dictated by the needs of the courts, the intraorganizational structure and organizational content is, I will argue, more directly responsive to the needs of its incumbents. At this level of analysis it will become clear that the public defenders' desire for respect and validation of their claims to being "real lawyers" (or, more specifically, real *trial* lawyers) is neither epiphenomenal nor unimportant. The lawyers' motives are the crucial key to understanding the public defender's office's structure and—as I explain in part 3—to explaining what makes public defending work as well as it does.

These lawyers don't work for me, I merely give them the
opportunity to serve.

J. J. Doherty, 1985, personal communication to author

There was a time when the presumption was that professionals and bureaucracy do not mix (Goss [1959] 1980; Gouldner 1954; Kornhauser
1962; Miller 1967; Parsons 1947). "The consensus seemed to be that
[professionals] require a kind of autonomy that is antithetical to Weber's
model of rational-legal bureaucracy. . . . The proper way for such men
to work is as members of a self-regulating 'company of equals'" (Friedson and Rhea 1972, 185).

More recently, observers have questioned the assumption that inte-
grating professionals into organizations is necessarily problematic. From
research that has focused primarily on the nature of different sorts of
health care facilities, a model of the "professional bureaucracy" has
emerged (Heydebrand and Noell 1973). While definite hierarchical and
impersonal bureaucratic structure exists within such organizations, it
performs a facilitating role and works *around* professionals who "play a
central role in the achievement of the primary organization objective"
(Scott 1965, 66). Those in the administrative bureaucratic structure may
be responsible for establishing and maintaining auditing and billing procedures, nonprofessional personnel policies, support services, and other

housekeeping functions, but, we are told, they leave to professionals the tasks of controlling, directing, and evaluating the work of professionals.

Still, even within the professional work groups, clear-cut hierarchies of control may exist. In hospitals, medical students and interns are supervised by residents, and residents are supervised by attending physicians or professors (Bosk 1979). In law firms, associates are supervised by senior associates and/or partners, and senior associates are supervised by partners (Stewart 1983). Within such organizations those who have not yet passed beyond being house staff or into the partner stage technically do not have their own clients and do not have final say over the course of treatment or type of intervention used in a case. Instead, they assist in caring for their seniors' patients or clients.

To an extent, the status of young professionals in these pyramidic organizations undermines traditional ideas about sources of professional authority. Often it is argued that, unlike corporate administrators who "ultimately gain legitimate authority to control work from their legal status of 'officer,'" professionals receive their authority from state licensing (Friedson 1975, 9), that their right to practice is legitimated by the state (Collins 1979, 133). Though medical students, interns, and, in some instances, residents are not fully licensed, associates in law firms are. Yet, notwithstanding their licenses, within institutions they are typically subject to close supervision from their seniors. Thus, within a firm, authority to control work is granted not just by official license but by other members of the firm—by elevating an associate to partner status. Within a professional bureaucracy, then, it is only the *senior* members who function as a company of equals. Though law firms may have senior partners and hospitals chiefs of staff, their function is primarily administrative and their authority is rarely invoked over partners or attending physicians (Friedson 1975). For seniors in the professional organization there is what one might call a presumption of competency; following from this presumption, professional etiquette makes it taboo to interfere in another's work. The presumption does not extend to juniors, however, and thus the relationships between juniors and seniors are governed by different sorts of conventions.

Within a particular professional pyramid, the relationship between juniors and seniors seems to depend, in the first place, on the style of the organization. For example, a national survey of third- and fourth-year associates in large law firms found that different firms tend to treat their associates differently. In some firms, associates are privy to more organizational decision making, inside knowledge about the firm's finances, and case management strategies. Thus, some firms were found to "do an excellent job of training associates and introducing them to their firms and to the profession. . . . [But] others don't—which may be why so many lawyers find themselves with few marketable skills even after several years of 'practice'" (Stewart 1982a, 37). The report concluded: "[In some firms] partners are clinging to the antiquated notion that associates are servants who should demonstrate their loyalty by following orders without complaint or question. A number of respondents told us that they feel like furniture" (Stewart 1982b, 44).

Beyond organizational style, the young lawyer or doctor must confront or adjust to the idiosyncrasies of the particular senior who supervises him or her. Even *within* firms or hospitals that have no reputation for "god-gopher" relationships between partners and associates or attendings and residents there are great differences. As Bosk found, the style of a particular attending physician gives a particular service or work group "color" and determines both the way in which patients' treatment is organized and the amount of freedom or input that is allowed the junior clinician.

However negative the usual assessment of bureaucracy, one of the most positive aspects of this form of organization is the fact that its members, to a large extent, are protected from the whims and capriciousness of superordinates (Perrow 1979; Weber 1978). Because of the autonomy granted seniors in a professional bureaucracy, however, fewer procedural protections are enjoyed by junior members than one might expect in a more traditional bureaucracy. A young associate in a New York law firm studied by Stewart relates how this lack of protection can lead to a great deal of perceived injustice:

> The highest level of achievement for an associate . . . was to take a deposition, and you were lucky to do that. I had prepared three volumes of Q's and A's for a deposition witness. I spent weekends, long hours, about six weeks on this set. My drafts were passed on by two partners, who made a few changes. Then this corporate partner got his hands on it. He reorganized everything. A few of his changes were valid, a lot were just stylistic, quite a few were mistakes. He didn't know the facts of the case well enough. Then I was told that a more senior associate was stepping in to take the deposition using my script. I was furious. (Stewart 1983, 96–97)

Though when the junior member of the team agrees with the decisions or style of his or her supervisor, this lack of freedom is felt to be less "chafing," both the surgical residents in Bosk's study and the associates interviewed by Stewart felt—as Bosk put it—"defenseless against the whims" of their seniors (1979, 66).

The Public Defender and Professional Bureaucracy

Given what has been learned from sociological accounts of how such organizations work, the public defender is a surprise or not, depending on what level of reality is inspected. At least on paper the structure of the office seems to fit the professional bureaucracy model. Closer examination of the structure and of its contents, however, suggests that the Cook County Public Defender's Office has a unique approach to organizing professionals.

A. Structure

The office is divided into seven divisions.[1] For the most part, lawyers in different divisions work in different courts. There are two trial divisions, one headquartered in the Criminal Courts building at 26th and California Streets and one at the 13th and Michigan Avenue facility. In addition, there is an appellate division, a juvenile division, and two municipal divisions. Lawyers in one municipal division represent clients in misdemeanor trials and felony preliminary hearings in the First Municipal District (Chicago), and lawyers in the other division cover the same types of cases in the remaining five municipal divisions of Cook County. As figure 8 suggests, the lawyers who work for this office are spread throughout the county. Finally, there is a seventh division called the Multiple Defendant Division. Created in 1984, this division represents clients who are codefendants. In cases involving more than one defendant, problems can arise when the defense of one conflicts with the defense of another. In the past, private attorneys would be appointed and paid by the state in order to avoid even the appearance that the interests of antagonistic codefendants were being compromised by their being represented by lawyers from the same firm. This new division provides public defenders from a separate office (headquartered at 13th and Michigan) to take the place of private attorneys. As figure 9 shows, the basic structure of the office follows that of the Cook County courts in which the public defender has statutory responsibility for defending clients.

1. *Administrative Structure*

Further bureaucratic expectations are fulfilled when one examines the public defender's organizational chart (fig. 9). At the head of the office is James J. Doherty, who, as noted in chapter 4, was appointed in 1972 to head the office. Aiding Doherty is First Assistant Public Defender Justine I. Knipper (who, in 1961, was the first woman hired to work as an as-

---

1. According to the 1984–1985 listing in *Sullivan's Law Directory,* there are now officially eight divisions in the office. In addition to the seven listed above, the office includes a Mental Health and Law Division. At present, there is only one lawyer in this division—Donald Paull, a psychologist, who, after some years teaching at the college level, returned to school and obtained a law degree.

sistant public defender in Cook County) and Second Assistant Public Defender Thomas J. Reynolds. At the next level of authority, each division is headed by a chief of division (formerly called assistant in charge). Divisions are divided into work groups called task forces. Each task force is headed by a supervisor or, in some cases, an assistant supervisor.

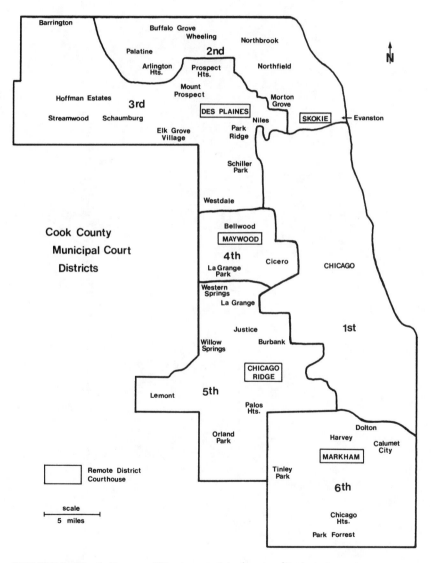

FIGURE 8. Cook County, Illinois, municipal court districts.

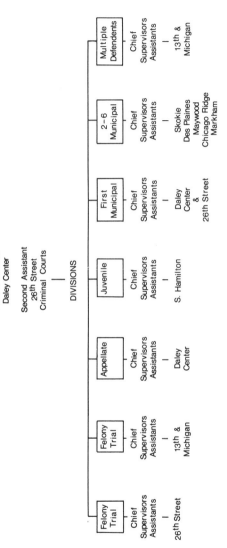

FIGURE 9. Organizational structure of the public defender's office.

2. Forms of Defense

The majority of assistant public defenders are assigned to what is called horizontal defense, meaning that these lawyers are assigned to specific courtrooms, not to cases or clients. In most instances, each task force is made up of attorneys who work in adjacent courtrooms. When a public defender is transferred to a different courtroom, even if it is one in the same division, he or she will often have to change task forces, supervisors, partners, and even desks.

Horizontal defense is zone defense. What it means to the indigent defendant in say, a felony case, is that at each stage of the process his or her case will be represented by different public defenders, and, although a file follows each client through the system, defendants will likely have to tell their stories to different lawyers at each stage of the case. Figure 10 shows the possible number of stages through which a felony case in the Cook County courts may proceed. At each step the defendant will not only have different public defenders but different judges and state's attorneys as well, for these too are organized horizontally.

There are important exceptions to the general rule of horizontal defense. Within the trial division at 26th and California, lawyers in two

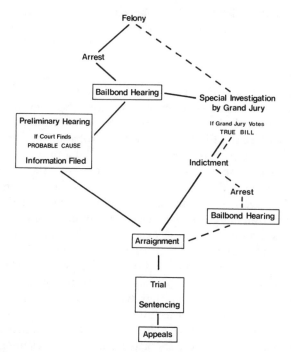

FIGURE 10. The felony justice process in Cook County, Illinois.

special task forces provide vertical or ongoing representation. In addition, a small vertical unit works in the juvenile division. These lawyers are assigned to clients, not to courtrooms. Lawyers in vertical units follow their clients from the preliminary hearing stage through arraignment, trial, and sentencing. At present, there are about thirty lawyers doing vertical defense work in the Cook County Public Defender's Office. These lawyers and the nature of their work are discussed in much greater detail in chapter 7.

B. Organizational Content

Where the office does not fit the expected model of the professional bureaucracy is in terms of its content. The first clue to this was the fact that no public defender even came close to complaining that he or she was treated—in the office—as anything less than a real lawyer, a competent, responsible, trustworthy professional. While attitudes of judges and clients may have been resented, to hear these lawyers tell it, within the office they work as a company of equals; there are no assistants in positions comparable to intern or associate. Each lawyer is presumed competent. Allegiance to this presumption, as I show below, is strong at both formal and informal levels of the organization. Indeed, it seems to be the major organizing principle underlying public defending in Cook County.

1. *Training*

The presumption of competency appears to apply to public defenders from the moment that they are appointed to the office—even if they have never before set foot in a courtroom. The Cook County Public Defender's Office has no official orientation or probationary or training period that lawyers must pass through before taking on real cases, before being given sole responsibility for a client's case. (It is not known whether this is typical of public defender offices. James Kunen [1983], writing of his experiences as an assistant public defender in Washington, D.C., did mention having a six-week-long training program.)

In Cook County, with rare exceptions, different attorneys related the same kind of stories about their first days on the job. Although each was a properly licensed attorney and thus in theory qualified to practice, however flattered they may have been, most were horrified to discover that they were to be treated as if they were actually qualified. Memories of their first days still evoked feelings of discomfort; during the interviews stories about those days were typically accompanied by a great deal of nervous laughter and punctuated with such disclaimers as "You won't believe this," "It was crazy," "I couldn't believe it," or "It was awful!" How do public defenders get trained? "I got trained by showing up there and they handed me a file and said, 'You are starting trials.' There was supposed to be, I remember [laugh], a lawyer there [laugh], but he wasn't there. I think he had already quit the office [laugh]; he never showed up" (005). Other attorneys related similar experiences: one said that he did not know what to do and that there was no one there to tell him: "No one ever told what they wanted. In fact, when I was sent to the branch court, I was plopped right down in the middle of the court-room with a heavy call. I was the only public defender there. In the courtroom next door there were two in there, and they were able to answer some questions, but I was all alone. Can you believe this?" (002).

Most of the other attorneys said that they had had some support from partners, but to many this seemed inadequate; in several instances, either the partner left after a short time or was himself also relatively new. One lawyer recalled his introduction to the misdemeanor court in which he began his career as a public defender: "I had a partner for one week and then I was put on my own. It was crazy, we used to do fifteen bench trials a day and I had, on the average, forty clients a day" (004). Even the exceptions to the rule of no training seemed unexceptional.

Q: Did you receive any training when you started?
R: No. Well, the first day, _____ _____, who was the supervisor there, had his supposed training program. He took you in his office and read aloud. He said, "Okay, you are to sit here, this is your training." It was 9:00 in the morning [when we started], and he closed the door and he just read. Literally. He said: "Okay, here is an interview sheet, you put the client's name there and you don't put your name there." I can't believe I sat there all day and just listened to him read! This went on until about 5:00 P.M., and then I said I had to go because [someone] was picking me up. And that was it. The next day they gave me [case] files and said, "Start talking." (008)

Some fared better. One lawyer related: "I never could have made it if my partner hadn't known what she was doing" (020). For the most part, though, public defenders did not report having been trained in the usual sense. One put it this way: "I certainly learned a lot, but not because the office planned it that way" (019). "Trial by fire" was a phrase often used by these attorneys to describe how they had learned their jobs. Many of the lawyers were uncomfortable with that. Several lawyers said that they had sought outside help; many had attended the National Institute for Trial Advocacy (NITA). Although the office does provide some schol-arship funds for such training purposes, it is often not enough. One lawyer told me that in order to finance his NITA tuition, he had hocked the silver that he and his wife had received as wedding presents.

103

It might well be suspected that the lack of training experienced by some public defenders was due to the rapid expansion of the office during certain years. Yet, on checking this, I found that even attorneys hired in years with relatively low turnover reported that they had received about the same amount of training—that is, essentially none.

2. Supervision

State statute requires that the public defender "keep a record of the services rendered by him and prepare and file monthly a written report of

COOK COUNTY PUBLIC DEFENDER

COURT)
JUDGE) _____ ASSISTANT _____ DISTRICT _____

Date	Total Ind or Inf	Total Defendants	Total Appearances

FIGURE 11. The Public Defender's Service Report Form.

such services transmitting a copy of such report to the Clerk of the Circuit Court for the judges thereof" (*Illinois Revised Statutes,* Chap. 34, sec. 5608). In figure 11, a facsimile of the form used by the public defender to gather information for his report is shown; assistants are required to fill out this form "regularly." What is most interesting about this form is that while it asks for the number of indictments or informations, defendants represented, and appearances filed by the lawyer, it does not have a query concerning case outcomes. In fact, many public defenders said that no one really seems to care about case outcomes, at least not officially. As one experienced public defender told me: "In the last year there was one stretch when I won ten cases in a row. And the people I work with knew it—'he's on a hot streak,' they would say, and that was kind of fun. But it wouldn't make a difference downtown. Doherty would be glad, I guess, but it wouldn't make a difference" (*002*). When I asked, "What if you had *lost* ten cases in a row?" he said that "would not have made any difference either: no one would care, no one would say anything." When I asked supervisors if they were required to fill out forms or make any sort of evaluation of their supervisees, they all said no.

One way to interpret this apparent lack of structured accountability is to argue that all that the office cares about is that the assistants handle a specific number of cases—that quantity, not quality, is what counts. But usually the lawyers read the situation differently. In theory, professional competency belies the need for supervision, and, in fact, supervisors in the public defender's office are treated as if they are redundant. When I asked, "What do supervisors do?" the answer from nonsupervisors usually began with a chuckle and ended with "Nothing" or "Not much." When prodded, some of the attorneys explained:

The way this Office is run—insofar as it can be said to be run—you're pretty much on your own. There is a supervisory structure, but mainly there is nobody, there is nobody looking over your shoulder, no one evaluating, no one correcting you, no one giving you feedback on what you do. (*001*)

There are supervisors in charge of sneezing on Tuesday or Thursday. They read the newspaper or they play bridge or whatever. They are *supposed* to take an interest in what their supervisees are doing; a lot don't. They collect their salaries. (*003*)

Your supervisors are there for support, research, that sort of thing. They are backup. You can ask them, "What would you do in this type of situation?" But I don't *have* to talk to anybody about what I am going to do. (*007*)

Good supervisors just happen to be around when you have a problem or a question. But, in general, a lot of them don't do that. They just show up for work. (*008*)

There was thus a widely shared perception among supervisees that though the best supervisors were there "just in case," no one in fact actually received much, if any, supervision. Most of the lawyers emphasized that there was really very little need for supervisors; the resentment that most felt toward supervisors did not exist because the latter failed to supervise but because many were seen as doing nothing at all to earn their keep. Most of the public defenders thought that, since there was nothing for a supervisor to do, he or she ought to be trying cases.

Findings of job enhancement and aggrandizement are common in the sociological literature; people like to make themselves seem to be more in control, more autonomous, and more important than they indeed are allowed to be (March and Simon 1958). Hence, I suspected that supervisors themselves might have a different sense of their role. I was surprised to find that apparently they did not. All six of the supervisors that I interviewed seemed to be uncomfortable with the idea that they were actually in charge of anyone. The first supervisor with whom I spoke turned out to be quite typical in this respect:

> **Q:** What does a supervisor do that a regular public defender does not?
> **R:** I do less [laugh]. It's not defined, it's not defined. It is whatever you make of it. I don't see myself as a cop. I don't see myself as an administrator, shifting papers and seeing that everyone is doing what they are supposed to be doing, being where they are supposed to be, that they are disposing of the right number of cases, or anything like that. I don't think that's our job.

The concept of the supervisor as being a supernumerary seems to be characteristic of professional organizations in which there are no junior members. When Friedson asked a chief of a service in a medical group what his job was, the latter responded: "Officially I am Chief of the department, but I do not meddle into treatment. I'm very reluctant to talk to a colleague unless it's something absolutely obvious. We have excellent people, and there are not many mistakes, really. . . . I do not go through the charts. It's not defined as one of my duties. The idea is to the contrary. I felt it was not my duty to have control over what people are doing. Everybody practices his own medicine" (1975, 116). In their study of a public defender's office, Platt and Pollock also found that, "compared to most workers," assistant public defenders "possess a relative degree of control over their work" (1974, 26). On the other hand, in

a study of Legal Services (civil) lawyers, Katz found that lawyers sometimes needed to "invoke the sanctity of professional canons to the at-
torney-client relation" in order to resist the efforts of superiors who
wished to meddle (1982, 111).

3. Transfers and Promotions

Although public defenders sometimes talked about getting ahead or
moving up in the office, they were more likely to speak of movement
simply as passing through or just being transferred. While it is clear that
there are entry-level slots in the office (as I discuss below), one must not,
public defenders cautioned me, assume that everyone in those jobs is
necessarily there because they are new and not competent to take on cases
in other courts. If you have not moved up, it may be because you do not
have the pull to get moved. As one supervisor explained: "Transfers? It
should be on merit, but it isn't always. There is sort of a schedule you can
count on, you know, spending a certain amount of time in misdemeanor
court. It's generally longer than you want to spend, because you have to
wait for a vacancy to open up, and you've got to hope that that vacancy
isn't filled by somebody with more clout than you have" (009).

For most assistants, the mechanics of being transferred are fairly
mysterious: "I was asking to be moved out for a year and a half before I
moved. I got a phone call one day. I don't know who makes the command decisions; I don't know how they do it. I'm just a soldier [laugh]"
(005).

An assistant who had been with the office for about four years and
had experienced four transfers shared his perspective:

Q: How do you get transferred?
R: You ask for it. Somebody thinks you are ready.
Q: Who makes the decision?
R: I don't know. I think there are certain viewpoints in the office, but I
   don't know exactly how these are made. (007)

Another assistant, with five years tenure, spoke (or tried to speak)
with more authority on the matter. He searched for rules but did not
seem very convincing: "Ultimately there are several ways you can get
transferred. The first is if the judge kicks you out of his courtroom.
Another way is if you have political pull, and your pull makes a phone
call and says 'It's time for him to be moved.' There are just so many
different reasons [pause]; I must admit that a lot of them are just caprice"
(001).

It is clear that most public defenders whom I interviewed had a
sense of when a move was, in fact, a move up—and that some of them

were proud of the speed with which they had moved through different kinds of courts. But most were careful not to claim too much credit, not to "pride themselves." It was as if these lawyers believe that getting moved is ultimately beyond the control of the individual. As they typically explained it, you might get moved because you deserve it, or you might get moved because "someone made a phone call" (or both). On the other hand, you might *not* get moved because there is "no room" or because some higher-up in the office "put a brick on your head."

Even more mysterious is how salary decisions are made.

> **Q:** What determines pay raises?
> **R:** Ouiji board, isn't it? I have no idea how they do it. (*006*)

Similar theories seem to circulate on how one gets promoted to supervisor—a move that usually does mean a salary increase for the lawyer. When I asked nonsupervisors, I was told that such promotions were usually the result of *anything but* merit:

> **Q:** How does someone get to be a supervisor?
> **R:** [Laugh] Well, I don't know [laugh]. I don't know. It's not the result of automatic tenure, it's office politics. (*002*)

> It's very mysterious, it's probably political. You probably have to be here a while. [pause] I guess I really don't know. (*003*)

> In some cases they are made supervisors because there is a need to get them out of a courtroom—or because they won't do any work. Well, maybe not very often, but sometimes. (*019*)

Supervisors themselves seemed equally unsure of—or perhaps reluctant to explain—how one generally gets promoted to a supervisory position, except that most of them said that it does take time.

> I think what happens is that some people leave at a crucial point and others stay on. And the ones that stay on beyond the crucial point, whatever that crucial point is, become supervisory material. And then you kind of wait your turn. Of course, there is politics. Does Justine [the first assistant public defender] know who you are? Have you caused any trouble in the past? Then you are not going to be a supervisor. (*006*)

> How did I get to be a supervisor? I think, longevity. Well [pause], maybe, if I want to pride myself, I'd say it's also because you do a good job. But more than anything else, I think it's just being there. I was made a supervisor sooner than others who have been here longer, but I think maybe that's just luck. (*004*)

One supervisor frankly admitted that his promotion came as a result of clout—and that this was true not only in his own case:

> **R:** I know someone six months out of law school who was promoted to supervisor. Now *he* was *connected.*
> **Q:** Clout can make *that* much difference?
> **R:** [Laugh] Now Lisa, what do you think? This is Chicago!

It is important to note that most public defenders spoke in relatively undifferentiated terms about clout, politics, and pull. Whenever I spoke with a public defender who clearly was politically well connected, I would receive some sort of caution about this: "There are two kinds of politics, two kinds of what people here will call 'clout.' The first has to do with the Democratic party. The second has to do with another kind of politicking—as when you make friends in the office who can help you out." Another lawyer said: "People do have different definitions of what is political. I don't know if you would call it political or not, but I know one person who got hired because his mother has the same hairdresser as Justine [the first assistant public defender]. Now maybe that's not *Political,* but it's political. It's like the difference between politics with a capital 'P' and politics with a little 'p.'"

Though most (66.7 percent) of the former public defenders agreed that most people used some clout to get hired, the majority (60.0 percent) *disagreed* with the statement, "Regardless of one's skill as a lawyer, having 'clout' was important to getting ahead in the office." Beyond simple agreement or disagreement, many comments in response to the latter statement indicated that once an attorney was in the office, in terms of getting the more coveted job slots in the office (though not necessarily the better-paying ones), skill was as important as—if not more important than—political clout. A few, however, did offer such comments as, "Others with less skills moved up faster than me in the office" (*032*).

For those *still* in the office, however, promotion to supervisor and other moves through the system were seen—at best—as more whimsical. Most believed such moves resulted from a combination of things: luck, seniority, clout (of some sort), tenure, and maybe skill. On the other hand, when explanations for pay increases or who got what salary were given, merit was not even mentioned. When the list of who actually was paid what was surreptitiously obtained by a group of public defenders, those who saw it found it difficult to make sense of. As one lawyer remembers it: "There really are great discrepancies. There are people who started together who are basically in the same group, but some are thrown in way above, and you can't really understand what their position is. *Some* of them you can understand that there are political reasons why they get as much as they do—'Oh yes, that's because it's so-and-so.' But many of them you can't understand how they rate."

If there was a slight tendency on the part of the successful to attribute their success to merit and that of others to clout or tenure, and if those who were not as successful attributed this to a lack of clout or tenure, these findings are not unexpected given contemporary theories of the attribution processes (Jones and Nisbet 1971, 2). Simply speaking, there is a tendency for people to want to take credit for their successes and to shift blame for their failures. What was less predictable was the weakness of these attributions. One former public defender, for example, attributed his success in the office to a case of mistaken identity! "To this day I believe Justine thought I was someone else. And that's why I advanced so quickly. My partner and I started at the same time, and left at the same time, but I made more money. There was no rhyme or reason for promotions or raises" *(031)*.

4. *Other Policies*

All 27,276 employees of Cook County (including the 487 lawyers, clericals, and investigators who work for the public defender's office), regardless of their affiliation or the nature of their work, are subject to certain policies set by the county board of commissioners. The range of county board policies that apply to public defenders is fairly narrow and concerns things such as insurance, health benefits, vacation time, and the like. Beyond these, the public defender has a great deal of latitude in establishing policy.

Each of the assistants interviewed in this research was aware of an office policy prohibiting public defense lawyers from doing any sort of private law practice.[2] Other than this, assistants and supervisors were unable to identify any other office policies for me. Many lawyers were, on the other hand, able to recall instances in which they had been frustrated by the *lack* of policy. For some, frustration was simply linked to uncertainty about promotions, transfers, and pay raises; others had been frustrated by the lack of policy in areas more directly related to their work as public defenders:

> There are a lot of things that we do where there is just no one, you know, to authorize things. Do we have an office policy about waiving transcripts?

2. Actually, this policy apparently was not created within the office but originated during the tenure of Judge Boyle; probably in response to his investigation of Getty's administration of the office (see chap. 4). The story may be apocryphal, but supposedly one month public defenders received a memo from the chief judge attached to their paychecks. In view of how public defenders feel, the wording of the message was somewhat unfortunate; it said simply, "Public Defenders are not allowed to practice law."

Do we have an office policy about subpoenaing transcripts? Do we have an office policy about this? About that? You don't know.

I had a case where a fellow was tried for murder and nine robberies. A private attorney was appointed to do the murder, but the state was going to use the robberies as part of their case. And this lawyer came to me and said, "Hey, I can't afford to do the investigation on all these robberies, will your office help me out?" Well, it made sense to me. So I went to my supervisor, and the supervisor above him, and they said, "There is no policy; there is no point of view. Do what you think is right."

But how can I commit our office to that much money? And nobody had any idea.

No public defender could ever remember having seen something like a public defender handbook or manual, or any document outlining office procedures and policies. Actually, there was such a document written in 1968 by Thomas J. Kelly, former chief of the public defender's trial division. It is called "Public Defender Manual and Trial Procedure." It begins with a short history of the office and then moves to substantive matters: a description of the trial process in Cook County, and a discussion of motions that public defenders are likely to make. The copy of this manual that I obtained from the Cook County Law Library is eight (typed) pages long.

Hidden Structure and Contents

When it comes to finding out about policy and structure in the public defender's office, the lawyers who work there are not necessarily the best ones to ask. In the first place, public defenders tended to discount the importance of—or gloss over—various day-to-day procedures. For example, public defenders are required to sign in when they come into the office and sign out when they leave. And when they leave they are supposed to tell the receptionist where they are going. After observing this process in the reception area of the office while awaiting an interview appointment, I asked a lawyer: "Isn't this procedure a form of supervision?" He said: "No. It isn't to keep track of how many hours we spend or anything, we are paid a salary. We sign out so they know where to find us in case of an emergency" (002). I suspect that he is correct, but, nonetheless, it *is* a policy, and the lawyers respect it, treating it—to an extent—as if it is a form of supervision. The lawyers seem loathe, for example, to leave any record that does not reflect well on them. During the day, public defenders usually sign out to a courtroom or the jail or simply note that they are going on an investigation. While there can be no doubt that investigations do take place, some, at least, are not work related. For example, the rate of investigation seems to pick up during

111

the holiday season—or at least that is what I guessed on the basis of my observations during a December afternoon spent in the waiting room at the public defender's office.

> **PD 1:** [To the receptionist] I'm gone now; I'm going on an investigation with what's his name [indicating PD 2].
> **PD 2:** I'm not going on an investigation with you, I'm going to check out a day-care center for my kid!
> **PD 1:** Well, I've got shopping to do.
> **PD 3:** I'm going on an investigation. I'm going with [one of the investigators], so it's a real investigation.

1. *Supervision and Training: Another Look*
Contrary to the nearly unanimous opinion that supervisors do not supervise, I found that at least some did. One supervisor who said during our interview that he did not interfere with his attorneys allowed (on another occasion) that he did, for example, "encourage" his lawyers to write their own motions instead of using "form" motions.[3] Another supervisor, who during our interview denied that he did anything that might be construed as supervising unless asked by someone for help, was accidentally caught out by me a few days later. One afternoon I happened on him in the hallways of the courts building, and when he mentioned that he was there "checking up" on someone, I jokingly accused him of supervising. In a low voice he responded that he usually dropped in on his courtrooms daily to make sure that all was well and that no one was having any problems. About a month later, I managed to observe one of these visits, which, I thought, was contrived to seem almost accidental. Another supervisor, who worked in the juvenile division of the office, was a little more up-front about his supervision. Often I would spot him chatting with his supervisees in the courtroom, looking for someone to handle a call during busy days, or helping out a lawyer in a courtroom, and so forth. Still, when I asked one of the lawyers assigned to this supervisor, "What does your supervisor do?" I was told: "Nothing."

When confronted with my evidence of their supervision, some lawyers remained adamant that what I had seen were exceptions to the general rule. Once, while I was in a supervisor's office listening to him remark that he really "didn't have anything to do as a supervisor," the phone rang. After he hung up, he said to me rather sheepishly: "I have to

3. In the photocopy room at the 26th street public defender's office, one can find copies of dozens of different types of motions. These are widely reputed to be among the best available for defense attorneys, and I was often told that private attorneys often come to borrow these, sometimes having been sent by judges to do so.

go now; one of my lawyers needs me over in the court. This rarely happens, though."

Similarly, when they talk about training, the lawyers underplay the fact that the office almost always places new lawyers in certain kinds of slots within the office; most newly appointed public defenders are assigned to the appellate division or to municipal or juvenile courtrooms. Some of the lawyers dismiss this as, if not accidental, then as owing to only the fact that there is room for new people only in these lower courts. In an important sense, time spent in these slots is considered a form of training necessary before the lawyer can move up to a trial court. The theory seems to be that the cases in these courts are not complicated and that after a few days of experience, the lawyer can handle himself at this level. The challenge at this level is not legal but related to the pressure of caseloads. An important consideration is that because the penalties that can be meted out in juvenile or misdemeanor courts are (relatively) minor, there is a limit to how much damage a neophyte can do to the clients. In the appellate division, new lawyers can work at their own pace on less difficult cases.

From these starting positions, the average assistant expects to move—after a time—through the various levels of horizontal defense. An attorney who begins in the juvenile division, for example, will likely move into a preliminary-hearing court before being assigned to a trial court; the attorney who begins in appeals may move into either juvenile or one of the municipal divisions—or both—before being given a trial courtroom assignment. But it is important to recognize that the paths through the office are not preordained, not routinized. As attorneys move through the office they may take many detours, and stops at the various levels may involve different amounts of time. Some assistants move up faster than others. The future of any newly hired attorney is therefore difficult to predict. He or she may spend only a year or two before being assigned to a felony courtroom, or a lawyer may take several years.

The training that public defenders receive does depend less on explicit policy than on other factors, but most public defenders do not seem to be as self-taught as they might have one believe. In the first place, as they themselves admit, public defenders rely a great deal on their colleagues for help and advice.

The thing that's great about being a public defender is that you can use others as a resource. Being able to share experience and information. Instead of being stuck in my office and having to look through ten books to find some point, I can walk into someone's office and get the point right away—that's what this is all about. (020)

Sometimes people just come up and say: "If you don't mind me being critical, I think you should do this and this." And I listen and learn. (007)

We say: "Hey, did you hear about so and so's case? Let's go watch." Or, "Hey, I found a case that reminds me of so and so's case, I'd better give it to him." Lawyers in private practice must really miss that. We watch and critique one another. (008)

I frequently observed more overt student/teacher sorts of interactions occurring when a less experienced lawyer was teamed in a courtroom or on a case with a more experienced one. In keeping with the egalitarian spirit of their enterprise and unlike state's attorneys, public defenders working horizontal defense in the same courtroom are assigned as "partners," and neither one is designated as "first" chair. One lawyer may be in charge of a particular case, but usually that is because it is his or her turn to be in charge. In some cases, however, especially when a lawyer from a vertical task force comes into the courtroom to do a trial, it is clear who is in charge and who is assisting. Often such pairings result when a vertical defense lawyer asks one of the horizontal defense lawyers permanently assigned to the trial courtroom to assist in a trial. This helps ward off any resentment that horizontal defense lawyers might have about vertical defense attorneys coming in and taking over. In some cases, a vertical defense lawyer will specifically ask a younger attorney to help because the younger lawyer is someone whom the more experienced lawyer believes has special talent and should be "brought along" more quickly. One lawyer recalled that his involvement in his first murder case came as the result of such a request: "We lost that case; it was a loser case. But that's one of the reasons why they asked me, because I didn't have much experience and they wanted to bring me along. If it had been a closer case, they probably would have asked someone with more experience. But this was more or less to indoctrinate me into things" (001).

One of the hallmarks of the public defender's office is the fact that, even when teaching is obvious, the tone remains collegial. With some allowances for personal style, when a senior lawyer becomes too abrupt or impatient while instructing a younger attorney, it makes observers uncomfortable. On one occasion, for example, I watched and listened to three lawyers practicing the line of questioning that they intended to pursue the next day with a hostile witness. It was accepted that the questioning of this witness was too important to be left to an inexperienced attorney, but Bob (the youngest lawyer) was nonetheless given his turn during the practice session. Below is an excerpt from my field notes. (Mark and Terry are the senior attorneys trying the case.)

Although it may have "sounded good," even I could tell that Bob was not very successful in getting the "witness" (played by another public defender) to discredit himself. He really did not seem to know what he was supposed to be going after, and he fumbled several times and got caught off guard by some of the "witness's" answers.

After his attempt, a postmortem was held. At first, Mark was very impatient with Bob's performance, and he roundly criticized the value of his approach. There was a period of silence after that; then Terry jumped into the discussion and argued that much of Bob's problem had been the fact that he (Terry) had been distracting him: "I was firing him notes, I was whispering in his ear. It was very difficult. Right, Bob? *Very* difficult. Very difficult to follow your own train of thought when I was plugging things into you. Wasn't it, Bob?" After a few moments of this, Mark finally backed down from his position that Bob "didn't really seem to *have* a train of thought" and agreed with Terry that the witness was a very "tough son-of-a-bitch." Then Bob admitted that he had done a poor job and said that he had felt "in over his head." Then both Mark and Terry jumped in and assured Bob that it really was no big deal, that "anyone can get frazzled."

There is, then, more supervision—and certainly more teaching—going on in the office than its incumbents tend to admit. But the tone of these is almost always matter-of-fact and collegial. How has this come about?

The Presumption of Competency as Myth

The presumption of competency has such force in the public defender's office that it can be called a fundamental organizing myth. Needless to say, here the term "myth" is not used in the colloquial sense (i.e., myth as lie or untruth), but as it has been articulated in a long tradition of social scientific work. Myth suggests a shared belief, a cosmological theory of the relatedness of things and people (Schorer 1959; Turner 1969). More specifically, the concept of myth used here follows Ferreira's characterization of myth in his study of family processes: "[Myth is] a series of fairly well-integrated beliefs shared by all family members concerning each other and their mutual position in family life, beliefs that go unchallenged by everyone involved in spite of the reality distortions which they may conspicuously imply. . . . The family myth is much a part of the way a family appears to its members, that is, a part of the inner image of the group, an image to which all family members contribute and, apparently strive to preserve" (1968, 457).

The myth of competency embraces public defenders from the moment that they are appointed to the office. Although there is a hierarchical structure in place, it is treated as if it is for purposes of show only: supervisors are believed to be redundant; public defenders work as a company of equals. Even when supervision or teaching and the like do occur, they are carefully done in a way that nurtures the myth and allows it to go unchallenged. Similarly, the lack of general policy identified by these lawyers suggests that, as far as they are concerned, the organization's hand rarely intrudes into their professional autonomy—and that when it does intrude it does so without interfering with the lawyers' claim that they are a company of equals: it transfers and promotes without rhyme or reason—and so, the official judgments that the office makes about who ought to be moved and who ought to be promoted are regarded as having little credibility by the lawyers.

While the policies (or lack thereof) of the office carefully nurture the myth of competency, one suspects that maintenance of the myth is also strengthened by the nature of the public defender's role within the courts. Most public defenders are assigned to courtrooms where they are very much subject to the supervision of their judges. As long as the judges have these attorneys under their thumbs, the office need not concern itself that disaster is around the corner. Parenthetically, here is where the role of the supervisor emerges, in part, as an important aspect of the latent structure of the organization. As it was explained to me: "If a judge gets mad because there is no public defender in the courtroom, or because a public defender did something to make him mad, then the supervisor is to go and smooth things over" (*002*). If the attempt to smooth over does not work, the supervisor is empowered to transfer the lawyer into another courtroom covered by his or her task force. The most dramatic role of the supervisor—I have been told—is to bail out public defenders who land in jail for contempt. This is a role that they are rarely called on to play.

It would be a mistake to assume, however, that the relationship between public defender and judge is analogous to that of an associate and partner in a law firm. As I noted in chapter 5, public defenders often feel that they are in an adversarial relationship with their judges, and, unlike junior members of a law firm, they do have access to procedures that give them defense against the whims of their judges.

Functions of the Myth

Some would have it that the existence of myth in an organization or group is symptomatic of an "organization neurosis" caused by pathological or dysfunctional management behavior (Kets de Vries and Miller 1984). It is obvious, however, that attempts to assess the personality of a corporate actor in this way lead to a too narrow perspective on their behaviors. Organizational myths, as Meyer and Rowan (1981) argue, can often be better understood as an organization's rational responses to demands from its environment. Myths, in this sense, belong under the rubric of institutional legitimating formulas (Berger and Luckmann 1967, 70).

Focusing on myth as a response to environmental (i.e., extra-organizational) demands, however, has its own bias. When it is viewed this way, one could argue that the only function of the myth of competency is to help legitimate the office in the eyes of the courts—and the courts in the eyes of the wider society. As I argued in part 1, the courts' legitimacy hinges on the requirement that defendants be represented by *competent* defense counsel. So, the most cynical assessment of the myth of competency is that it functions to mitigate for the courts the costs and consequences of right-to-counsel rules: having inexperienced and untutored lawyers is similar to having no lawyers at all, except perhaps that it is more efficient—public defenders work cheap and they lose. The supervisory structure that insiders allege has no real meaning can, in this tradition, be seen as important for what Meyer and Rowan call its ceremonial value: it functions to create an impression of the office as a rational structure. One expects bureaucracies to have hierarchies, so the office creates a hierarchy.

The problem with this viewpoint is that it ignores the fact that while public defenders do work (relatively) cheaply, they have been shown to do about as well as private lawyers do in these courts. More important, focusing only on the institution's relations to its environment obscures the importance of the institution's negotiations with its incumbents. One must not, I think, overlook the importance of the myth to those inside the office. As I have noted above, because of this myth, public defenders treat each other in particular ways, according one another a degree of respect and deference that they cannot find elsewhere. In other words, because of the myth, the office is a kind of psychic haven from outsiders who treat public defenders callously, gainsay their respectability, and deny their claims to being real lawyers. The myth and the concomitant autonomy that is provided the lawyers is, in a very real sense, the public defender's biggest reward for service.

Not unexpectedly, many public defenders revel in the structure (or lack of structure) that goes along with this myth, taking it as proof not only of their competency but as an acknowledgment of the validity of their claims to professionalism. The gratification that they receive from working in this structure is enhanced when they compare their situation (as they often do) to that of their counterparts in the state's attorney's office.

117

As in any big prosecutor's office, they have their quotas, and they have a lot more accountability to the top. If I couldn't have more control than they have, I wouldn't do it. [During plea bargaining sessions] they can't just say "I'll reduce this" and judge a case on merits. They have to say: "I'll have to talk to my supervisor and see what he says." *(011)*

In the State's Attorney's Office it is *very* structured. They have supervisors who can actually tell a lawyer what to do! They have supervisors who will sit down with you and go over your case files! We don't need that. Here supervisors are a backup; you *can* ask them: "What would you do here?" But the final decision is yours. *(007)*

For many public defenders the freedom that they find in the office is more than just something that they can enjoy; it is an essential part of being able to do a good job. Good defense work, they say, is not something that can be routinized. As a lawyer of eight years' experience explained to me, "the state's attorneys sometimes have you take all your files and your supervisor says, 'Have you done this?' 'Why did you do that?' We *never* do anything like that! I just don't see how it could work. It is a kind of crazy, creative, arty thing we do here" *(008)*.

Thus, some lawyers suggested that public defending cannot be truly rationalized, that defense lawyers cannot be supervised in the usual sense, because you just cannot do *good* defense work that way. Whether or not that is true is difficult to say for sure; certainly one could envision a defender's office in which more structured training opportunities existed, where regular meetings took place in which attorneys could discuss how they approached their cases, and so forth. But this sort of envisioning does bring to mind an additional point: one important function of the myth of competency is that it allows public defenders to be competent inasmuch as it means that they are not shackled to supervisors or administrators who conceivably might have vested interests that are contrary to those of defendants (i.e., keeping costs down, appeasing judges, etc.). The myth makes it difficult for supervisors and administrators who would meddle in the lawyers' decisions about what cases ought to be pursued vigorously. While in the absence of any meaningful supervisory structure there are no institutional guarantees that public defenders will provide quality representation, at the same time this state of affairs means that these lawyers are relatively free from potential institutional corruption of their mission. The myth makes it difficult, for example, for anyone to make a phone call and put pressure on a lawyer who might be embarrassing the state by calling into question the tactics of the police or prosecutors in any particular case. In this sense, the myth responds not only to the needs of the lawyers to be free to act as real professionals but also to the concerns that many have about the indebtedness of the public defender to the system that pays his or her salary. It would seem that this latter aspect is important, at least as long as public defenders "have a sense that the judges would like you to lose, no matter what sort of case you have" (*002*).

Although gathering data on the actual quality of public defending was beyond the scope of the present research, I found some evidence that public defenders, in general, do live up to the standards suggested by the myth of competency. The Cook County Court Watching Project (begun by the League of Women Voters but now functioning as an autonomous group) has, since 1974, been placing observers in the Cook County courts. Each court watcher is asked: "Would you feel confident having a public defender defend you?"

In their 1983–1984 report, on the basis of observations made of 53,202 proceedings in 108 courtrooms, the court watchers gave public defense lawyers relatively high marks, as is shown in table 4. On the other hand, the court watchers were more critical of the performance of assistant state's attorneys. Although from all sources it was heard that lawyers in the state's attorney's office are subjected to much more supervision than are lawyers in the public defender's office, the court watchers reported that, based on their observations, "it is obvious that appropriate supervision of [assistant state's attorneys] in the courtrooms is not taking place" (Cook County Court Watching Project, Inc., 1983–1984, 30).

There is irony in this situation, however, for as I shall explore in the

Table 4   Court Watchers' Responses to Questions About Assistant Public Defenders and Assistant State's Attorneys

	Would You Feel Confident Having the Public Defender Defend You?		Except for Cases Up for the First Time, Was the State Always Prepared?	
	% Yes	% No	% Yes	% No
Municipal divisions (misdemeanor courts)				
District 1 (Chicago)	72	28	67	33
District 2 (suburbs)	69	31	57	43
District 3 (suburbs)	88	12	65	35
District 4 (suburbs)	79	21	70	30
District 5 (suburbs)	79	21	83	17
District 6 (suburbs)	69	31	70	30
Criminal division (felony courts)	85	15	76	24

Source.—Cook County Court Watching Project, Inc. 1983–1984, 27, 30.

119

next chapter, there are costs to the public defenders stemming from their allegiance to the myth: unlike state's attorneys, who are believed to be heavily supervised, public defenders have the freedom to act as real lawyers, but they pay a price in terms of the amount of respect that they can earn from others.

Myth and Antistructure _____ 7
in Public Defending _____

Public defenders, like senior members of law and medical firms and attending physicians and professors in hospitals, work in a carefully fashioned environment, what one might call antistructure or *communitas:* an environment in which hierarchical orderings of relationships are tacitly avoided or ill defined, an organization of "concrete idiosyncratic individuals who, though differing in physical and mental endowment, are nevertheless regarded as equals" (Turner 1969, 117). Thus, the office of the public defender has a hierarchical structure, but its incumbents deny that that structure has any force or impact. Supervisors (it is alleged) do not supervise, but are a joke.[1] No one, it seems, tells a public defense lawyer how to do the job, how to manage files, cases, or clients. No one imposes or interferes unless asked. Although, much like other professionals, they will often ask colleagues to consult, public defenders func-

---

1. The value of this joke as humor was illustrated by the fact that during a dinner honoring Public Defender Doherty, one speaker (Judge Warren D. Wolfson) earned a big laugh when he prefaced his remarks by quipping as he looked out over the large crowd, "This looks like a meeting of the supervisory staff of the public defender's office." (*062*)

tion autonomously. If there is an office viewpoint, it is, as one supervisor told me, that "they are all adults; they are all attorneys" (006).

Notwithstanding the fact that, as noted in the previous chapter, public defenders enjoy and believe the antistructure to be a necessary and essential resource, many also betray a large degree of ambivalence about the freedom and autonomy that they have. When I asked public defenders, "What sorts of changes would *you* make if you were appointed to be the public defender?" even lawyers who had spoken glowingly of the amount of freedom and autonomy that lawyers in the office have, answered that, given the chance, they would add structure and rationalize procedure in the office:

> I think there should be more control, more support. I think there should be more overseeing, more of a training program. Supervisors should be in trial courtrooms more often watching the people under them. (001)

> I think the office needs more structure. We can still be creative, but we need more structure. Have supervisors more involved with cases and more involved with their people. I would also have a much more detailed structure of promotion. (008)

> I would change the hiring, transferring, and promotion procedures, to make things more understandable. I would institute more training. I would make sure that supervisors actually worked and actually supervised their people. (009)

> I would clean this place up, get some control over who goes where, set the mechanisms in order and have a merit system for who goes where. And have some substantive law seminars. Mostly *I* would have some idea of what the fuck goes on around here. (003)

In order to understand the nature of their ambivalence, this desire for structure and antistructure—and, as well, the consequences of the myth of competency and the antistructure that has grown up around this myth—it helps to look more closely at one kind of differentiation that *has* emerged in the office.

The Rise of the Special Task Force

In 1974, a group of lawyers in the Cook County Public Defender's Office was organized into a special unit called the Homicide Task Force. Lawyers in this unit would provide vertical rather than horizontal representation to clients charged with homicide. In other words, instead of being assigned to particular courtrooms, these lawyers would be assigned to clients whom they would represent as their cases moved from the preliminary hearing stage through trials and sentencing. Public Defender James Doherty conceived of the task force as an experimental response to criticisms that the balkanized horizontal defense generally provided to indigent defendants in Cook County was too fragmented and therefore inadequate (Meyers 1977). The idea of vertical representation itself was not new; other defender agencies around the country were at the time offering this sort of ongoing representation (Dahlin 1974).[2] What *was* new was the fact that these lawyers would specialize in murder cases.

To lead the new unit, Doherty approached William Murphy, who had been a public defender for several years and was then working as a supervisor in charge of "special defenses" (representing clients in well-publicized cases). Murphy, who would ultimately be called the father of the Homicide Task Force, ended up supervising and shepherding lawyers through the first six years of the unit's existence. But Murphy, though willing to make an attempt, was at first unenthusiastic. He remembers telling Doherty, "It won't work, but I'll try it" (Murphy, personal communication to author).

In spite of his lack of enthusiasm, from the beginning Murphy had a particular sort of lawyer in mind for this new unit, "I was looking for people with competitive spirit. . . . I didn't want people who would get into the courtroom and get pushed around. I wanted winners" (Cohen 1982, 87).

To get his winners, Murphy could have sought out the more experienced, proven trial lawyers in the office. He did not. Instead, as one of the original members of the task force recalls, "Murph's idea was that he wanted young lawyers, people who were relatively inexperienced, but people he had heard about or got recommended to him as being aggressive lawyers. These are the lawyers he wanted to mold into this homicide unit."

At least some of the original task force members wondered why Murphy had selected them, relatively untrained in trial advocacy, instead of those who had already shown themselves to be competent (or better) trial attorneys. Murphy acknowledges that "there were a lot of great lawyers in the office" but notes that he had wanted inexperienced law-

---

2. Vertical representation is more characteristic of smaller defense offices than of larger ones. A national survey found that only 4 percent of public defender agencies offer only horizontal defense; but of agencies that serve large jurisdictions (more than a million people), 82 percent offer only horizontal defense. According to the survey, most small defender organizations, the ones that typically do offer vertical defense, "consist of fewer than 3 staff attorneys" (Singer and Lynch 1983).

yers so that he could, as he put it, "train them to do it my way." But Murphy also betrayed another sort of concern, for he implied that what he wanted most were lawyers untainted by the PD image of being losers: "Because of that 'I don't want a PD, I want a real lawyer' and 'I don't have a lawyer, I have a PD,' I went into it; well, I was accused of being image conscious, and I guess I was. I wanted us to be *different.*"

One might guess that, within an office organized on the principle of the myth of competency and the resulting antistructure, creating a group of lawyers who would be different would be fraught with difficulties. In fact, Murphy said, at first it was not at all difficult. The more experienced lawyers, he said, "didn't want to have anything to do with it." But, "as we became more successful, started getting more publicity, and becoming more visible, they *demanded,* they didn't ask, they demanded to be on it." As another lawyer, a former task force member recalls, the problem was that "some of the more experienced lawyers felt that if this elite type of group was going to be, the lawyers should be picked from those who had experience and who had proven themselves."

Murphy said that, after a meeting of all concerned, he compromised and the Homicide Task Force came to include the best of the experienced lawyers and the most promising of the younger lawyers.

The Homicide Task Force quickly lived up to expectations that its lawyers would be perceived as special, as different from the average public defender. Murphy believes that this was proved not only by the media attention that they received but by the number of requests that he received "from lawyers around the country, lawyers who wanted to be on the Task Force, to watch us, and to talk about what we were doing." He added: "I must have had hundreds of requests a year! We were a showcase!" In time, "every lawyer worth his salt wanted to be on the Task Force."

Murphy said that, owing to the stress of doing "death cases," membership in the task force became less appealing to some lawyers after reinstitution of the death penalty law (one that would hold up against constitutional challenges) in 1979. Nevertheless, within the ranks of public defenders, Homicide Task Force lawyers continue to be seen as special. No longer are relatively inexperienced lawyers accepted as task force members; instead the lawyer must prove him or herself worthy of serving on the task force. To a great extent, being asked to join remains a "symbol of approval, an acknowledgment of talent" (Meyers 1977, 19). As attorney Bob Gevirtz, who served a number of years on the Homicide Task Force, once told a reporter: "There is a lot of pride here. . . . You feel you've been selected for a reason. A lot is expected of you, but people in the Murder Task Force are very confident of their abilities" (Meyers 1977, 19).

In 1980, another special task force was organized. This unit too would provide vertical representation to clients—but with an important difference: its caseload was not limited to a particular type of crime but encompassed a variety of serious felonies. Officially the unit is called the Vertical Representation Task Force, but it is commonly referred to simply as "Vertical." That the Homicide Task Force remains the exemplar of special units is suggested by the fact that, within the office, it is most often referred to as "the task force."

Finally, a smaller group of lawyers who work in the juvenile division of the office make up what one lawyer called a "mini–task force." At the time of its creation (in the early 1980s), this group specialized in handling the cases of habitual offenders and older juveniles who, because they had committed serious offenses, the state wanted to have transferred to the adult system for trial. Until recently, such transfers could only take place after a special hearing. Members of the Juvenile Task Force represent youth at these transfer hearings.[3] If necessary, a lawyer from the Juvenile Task Force will follow the youth to the criminal court where he or she will assist Trial Division lawyers defending the juvenile. Since September of 1982, however, state law has required that all youth of fifteen years of age or older who are charged with serious offenses (e.g., murder, rape, deviate sexual assault, or armed robbery with a gun) must be tried as adults. Since this automatic-transfer law took effect, transfer hearings have been relatively rare in juvenile court. The four members of the Juvenile Task Force do continue to represent habitual offenders whose cases are heard in juvenile court.

Functions of Special Units

Though the majority (85–90 percent) of assistant public defenders continue to provide horizontal representation, it is fair to say that today the special vertical units are no longer considered experimental by those in the office. When asked why these units exist in an office still organized primarily in terms of horizontal defense, the usual response is that vertical representation exists because certain cases present special challenges; the nature of these challenges is such that special expertise on the part of the defense lawyer is required.[4] Does the special expertise theory account for the persistence of these units?

3. Technically these hearings are called "702 Hearings," owing to the fact that the transfer of juveniles to adult criminal court was covered in paragraph 702 of the Juvenile Court Act (chap. 38 of the *Illinois Revised Statutes*).
4. It is important to note that although the state's attorney's office in Cook County does have units that offer "vertical prosecution," these are targeted differently. For example, in the state's attorney's office there is no vertical unit that prosecutes homicides.

The theory is persuasive with respect to the Homicide Task Force, although I would argue that this has not always been the case. As noted above, when the Homicide Task Force was created, Illinois had no death penalty (and most did not foresee that one would soon be created that could stand up to constitutional challenges). Thus, the maximum sentence that a convicted murderer might receive was life imprisonment. Because of this, defending a client against the charge of murder was, for all intents and purposes, much the same as defending a client against any serious felony charge.[5] Since the reinstitution of the death penalty law, however, the special expertise theory has can be seen to have greater merit. In capital cases there are different issues to be raised and additional procedures to carry out:[6] because "death is different," the courts have ruled that "there is a corresponding difference in the need for reliability in the determination that death is the appropriate punishment in a specific case" (*Gardner v. Florida* 430 U.S. 349 [1977]).

The special expertise theory also fits as a justification for the vertical unit in the juvenile division, although it can been seen to fit less well since the passage of the automatic-transfer law. Currently, the four lawyers doing vertical defense in juvenile court concentrate their efforts on handling habitual offenders who have committed serious crimes—murder, sexual assault, and aggravated arson. But to the extent that juveniles tried as juveniles can receive as a maximum punishment only time in the De-

---

5. One hesitates, on the other hand, to go further and argue that murder cases are any *less* difficult to defend than other serious crimes. This was asserted, however, by former Chief Deputy State's Attorney Kenneth Gillis, who in 1977 refused to be impressed with the Murder Task Force, saying that their's was the easiest defense job. In murder cases, Gillis argued, the defense has an obvious advantage over the prosecution. With respect to most homicides, he said, "There's an old saying that the state's best witness is dead" (Meyers 1977, 20).

6. For example, in order to serve as a juror in any case, one must—as the saying goes—"be willing to follow the law." In cases in which jurors may have to decide whether the defendant deserves the death penalty, jurors are required to be "death qualified." In other words, in order to serve as a juror in a case in which the state is asking that the death penalty be imposed, one must believe that, in some cases at least, the death penalty is appropriate. Jurors who are not death qualified, who are adamant in their moral or conscientious scruples against capital punishment, cannot serve in such cases. Of course, having jurors with such scruples is exactly what the defense attorney wishes for his case. Thus, one of the tasks of a defense counsel in a capital case is to try to "rehabilitate" prospective jurors who say that they are against the death penalty. If a potential juror (venirman) can be made to admit that he or she could see imposing the death penalty in some cases, then he or she is rehabilitated and—the defense lawyer will argue—should be admitted to the jury (*Witherspoon v. Illinois* 391 U.S. 510 [1968]). Recent Supreme Court decisions have made successful rehabilitation much more difficult, however.

partment of Corrections until they turn eighteen, the special expertise theory is not as appropriate.

The special expertise theory makes very little sense as a justification for the existence of the Vertical Task Force. As noted above, Vertical defense lawyers represent clients charged with a variety of felonies—burglary, aggravated battery, serious theft, forgery, robbery, armed robbery, and rape. Generally, with the exception of rape cases, all that the cases represented by Vertical Task Force lawyers have in common is that their preliminary hearings are held in a courtroom known as Branch 44. This is the preliminary hearing court for the West Side (and a little of the South Side) of the city of Chicago. In other words, if someone commits an armed robbery in another part of the city, he or she has very little chance of receiving vertical representation.[7] Vertical lawyers generally "pick up" their rape cases in Branch 66 (otherwise known as "violence court"), which does cover the entire city (but not the county).

Conceivably, a case could be made for the notion that there is something about felonies committed on the West Side of Chicago that requires lawyers with special skills. Because the West Side has a large Hispanic population, for example, could one of the vertical defense lawyers' special skills perhaps be fluency in Spanish? In fact, very few Vertical defense lawyers admit to speaking much Spanish. Even if there were some other factor shared by cases heard in Branch 44, the special expertise theory would still be undermined by the fact that not all cases heard in this branch court are picked up by Vertical defense lawyers. There are two horizontal defense lawyers stationed in Branch 44 as well. How is it determined which cases are to receive horizontal and which vertical defense? I discussed the selection process with the supervising lawyer of the vertical unit:

> It's just random, more or less. You are there and the judge calls each case, and as they are passed for workup . . . the judge puts them on a pile. And when you are free, you go up to the pile and take a case—whatever is on top.
> **Q:** So let me get this straight. In order to get a vertical lawyer, I want to be brought to Branch 44 and not some other court—like Branch 22?
> **R:** Yes.
> **Q:** And once my case does go to Branch 44, since there are two vertical

7. There is *some* chance, however. I observed that, when they realized that they had time to pick up another case but it was not their turn to cover Branch 44, some vertical defense lawyers went to a branch court that does preliminary hearings for serious felonies in another part of the city or county.

lawyers and two horizontal lawyers there every day, my chances of
getting a lawyer from vertical would be two in four?
R: Yes, that's it.

Vertical defense lawyers also take turns covering Branch 66, where
preliminary hearings for rapes (and murders) are held. Here—for rape
cases—the ratio of vertical defense to horizontal defense lawyers is 1:3,
so one's chances of getting vertical representation is less in Branch 66
than in Branch 44.

Special Task Forces as Co-optation

Arguably, a stronger case can be made for the idea that vertical representation units exist more to serve the needs of the public defender's office
and the courts than the needs of indigent clients. Certainly such an argument gains credence when it is remembered that the Homicide Task
Force *was* instituted in response to criticism of the horizontal system of
defense. The institution of one or two small vertical units in the office
could thus be seen as an attempt to co-opt system critics. Enhancing the
value (and economy) of this maneuver is the fact that providing vertical
representation to those accused of murder—perhaps the most visible of
all crimes—guaranteed that the most visible of all defense work could be
done vertically. As an attempt to co-opt, this ploy (should one wish to
call it that) certainly seems to have worked. As William Murphy remembers the impact of the Homicide Task Force: "Well, I think we became
almost the image of the public defender services, all over the country.
We really had good trial lawyers and the most visibility. . . . It certainly
made the [Cook County] Office seem like it was working harder" (Murphy, personal communication to the author). One could add that bring-
ing the best lawyers into one unit, a unit assigned to defend the most
difficult cases, helped to minimize the "damage" that these lawyers
could do. They would provide great defenses, but, ultimately, because
most of the clients were factually guilty and because the state tried very
hard to win such cases, the lawyers would lose. This sort of scenario, as I
suggested in the conclusion of chapter 4, shows the courts at their best—
and most legitimate.

A more interesting and potentially revealing question is, what have
the other vertical units done for the office? Why were these units created
and why are they maintained? In order to answer such questions, it is
helpful to look more closely at the nature of antistructure as well as at the
needs of the lawyers who work in the office—especially with respect to
their feelings about their respective places in the public defender's
antistructure.

The Nature of Antistructure

Antistructure is not an unknown or even unusual phenomenon in society. Leaving aside for the moment the antistructural *communitas* characteristic of professionals within their organizations, Mardi Gras, New Year's Eve parties, and Halloween immediately come to mind as examples of antistructure in our society. But antistructure, in its various manifestations, is generally confined to periodic social upheavals (often intended, in the Durkheimian sense, to celebrate society and not to destroy it). One does not expect antistructure to persist, for it is notoriously unstable.

It is mainly in terms of its persistence that the antistructural *communitas* or social leveling seen among senior members of law or medical firms seems anomalous. But when one carefully sifts through the levels of analysis under study, the antistructure is shown to be an illusion—and thus the anomaly disappears. The example of the professional *communitas* as illusion, however, helps to explicate both the source of the public defenders' ambivalence about the antistructural *communitas* in which they work and the emergence (and persistence) of the special task forces.

In the sociological literature the most obvious referent for the ephemeral quality of antistructure is Weber's discussion of charisma and the inevitability of its routinization. A group of people who are followers of a charismatic leader, Weber argues, cannot sustain interaction in the absence of routinized differentiation of some sort: "Charismatic authority has a character specifically foreign to everyday routine structures. . . . If it is not to remain a purely transitory phenomenon . . . it is necessary for the character of charismatic authority to become radically changed. It cannot remain stable, but becomes institutionalized or rationalized or a combination of both (1978, 246). In this respect, the routinization of charisma exemplifies the natural course of other forms of antistructure.

Even within groups or movements based on ideals of social leveling (e.g., brotherhood, etc.), some sort of hierarchical ordering of individuals seems to be an inevitable part of the routinization process (see, e.g., Kantor 1972). As Turner notes, even the Hell's Angels, whose members call themselves "the one percent that don't fit and don't care" and have thus "opted out of the structural system," have nonetheless reconstituted themselves as an organization, "with complex initiation ceremonies and grades of membership emblematized by badges. They have a set of by-laws, an executive committee, consisting of president, vice-president, secretary, treasurer, and sergeant-at-arms, and formal weekly meetings" (Turner 1969, 193–194).

It is perhaps tempting to explain this urge toward hierarchy as merely a response to the general problems of control and coordination that groups experience, especially as they increase the size of their memberships (see, e.g., Turner and Killian 1972, 404). But Turner (1969) cautions that the growth of structure, especially in terms of the levels of hierarchy, is a response to neither numerical strength nor task needs alone. As an example, Turner cites Allen C. Spiers' work, in which he "describes a Mormon separatist sect numbering not many more than two hundred souls," which had "a complicated hierarchical structure somewhat similar to Mormonism . . . having such positions as First High Priest, Second High Priest, President, First Vice-President, Second Vice-President, Priests of Branches, Bishops of Councils, Teachers and Deacons" (Turner 1969, 192).

While it is doubtful that there exists a primordial human instinct that compels individuals to join or create elaborate hierarchies, it is plausible that one impetus toward routinization and hierarchization is the individuals' needs to stabilize their access to rewards. Thus, Weber argues that beyond the interest that group members have in the "continuation" of the community, a "principle motive" underlying routinization is the "still stronger interest" in stabilizing the "appropriation of powers and economic advantages to the followers," the majority of whom, Weber notes, "will in the long run" seek "to make a living out of their calling" (1978, 249).[8]

Professional *Communitas* and Antistructure

The question is, Do the professions, these "companies of equals" contradict the idea that routinization and hierarchical ordering of individuals are inevitable?

On the whole (even if we count only the senior members), it is quite clear that any idea that the membership of an entire profession constitutes a company of equals is patently false. For example, not just differentiation but stratification within the field of law has long been obvious (Bucher and Strauss 1961; Heinz and Laumann 1982). In her important study, *The Rise of Professionalism,* Magali Sarfatti Larson (1977) argues that, notwithstanding the persistence of the ideological conception of the professions as companies of equals, the professions

---

8. Given its nature, the chance of making a living out of charisma is, in the long run, not a good bet. Not only is its persistence doubtful (history is replete with examples of charismatics forsaken by their gods), but even should it persist, it is exhausting. The charismatic must work miracles, must perform heroic deeds, to prove him- or herself— not once but continously. Pure charisma, Weber reminds us, "does not recognize any legitimacy other than one which flows from personal strength proven time and time again. Charisma is gained and retained solely by proving [its] power in practice (1978, 249).

have become increasingly stratified. An important factor in this process, Larson argues, has been the increasing number of professional organizations. The growing dependence on this form of organizing as a medium through which professional services are delivered, Larson says, "stratifies the professions from the outside, putting chosen professional institutions and chosen professionals toward the centers that control power and resources, while relegating others to marginality" (1977, 205).

The strength of this stratification process is enhanced by the fact that while the state, as it hands out licenses, may not choose to discriminate between the professional educations received from schools A and B, those who recruit for professional organizations do. Their ability to discriminate is, in turn, facilitated by the fact that "at the gates of the professional world, the professional minorities who control a field do not receive an undifferentiated mass of entrants, but a superfiltered, superclassified and hierarchical cohort" (ibid.).

Thus the stratification not just of the organizations in which professionals work but of their feeder institutions as well augments the hierarchical aspect of the profession without destroying the illusion of *communitas*. Within the professional communities, then, stratification is not by individual but by clumps of individuals or "professional segments" (Bucher and Strauss 1961); this sort of stratification allows individuals within those clumps to stabilize their access to power and economic advantages. At the same time, because the stratification takes place one step removed from the individual, the individuals themselves can maintain the ideological conception (or myth) of the entire profession as a company of equals. This allows professionals to enjoy the benefits of *communitas* (freedom and autonomy) without the costs of having to prove their talent, work miracles, or do heroic deeds time and time again.[9]

Why then do public defenders feel ambivalent about the antistructural company-of-equals aspect of their organization? Why, while enjoying the benefits, do many of them want to add more structure? The answer has to do with the lack of legitimacy that the public defender's office has as a professional organization.

Looked at as a whole, Larson argues, the institutionalization of the professions in society has meant that professionals—regardless of their rank *within* the profession—do belong to a company of equals with respect to nonmembers of the profession: "The visible professions [e.g.,

9. The rare individual practitioner who ranks high in status, I believe, does so only because he or she constantly proves his or her talent. In this sense, F. Lee Bailey's access to rewards is much more dependent on ongoing and visible proof of his charisma or talent than is that of the senior member of a prominent law firm.

law, medicine, etc.] which have a clear monopoly of competence—and not only a monopoly of practice—have authority over a kind of knowledge that is important for every man's life. The gap in competence between professionals and laymen, institutionalized by monopolies of training and certification, ipso facto sets *every* professional apart: he belongs to a privileged society of 'knowers' " (1977, 231; see also Smith 1958, 414). In this, Larson is quite wrong. If the experience of the public defense lawyer teaches us anything, it is that the mere acquisition of technical training and certification does not guarantee that one will be perceived as apart and deserving of "deference in the nonpolitical circumstances of everyday life" (Larson 1977, 231). That public defenders are not accepted as deserving of the deference usually accorded professionals is proved by the lament, "I don't want a PD; I want a *real* lawyer!" Public defenders will protest that they *are* real lawyers, but for an individual to be given the deference that comes from having a high rank, it is not enough, as Homans put it, "that he should evaluate himself highly. . . . [The] group must also accept his evaluation" (1950, 140).

By mere affiliation with a group that lacks legitimacy as a professional organization, the public defense lawyer is barred from legitimacy as a lawyer—and, in consequence, his or her title to the deference and respect given "real lawyers" is clouded.

Playing an important part in maintaining the myth of competency—and hence the *communitas* found in most professional organizations—seems to be the implicit trust (shown by both its incumbents and their clients) in the organization as a "gatekeeper." There is no need to believe that all professional credentials are equally worthy (a belief that would be difficult to sustain); within legitimate professional organizations, *communitas* is sustained by the shared belief that one would not be there in the first place if he did not have the qualifications. In other words, as Friedson found in his study of the medical groups, "the very fact that the medical group had hired a physician was itself held to be a testimony of the competence of all its members" (Friedson 1975, 140). Because the public defender's office lacks legitimacy—or, more accurately, as one of the reasons why the office lacks legitimacy—there is no shared understanding that the office performs the requisite gatekeeping functions. Thus, in a way that is unusual among professional groups, the myth of competency has no believable roots.

While some public defenders may revel in the antistructure, others, as noted above, are made uncomfortable by it. This is due to the fact that the myth of competency does nothing for lawyers who believe (perhaps rightly) that, given the quality of their work, were it not for their affiliation with the office, their claims to professionalism would be accepted. The public defender's antistructure becomes a burden to lawyers when it denies them the chance to be acknowledged as better than the average public defender. Compounding this is the fact that both promotion to supervisor and salary increases, which in other contexts might be regarded as official sanction of superior skills, are tainted in the office of the public defender because they appear to be unrelated to either merit or consistent, rational policies. Moreover, the one official public defender policy that can be found forbids lawyers to practice law privately and thus denies individual public defenders the opportunity to negotiate legitimacy as lawyers in the private sector.

The lawyers' desire for more structure can be accounted for by their belief that more structure would play a gatekeeping function. If transfers, promotions, and pay raises were based on merit, then these would more likely validate the lawyers' claims to being "real" as they moved up in the office (much in the way that movement from associate to partner does in a private law firm).[10]

The persistence of special task forces within the office seems to be best explained as a response to the lawyers' ambivalence toward the office's antistructure. Perhaps because membership in a task force brings no automatic pay raise, the general feeling is that transfer into a task force is based on merit. In fact, this seems to be a valid assessment. Although the supervisor of one vertical task force allowed that, very rarely, he is obliged to accept a lawyer because of political considerations, he was firm in his assertion that almost all selections are based on merit. Importantly, in one of the task forces, members reportedly have to pass on prospective members before they are allowed to join the unit.

In effect, the vertical units, especially the two within the felony trial division, constitute separate law firms within the office of the public defender. The members of these units not only treat each other as members of a community of equals but tend to regard the average task force member as a better attorney than the average non–task force member. Because of the myth of competency, however, such comparisons are

---

10. Lawyers unsatisfied with their status as public defenders can, of course, leave the office, set up private practices, and attempt to validate their claims to professionalism on the open market. Or they can join a "real" law firm. This is, of course, what most public defense lawyers eventually do, and indeed it seems to work. One former public defender said that when he left the office, he was in the middle of working on a case. As is the custom, he took the case with him to private practice. What he especially remembers is that, "in the eyes of the trial judge, right in the middle of that case, I had suddenly become a genius! Just by leaving the office, I became a genius" (042). But while retiring from the office may be an attractive option for some, for many it is not something to rush into. Even after they have gained the experience that they believe is necessary to succeed on the outside, many continue to enjoy (as I noted in chap. 5) what they are doing—that is, practicing criminal law without being distracted by the business end of it.

overtly regarded as invidious; and often when such judgments were shared with me, I was cautioned that they were to be considered as definitely off-the-record. Nonetheless, among task force lawyers, the feeling of being special is common. As one lawyer, newly elevated to the Homicide Task Force, informed me when I commiserated that he would have to start working long hours on a difficult caseload, "lawyers don't work hard because they're on the task force; they're on the task force because they work hard."

Because no increase in either pay or power attends membership in a task force, it might be argued that these lawyers are "playing" at hierarchy (Turner 1969, 194), that theirs is a hierarchical distinction without instrumental value. This is, in effect, what some horizontal defense lawyers told me. For example, according to a lawyer who supervises a horizontal unit, "the differences between horizontal representation and vertical representation are totally overblown." But many more horizontal defense lawyers allowed that, regardless of any other benefits, the vertical lawyer can more easily do a more thorough job:

> I'd like to work on the vertical representation unit. It is like what I am doing now, except that I would get the case through the preliminary hearing and stuff. The first thirty days, when you first pick up the case, there's a lot of discovery or investigations you can go on. Say there's a 911 flash tape—you can get that subpoenaed. And you can see if, say a witness says, "I gave a complete description to the police," well you can check the tape and see if in fact there was a description. When I get a case [at the trial stage] after thirty days, it's already too late to get those types of things, and if the lawyer at the preliminary hearing court didn't follow through, they are lost. Sometimes it's already too late to get some witnesses (*007*).

Another tangible reward, according to vertical defense lawyers, is that clients often treat them better. When I asked vertical defense lawyers about the "I don't want a PD; I want a real lawyer" attitude, I was told: "Vertical representation helps that a lot. When you meet a guy when he is just off the street, and he's kind of claustrophobic and frightened, and you are the only one there, you make a quick bonding. And because you stay with his case, you get a different kind of relationship with them" (*008*). But most of all (as many commented with great enthusiasm), a vertical defense lawyer can be just like a "real lawyer": "You are on your own. You aren't under one judge's thumb. You don't have to report to the same courtroom every day, you keep a diary, you have your cases, and you go from court to court. And mostly, it's like being a private lawyer. You deal with different judges, with different state's attorneys, clients, different places, things like that" (*004*).

It is likely that it is not only those defendants who actually receive vertical representation who benefit from the special task forces. Because of the examples that vertical defense lawyers set, because of the prestige of being selected as a member of one of these special units, the existence of these task forces represents a crystallization of incentives for other public defenders and a standard against which they can measure their own skills. One lawyer remembers his early impression of these lawyers: "They seemed millions of miles away. The task force stood out in my imagination. They were wonderful lawyers who cared and were involved and loved their work. And that was what I needed to see. . . . I needed a sense that there was something I could aspire to, other than just aspiring to be a competent trial attorney." Having these units in the office gives the younger attorney something to strive toward. The belief that membership is based on merit means that, regardless of one's clout, all lawyers have an equal chance if they work hard. The important thing is that membership in a task force is accepted as visible proof of being apart, of being more than just a regular public defender.

Concluding Comments

What the experience of the public defender teaches is that the professional's place in society—and his or her rights to the respect and deference accorded to those who occupy high status—do not follow automatically from mere credentials. Because the public defender's office exists in the shadows and avoids negotiating legitimacy with the broader society, it denies its incumbents the shelter that legitimate institutions can offer workers. Although public defense lawyers are properly educated, credentialed, and licensed attorneys, their standing in the community is tainted by their affiliation. Although they have the necessary freedom and power to defend their clients well, they are not considered real lawyers—and thus they are not accorded the respect usually given "real lawyers." In the courtroom, at least, they could perhaps demand this, but they are constrained from such clearly (or so they think) self-serving action by the fear that being uppity will injure their clients (see, e.g., Platt and Pollock 1974, 26–27).

But, as an inside view shows, the organization is not unresponsive to the needs of its lawyers. Lawyers join the public defender's office because they want to become trial attorneys. For their service they are rewarded with the opportunity to learn the trial skills that this sort of advocacy demands. They are rewarded, moreover, by being treated—in the office—as adults and as attorneys, by being given more freedom of action than some of them perhaps deserve. Certainly they are rewarded with more freedom than are young lawyers who join either the typical private law firm or the state's attorney's office.

For many of them, the fact that public defending is not expected to be a life-time commitment probably eases the frustrations that come with not being regarded as "real." But for many of them, once they have acquired the skills that make them (in their own estimation, at least) as good as or better than the private lawyers that they encounter, the stigma of being a public defender is not compensated by the freedom of action that they receive. There is a desire on the part of many of them to be something better than just a P.D. Being one of a company of equals is all very well and good—but not when you believe you are superior. It is likely that it is at this point that many lawyers leave the office and begin private practice, where, unhindered by the stigma of being a public defender, they can receive the respect and deference normally accorded professionals.

For many lawyers, the benefits of public defending, including the freedom to practice criminal law without being distracted by the business end of it, makes leaving the office something to be postponed. Among these lawyers there has evolved a form of organizing within the office that runs counter to the egalitarian currents that govern the office. The special vertical task forces have become, in effect, separate entities within the office, and the lawyers who work within these have managed to negotiate for themselves a reputation of being better than the average public defense lawyer. Although there is some resistance to this situation on the part of their unchosen colleagues, these units are a source of incentive for many of the younger lawyers.

Three

Public Defense Lawyers and Their Society

"But How Can You _____ 8
Sleep Nights?" _____

Hardly anyone will take issue with the idea that everyone, guilty or innocent, is entitled to a fair trial. But beyond this, the views of lawyers and
nonlawyers diverge. To the nonlawyer, a fair trial is one that results in
convicting the defendant who is factually guilty and acquitting the defendant who is not. But it is the lawyer's job to do every possible thing that
can be done for the defendant, even when that means getting a criminal
off scot-free. Loopholes and technicalities are defense attorneys' major
weapons. Lay people are inclined to feel that using legal tricks to gain
acquittals for the guilty is at least morally objectionable, if not reprehen-
sible. What many people want to know is how defense attorneys can live
with themselves after they help a guilty person escape punishment.

It might be supposed that lawyers are unimpressed by what, to the
rest of us, is the core dilemma of their profession—that is, how to justify
defending a guilty person. It might be reasoned that lawyers escape this
quandary because their legal training has taught them that it does not
exist. In law school everyone learns that a defendant is innocent until
proved guilty. Lawyers believe this—and can act on it—because they
have been taught to "think like lawyers." Legal reasoning, "although

not synonymous with formal reasoning and logic . . . is closely tied to them. Promotion of these skills encourages abstracting legal issues out of their social contexts to see issues narrowly and with precision" (Zemans and Rosenblum 1981, 205).

Simply put, legal reasoning depends on a closed set of premises; some propositions are legal, others are not. The nonlawyer can scarcely be expected to appreciate or understand the difference, for it takes "trained men" to "winnow one from the other" (Friedman 1975, 245). But lawyers, by virtue of this training, are expected to cope with complex issues, to detach themselves from difficult moral questions and focus on legal ones, to take any side of an argument while remaining personally uninvolved, and to avoid making moral judgments about their clients or their clients' cases. Thus—and this is a surprise to non-lawyers—the factual guilt or innocence of the client is *supposed* to be irrelevant. A lawyer is expected to take a point of view and argue it; a criminal defense lawyer is expected to put on a vigorous defense even when the client is known to be guilty.

On the other hand, however much their training sets them apart, there are some attorneys who cannot detach themselves, cannot overlook the social and moral meanings and consequences of their jobs. There are lawyers who in fact see the issues very much as nonlawyers do. Ohio attorney Ronald L. Burdge explained to columnist Bob Greene why he had given up defending criminal cases: "If your client is guilty and you defend him successfully, then you have a criminal walking the streets because of your expertise. I have a couple of children. I just didn't like the idea of going home at night knowing that I was doing something so— unpalatable. I found it difficult to look at my kids knowing that this was how I was making a living" (Greene 1982, 1).

A former assistant public defender who spent five years in the Cook County Public Defender's Office echoed Burdge when he explained his disenchantment with the job: "The public defender's cases are thankless: if you lose, society wins; if you win, society loses. I really began to feel as if I was doing a bad thing when I got someone off. They were dangerous people" (*049*). Today, almost all of this attorney's clients are indigent, but criminal cases do not intrude into his practice.

In spite of their training, lawyers may find it difficult to focus only on the narrow legal aspects of their cases because they are rarely isolated from others who question the morality of the defense lawyer's job. Seymour Wishman, in his book *Confessions of a Criminal Lawyer,* says a chance encounter with one of these "others" marked a turning point in his career, made him rethink how he was spending his life. It happened in a hospital emergency room:

Across the lobby, a heavy but not unattractive woman in a nurse's uniform suddenly shrieked, "Get that motherfucker out of here!" Two women rushed forward to restrain her. "That's the lawyer, that's the motherfucking lawyer!" she shouted.

I looked round me. No one else resembled a lawyer. Still screaming, she dragged her two restrainers toward me. I was baffled. As the only white face in a crowd of forty, I felt a growing sense of anxiety.

I didn't know what she was talking about.

"Kill him and that nigger Horton!"

Larry Horton . . . of course. Larry Horton was a client of mine. Six months before, I had represented him at his trial for sodomy and rape. At last I recognized the woman's face. She had testified as the "complaining" witness against Horton. (1981, 4)

Wishman remembered how he had humiliated this woman when she testified against his client, how by cross-examination he had undone her claim that she had been raped and had made her seem to be little more than a prostitute. Seeing her rage started him thinking that society—and, more specifically, the victims of those whom he had defended—were "casualties" of his skill as a defense lawyer. After years spent preparing for and practicing criminal law, Wishman believed that he had to change: "I had never turned down a case because the crime or the criminal were despicable—but now that would change. I could no longer cope with the ugliness and brutality that had for so long, too long, been part of my life" (241).

Encounters between defense lawyers and those who question the ethics of their work are seldom as dramatic as the one experienced by Wishman. But it is certain that such encounters occur with great frequency in the lives of defense attorneys. All of the current public defenders with whom I spoke and nearly all (93 percent) of the former assistants interviewed in my research agreed that people "constantly" ask public defenders, "How can you defend those people?" But the disenchanted public defender quoted above seems to speak for only a minority of lawyers. The overwhelming majority (97 percent) of former public defenders interviewed agreed that they had believed that they were putting their legal skills to good use by working as public defenders. Only five (8 percent) said that they would not join the office if they had it to do over again.

Given that the public defender's goal is to zealously defend and to work toward acquittal for his or her clients (even clients whom they themselves believe are guilty of heinous crimes), how do these lawyers justify their work? As I explain below, it is not as if public defenders harbor any illusions about the factual innocence of the usual client; on the contrary, most will openly admit that the majority of their clients are factually guilty. If conventional morality has it that defending guilty people is tantamount to an obstruction of justice, how do public defenders justify their rebellion? How *do* they defend those people?

How can you defend people whom you know are guilty? Public defenders say that question is incredibly naive, that for the most part they have little patience with that question and little time for anyone who asks it. One suspects that they would like to answer with shock and outrage when asked how they do what they do—and sometimes they do answer like that. But usually they respond in a manner that is more weary than indignant:

> Oh God, *that* question! How do you represent someone you know is guilty? So you go through all the things. You know, "he's not guilty until he's proven guilty, until a judge or a jury say he's guilty, until he's been proved guilty beyond a reasonable doubt." I think everyone deserves the best possible defense, the most fair trial he can get. It's a guarantee of the Constitution, no more, no less. (*004*)

I tell them it's easy, and I give them a whole list of reasons why it's easy. . . . Everyone has a right to a trial, and with that right to a trial you have a right to a lawyer. I'm that lawyer. That's the American way. (*009*)

> I get asked that all the time, even by my family, even by my wife! The only answer I can give is just that everyone deserves somebody to stand up for them; everyone deserves a trial, a fair trial. They aren't going to get a fair trial unless they have someone like me. (*011*)

Without exception the public defenders whom I interviewed all had spiels prepared for that question—another testimony to the fact that answering it is part of their routine. As a reporter who interviewed Public Defender James Doherty in 1983 observed, "If you don't ask him soon enough, he'll preempt you" (Spencer 1984, 1). Some lawyers even had two spiels, one for people who phrased it *as* a question and another for those who made it an accusation: "I have developed a patter that depends on how aggressively I am asked. When asked aggressively, I respond aggressively—'How can you possibly ask me such a question? Have you never read the Constitution?' It gets meaner. When I am asked, well, you know, in a relatively dispassionate way, a neutral sort of way, basically the response is, 'It makes no difference to me whether they are guilty or not, whether they have committed the offense or not, the person is entitled to have representation to protect his Constitutional rights'" (*014*). Simply put, public defenders believe that they come not to destroy the law but to fulfill it.

The sincerity of the public defenders' beliefs is compelling, but the persuasiveness of their arguments is less so. The litany of constitutional ideals rarely convinces the hearer any more (as I will suggest) than it emotionally empowers public defense lawyers to act zealously in the defense of their clients. Attorney Burdge, for example, states unequivocally that *he* still *believed* in the constitutional rights of defendants, that all he was abandoning was his personal protection of these rights: "I just think I'll let other lawyers defend them" (Greene 1982, 1).

Making a Case Defensible

Sociologist Emile Durkheim pointed out that conformity to and rebellion against conventional morality have much in common. The individual, he argued, can free him- or herself partially from the rules of society if there is a felt disparity between those rules and society as it is: "That is, if he desires a morality which corresponds to the actual state of society and not to an outmoded condition. The principle of rebellion is the same as that of conformity. It is the *true* nature of society which is conformed to when the traditional morality is obeyed, and yet it is also the *true* nature of society which is being conformed to when the same morality is flouted" (1974, 65). If Durkheim is correct, public defenders who daily "flout" conventional morality by defending guilty people are perhaps no more focused only on the narrow legal issues than are those who are troubled by what public defenders do. In fact, if pursued (tactfully) beyond the obvious constitutional justifications, the question, How can you defend someone you know is guilty? uncovers the fact that other sorts of rationales are used. Although none of the lawyers went so far as to say, "Yes, I like putting guilty people back on the streets, and I am proud of myself each time I do it," they find justification for doing defense work precisely where Burdge and Wishman found justification for abandoning it—that is, in its social and moral (rather than simply legal) context. Of course, as one might expect, most public defenders stress a different kind of moral and social context than Burdge and Wishman emphasized.

Under some circumstances, mere empathy with the client's situation permits lawyers to feel justified when defending someone whom they know is factually guilty:

> Especially when I was in misdemeanor courts, I could see myself as a defendant. Sometimes you get angry enough at somebody to take a swing at them—if you had a gun, to take a shot at them. I could see myself doing that. . . . Just because somebody was arrested and charged with a crime doesn't mean they are some kind of evil person. (*009*)

143

Look, kids get into trouble, some kids get into serious trouble. I can understand that. In juvenile court our job isn't to punish, the result is supposed to be in the best interests of the minor. Here you've got to keep them with their family and give them all the services you can so they don't do this again. (*016*)

Not unexpectedly, at some point the ability to empathize breaks down. This is especially true for public defenders who have passed through juvenile or misdemeanor assignments and into felony trial courts, where they are less able—or maybe less willing—to see themselves as being like their clients:

They [the clients] are seedy and they tend to be, compared to the general population, they are seedier, dirtier, less intelligent, have less conscience, are more sociopathic, more inconsiderate of others, more violent, more poverty stricken and more schizophrenic. (*002*)

Your clients have no funds, they know witnesses who only have one name and not even an address because they all hang out on the streets. They don't have phones. They just don't have a life like the rest of us. (*007*)

They don't make their appointments; they aren't articulate enough to take the stand. All those things make it hard. (*008*)

While the differences between attorney and client mean that the attorney sometimes has a hard time understanding his or her client (and especially the client's motive), *it does not mean* that the client cannot be defended:

A guy hits somebody over the head and takes a wallet—no problem. A guy that gets into a drunken brawl—no problem. I understand that. Somebody that goes out in the street and commits a rape—I still don't know what goes on his mind. No, it doesn't make it harder to defend. There is *never* any excuse for a rape, but you don't have to understand what makes a rapist tick to defend him effectively. (*012*)

Sometimes I would question their motives—if it [the crime] seemed senseless, if it seemed particularly brutal or something like that. Then I realized that those were really, for me, irrelevant questions. I still wonder, of course, but I don't ask anymore. (*014*)

But the alien character especially of the crimes that their clients are alleged to have committed—and the sorts of attributions that they make about their clients because of their crimes—often mean that "you have to care more about your clients' rights than you can usually care about your clients" (*030*).

A. The Moral Context of Public Defending

> Why do I do it? I do it because the day that I start laying down and not doing my job is the day that people who aren't guilty are going to be found guilty, and that person might be you because the whole system will have degenerated to the point where they can arrest and convict you on very little evidence. So I am protecting you, I am protecting the middle-class. (*006*)

On the surface, what a defense lawyer does is simply protect the client's rights. But many lawyers transform the nature of the battle. They are not fighting for the freedom of their client per se but to keep the system honest: "It doesn't mean that I want to get everybody off. It means that I try to make sure the state's attorneys meet up to their obligations, which means that the only way they can prove someone guilty is beyond reasonable doubt, with competent evidence, and overcoming the presumption of innocence. If they can do that, then they get a guilty. If they can't do that, then my client deserves to go home" (*004*).

The lawyers' way of "bracketing" their role (Weick 1979), of focusing not on the guilt or innocence of their client but on the culpability of the state, transforms circumstances of low or questionable morality into something for which they can legitimately fight. They do not defend simply because their clients have rights but because they believe that those rights have been, are, or will be ignored by others in the criminal justice system. That their adversaries often cheat is taken for granted by public defenders. As one put it, "I expected a fairly corrupt system, and I found one. Here I am representing people who cheat, lie, and steal, and I find the same intellect represented in the police who arrest them, in some of the prosecutors and some of the judges as well" (*001*). Even when not asked to provide examples, every public defender with whom I spoke offered examples of cheating. There was cheating by the police:

> When I was [working] in the state's attorney's office, I would have cops walking up to me as I was preparing a case and I would say, "Officer, tell me what happened." And they would say, "Well, how do *you* want it to have happened?" (*017*)

> The biggest form of police dishonesty was this street files thing. They were hiding evidence that would get people off—or get the correct person. But they had decided in their own minds, "This guy is the guy I'm going after," instead of letting the court system decide who was right. (*011*)

And there was cheating by state's attorneys:

Sometimes you know it; sometimes you just suspect that they are kinking the case. One guy, fairly high up in the state's attorney's office, described one of their lawyers as naive because he'd been shocked to find a state's attorney had kinked the case. He said of the lawyer, "He thinks this is for real?"

Q: Kinked the case?

R: You might call it suborning perjury; you might call it jogging the memory. (*012*)

Q: Are you saying that state's attorneys are sometimes a little unprofessional?

R: Yes, yes, yes! Lying, having witnesses lie; they lie themselves on the record, they make inferences that I'm lying. It's just a basic matter of cheating, of not being professional. Because they feel they *must* win the case and will do anything to win the case. . . . Their obligation is *not* to win; it is to make sure the law is upheld—and to make sure that my client gets a fair trial. And to them, *that* is a fallacy. (*004*)

I remember in that case the prosecutor basically pulled every trick she could: she argued things that were outside the record; she told the jury that [my client] had a record, that he had put a contract out on the witness. She would stop at nothing to win. (*011*)

This is not to say that one can walk into a Cook County courtroom and expect to see public defenders and state's attorneys at each others' throats. That does happen (at least verbally) on occasion (as I illustrate below), but most public defenders say that they try to maintain a good rapport with their opponents—if only because it helps them do their jobs. And I was cautioned by some lawyers not to listen to those who would condemn state's attorneys universally. As one lawyer told me, "Most of them are not unreasonable; most of them are not [pause] dirty. Most of them are just doing their jobs as best they can" (*010*).

Yet, scratch the surface just a little and it is likely that a great deal of tension will be uncovered. It can be noted too that this is not unique to Cook County. A study conducted in Alameda, California, found that relations between public defenders and prosecutors were "often characterized by hostility, suspicion, and conflict" and that "relations between public defenders and judges were not much better" (Lydon 1973; cited in Utz 1978, 215).

Actually, public defenders in Cook County seem to be of two minds about their judges. On the one hand, they seem willing to trust the judges to do the right thing.

If the facts are on your side then you usually take a bench trial. Because you know if you take it before a decent judge, he'll give you a not guilty. *(008)*

We win most of our bench trials; at least we get what we think the case is worth in most of our bench trials. *(011)*

I think if you stand up there and talk like you know what you are talking about, judges who don't know the law tend to listen to you. If you can present it in a fair-minded way and not ranting and raving and saying, "You idiot, you can't do that and you can't do that!" Sometimes it doesn't work, but, for the most part, it is better if you rationally and calmly explain why you are right. *(010)*

On the other hand, one gets a definite impression that what public defenders trust about judges is not their fair-mindedness and good-will, but rather, in many cases, the judges' desire not to get into trouble by being overturned by a higher court. In any case, many public defenders told me that they just do not trust the judges' "instincts":

Knowing legal theory is important, I guess, but it doesn't do any good in Cook County courts, because the question is not Does the law apply? but Can you get the judge to obey it, even though his instincts are to fuck you? *(003)*

Oh, I wised up real quick and found that judges don't care about the law; they don't always follow the law.
Q: Do they know the law?
R: Sometimes . . .
Q: But there's always a public defender there to teach them?
R: Yea [laugh], but they don't usually care. *(009)*

I view judges as another state's attorney. I see judges as essentially enemies I have to deal with . . . most of them are just bangers.
Q: Bangers?
R: Someone who gives heavy sentences—oftentimes regardless of the facts of the case.

The sort of cheating to which public defenders attribute their hostility toward police, prosecutors, and judges is something that public defenders say they see a lot. And though such cheating may be expected, public defenders find it unacceptable—and are not afraid to say so. It is ironic, but listening to public defenders talk about their cases and why they do what they do is like listening to someone who has just been mugged. Public defenders do feel as if they are often mugged—by the legal system. There is a lot of real and passionate anger: "Some people said I'd become cynical after a while. Well, I might be more cynical about some things, but I don't think I have really changed my attitude. If anything, I might have become a little more gung ho. You see that there really is an awful lot of injustice. It becomes very real and it's scary. I find myself becoming very angry in this job, all the time" (*009*).

There is good evidence that the things that public defenders cite when they complain about police, prosecutorial, and judicial misconduct do happen (and not just in Chicago [see, e.g., Alschuler 1972; Dershowitz 1983; Dorsen and Friedman 1973; Friedman 1975]), but it would be difficult, of course, to determine just how widespread such behaviors actually are. Yet, the real frequency of misconduct is beside the point. The point is that most public defenders *believe* that such things do happen "all the time. It's something you really have to watch for" (*019*).

Whether or not public defenders are correct in their assumptions that police lie, that prosecutors will often do anything to win, and that judges do not really care or know enough to be fair, it is quite clear that the way in which the public defenders see the world not only excuses their work but makes it seem important. Their rationales are enabling mechanisms for the public defenders. But what ultimately pushes the lawyer to do the job is, I believe, something even more personal—the desire to win.

B. "Adversariness"

Perspectives on the criminal justice system sometimes make use of two ideal type models: the classic adversarial model, which is "couched in constitutional-ideological terms of due process" (Blumberg 1979, 291), and the "dispositional" or "bureaucratic" model, which serves only "bland obeisance to constitutional principles. It is characterized by the superficial ceremonies and formal niceties of traditional due process, but not its substance" (*Ibid.*, 145). (See also Eisenstein and Jacob 1977; Packer 1964.) The difference between the two models is the difference between the presumption of innocence and the presumption of guilt.

It is significant that social scientists who study public defenders tend to discuss their findings only in terms of the second model—the bureaucratic or plea-bargaining model. Never is the matter of how public defenders measure up as trial attorneys studied. The stereotype of the public defender as plea bargainer is, to put it mildly, firmly entrenched in the literature (see, e.g., Blumberg 1967, 1979; Eisenstein and Jacob 1977; Heumann 1978; Jackson 1983; Nardulli 1978; Sudnow 1965).[1]

1. Importantly, not all who study plea bargaining necessarily regard it as a nonadvocacy—or even nonadversarial—process. Feeley, for one, has cautioned us that

It is a fact that most cases that come into the criminal trial courts are disposed of through pleas of guilty; many of these are negotiated—that is, based on a reduction of charges or sentences. Kalvin and Zeisel's (1966) estimate that 75 percent of total criminal prosecutions are disposed of through pleas is now seen as conservative; more often the estimate is between 85 percent and 95 percent (depending on whether misdemeanor cases are included in the count)(see Blumberg 1979, 168). The National Advisory Commission on Criminal Justice Standards and Goals (1974, 42) has estimated that in many courts the rate of guilty pleas is 90 percent.

Public defenders do not deny the importance of plea bargaining in their work; they openly and easily acknowledge that the greatest majority of their cases are ultimately disposed of through pleas of guilty. But, they stress, plea bargaining is not their reason for being there but is just a tool:

> **Q:** Now here you are telling me that you are a "trial attorney." How can you say that? To be fair, isn't most of your work really plea bargaining?
>
> **R:** Plea bargaining is just part of procedure. Just like I wouldn't say, "I'm a procedural attorney." . . . It's part of what you go through, and it's one of the options available to my clients. You know, "If you in fact did this, and you want this deal, and you understand what you are offered, here is the deal." (016)

In some cases, I was told, the structure that ostensibly exists to handle plea bargaining is used in the lawyer's trial strategy:

> In most courtrooms you have a conference before the trial and lay out your case and say what you are going to do. This happens before the judge. Part of this is a function of State's Attorney Daley's office. The state's attorneys are very rarely giving very reasonable offers. They are putting it all on the judges; they make the judge make the decision.
>
> So, in general what you do is ask for a plea conference. You go back with the state to the judge's chambers.
>
> Supposedly, you are there for the state to say their side, for you to say your side, and for the state to make an offer.
>
> What I'm finding though, is that you are trying your case that way—for the judge. We [public defenders] are stronger, better prepared. Even if

---

"preliminary hearings, probable cause hearings, and informal discovery may serve many of the functions of a trial—to obtain and test crucial evidence and challenge assertions of fact and law—which may in turn lead to nolles, dismissals, or pleas of guilty in the face of an overwhelming case. To infer the lack of an adversarial stance and the existence of bargained settlement—for the pure purpose of administrative convenience—from the absence of trials is to ignore altogether the importance of these other 'truthtesting' and highly combative processes" (Feeley 1979, 29; see also Maynard 1984, chap. 5).

I'm not getting an offer that my man is going to plead guilty to, I'm taking the case in front of the judge. It gives me an advantage in the trial. *(008)*

The Role of Trials in Local Justice

The majority of their clients do plead guilty, but trials are not unimportant in the world of the public defender. They are important, on the one hand, because what happens during trials helps determine the outcome of cases that are plea bargained. For example, prosecutors wish to maintain a strong record of conviction at trial or else defendants who might otherwise opt for a plea bargain will seek acquittal at a trial. Rulings on evidence made by judges during trials also have an impact on the negotiating process. Attorneys from both sides will evaluate the strength of their positions by the standards evolved through trial court and appellate hearings; these rulings made by trial judges, as well as the sentences given to defendants found guilty, help parties in a plea bargain to determine what their respective cases are "worth" (Jacob 1980, 80).

But more fundamentally, trials are important in the public defender's world (and hence are stressed here) because, at least in Cook County, public defenders first and last define themselves as trial lawyers. As I noted in chapter 5, lawyers become public defenders primarily to gain trial experience; once they have become public defenders, performance at trial is much more crucial to attributions that they make about themselves and each other than one could ever guess given the relative frequency of these performances.

Public defenders often said that they like the trial work more than any other part of their job. Each one will admit, however, that there are some who do not feel that way.[2] These were pointed out to me as examples of bad public defenders or "kickers." "Sometimes we get a public defender that does not work. He'll force his guy to take a plea, finally on the last day before trial: 'Listen guy, you can take a plea which is the best thing you could do or you can go to trial. But I'm not prepared for trial and you're going to lose because you are *supposed* to lose this case—you know that too'" *(001)*. Some public defenders are labeled as bad lawyers because they cannot hack it in the courtroom; the reason that they cannot

2. At some level public defenders seem to understand clients who think that public defense lawyers are unwilling to go to trial, are just "penitentiary dispatchers" interested in making deals for clients. Appearances can sometimes be deceiving—even to some lawyers: "Now _____, he was to me the epitome of the worst kind of public defender. From a distance, I got the feeling that he was just there to cop people out, and to run through cases with no sense of the client, no empathy with the person. I know now I was making a childish sort of judgment. It's a show he puts on, maybe to protect himself. In reality he practically weeps when he loses, not for himself, but for his client" *(008)*.

hack it (it is said) is that they are afraid. As many pointed out, being "on trial" is scary. One veteran lawyer told me: "We lose a lot of public defenders because they can't handle being on trial."

But all of them, even the lawyers who love trial work, are ambivalent about it. Trial work, or so most of them acknowledge (in words, if not by deed), is as terrifying as it is exhilarating.

> You know [a lawyer who is now in private practice]? Now he is one of the better trial lawyers. But he used to throw up before final arguments. Once he did it right in front of the jury; he just went over to the wastebasket and threw up. (*009*)

> Trials? *That's* when I can't sleep well at night; I'm too busy thinking. A trial is not one issue, it's many. It's win or lose; it's deadlines, organizing things, making sure your witnesses are ready, looking good in front of the jury, looking confident in front of the judge, watching everything you are doing, being alert, keeping a lot of things in your mind at once. And remembering that your client's freedom depends on your polish, how well you can bring it off. (*001*)

Doing Trials

On television a defense lawyer confronts his clients with demands for the truth: "Okay, I'm your lawyer and you gotta trust me. If I am going to do a good job I need to know exactly what happened. Don't be afraid to tell me, I can't defend you unless you are perfectly straight with me." The client is thus persuaded to tell all to his lawyer.

This sort of dialogue may appeal to the viewer's common sense—that is, of course the lawyer needs to know what happened and whether the client is guilty. But in real life, things do not happen that way—at least they do not happen that way when the lawyer is a public defender. Public defenders are quick to admit that they usually *do not* ask their clients whether they are guilty or innocent. Why not ask? The lawyers claimed that it was simply not relevant, that it was something that they did not need to know.

> I don't ask "Did you do it?" anymore. I realized it was irrelevant. (*008*)

> I say to them first thing: "I don't care if you did it or not." (*007*)

> I say: "I don't give a damn whether you did it or not. I'm not your judge, I'm not your priest, I'm not your father. My job is to defend you, and I don't care whether you did it." (*002*)

151

It might be that public defenders do not ask because they know that their client is probably guilty and because, as one said, "they will all lie anyway" (*011*). But there seems to be more to it than that. Many said that, when it comes down to it, they do not ask because they are afraid that the client will tell them the truth!

Q: Don't you ever ask your clients if they are guilty or innocent?
R: Never!
Q: Why is that?
R: Because, in the first place, it is irrelevant. It's not my role to decide whether they are guilty—in our sense of the term guilt.
Q: What about the "second place?"
R: Well, it is my role to fashion a defense and to be creative. If the person says to me "This is how I did it," it's pretty hard for me to come around and try to do something for them. In general, I fence around with some of my questions. I ask them about an alibi or something like that. But the more I think they are guilty, the less I will ask. (*008*)

Public defenders do not begin their relationship with a client by asking awkward questions (e.g., Did you do it?) because once the client admits guilt, it limits what the public defender can ethically do:

I don't ask them because you put them at a disadvantage if you ask them and they say they did it.

I had a client once who was charged with battery, and he said, "Yea, I hit him, and I've been meaning to hit him for a long time. But it's just his word against mine, and I'm gonna say I didn't do it."

And I said: "*Not* with me as your lawyer you're not! You are not going to say anything like that."

So it's important to get the transcript [from the preliminary hearing] and look at the police reports and say "Look, this is the evidence against us" and then let him make up his own story. It's the only way to do it. (*002*)

Being honest, ethical, and "scrupled" in a system that many of them believe is corrupt is very important to the lawyers with whom I spoke.[3] Although some (naive observers) may wonder at the fragility of this honesty, it is something in which the public defenders take pride:[4] "There aren't many public defenders—if any—that I can point to and

3. For discussions of such ethical positions see Freedman (1975, chap. 5) and Hazard (1978, chap. 9).
4. On the other hand, most of the lawyers admitted that, as public defenders, they are relatively protected from temptations to cheat. Whenever I asked them about this, the

say: 'that man is dishonest. He lied and distorted everything, just to get a client off.' That just doesn't happen. The same cannot be said for lawyers in the state's attorney's office.

You test the state's evidence, you doubt it, you put it into its worst light. But that is not dishonest. Quite the contrary, that is how you get at the truth!" *(011)*.

Public defenders learn quickly that the tell-me-the-truth approach will only help defend an innocent person—the exceptional client. Public defenders argue that it is not their job to decide who is guilty and who is not. Instead, it is the public defender's job to judge the quality of the case that the state has against the defendant. If the lawyer does decide that the state has a case that cannot be called into reasonable doubt, then the lawyer will probably try to get the defendant to admit guilt so that pleading is more palatable—but usually *only* then.

Bad Cases and Good Lawyers

> There is a saying in the office: "Good facts make good lawyers." A good lawyer, I think, is one who doesn't screw up a case. Someone who takes a case that's a winner—one that should be won—and wins it; gets a not guilty. A bad lawyer is a person who takes a case that should be won and loses it. A good lawyer isn't necessarily one that wins a loser case. You get lucky; you get a good jury and win a case that no one could possily win. That doesn't prove anything; that is very often luck, and it doesn't mean anything. *(004)*

In practice, a more diffuse yardstick is used: "competency is taking the right cases to trial and winning them." As I show below, the lawyers following this logic are in peril of succumbing to a painful tautological trap.

Public defenders try not to go into a trial with cases that cannot be won. Unfortunately, most of their cases are of this type—loser (or "dead-bang loser") cases, cut-and-dried situations in which the client was caught red-handed and "the state has everything but a video tape of

---

typical response was "Who would want to bribe a public defender? Anyone who could afford to bribe someone would have a private lawyer."

Once in private practice, these lawyers may not find it so easy to avoid what may be called the near occasions of sin that are apparently relatively common in Chicago. Recently, a former public defender was indicted for attempted bribery. He got a not guilty on a "technicality." Furthermore, five of the twenty lawyers alleged by the *Chicago Lawyer* magazine to be "Hallway Hustlers" were former public defenders. This label is applied to lawyers who hang out in misdemeanor courts and prey on unwary defendants—that is, take their money and render no or only dubious services.

the crime" *(006)*. In the face of overwhelming evidence, the lawyers will try to talk the client into taking a plea or "copping out." One reason for this is the knowledge that taking a loser case to trial will hurt the client:

> My philosophy is that if you are going down and you know it, you should get the best deal for your client that you can. And you should try and make your client see the wisdom of that. It's better for your client. I could say "Sure, I'll take this to trial, sure I can use the experience," but that doesn't do your client any good if he's going down for more time.
>
> I have a client who I have been dealing with just recently who, ah, I was his attorney and I told him he ought to plead guilty. I told him I got this *great* deal for him: I had packed up several cases he had pending in several courtrooms and got him two years. And he had been convicted before!
>
> But he didn't like it. He got himself a private attorney who gave him a guarantee of probation or something. He calls me up and said the private attorney had come back to him with an offer of *six* years. He said to me: "You were right!" *(009)*

In large part, being competent is being able to convince a client that it is not in his or her best interests to insist on a trial that cannot be won. One lawyer explained how he had learned this lesson back when he was assigned to a preliminary hearing court:

> "Well, pal, listen. They caught you inside this guy's home, this guy held you down while his wife called the police. You are not going to get a chance to beat this case. You say you were drunk, but being drunk just isn't a good excuse anymore. It's up to you. The state is making you an offer and if you take it, you'll be better off than if you go upstairs [to the trial court]."
>
> Everybody told you to say things like that and sure enough, when I got up to the trial courts, I realized it was true. The offers *are* much better in preliminary hearing courts.
>
> But to confront those guys with that decision. It was incredible, it was so hard.
>
> Now I can do it fairly routinely because I have been doing it long enough to have confidence in what I'm saying. I know it is true. And I learned that you aren't doing anyone a favor when you bring a loser case upstairs—it's no good for the client, it's no good for the lawyer. But then I felt incredibly guilty.

Once it is decided that they have a loser case, different attorneys have different ways of trying to "cool out" clients who want to go to trial. However, all of the attorneys with whom I spoke and all of the public defenders that I observed with clients seemed uncomfortable with the idea of forcing anyone to take a plea.[5] Most emphasized that they always tried to reason with their clients:

> Most of our clients do feel that if you are a public defender you are not going to give it your all, because you have so many cases, or you just don't care, or whatever. They feel that you are just there to cop them out.
> But my partner and I sit down with a guy and say: "Look, we are lawyers, and we are paid to analyze facts. After we have analyzed the facts we might say to you, 'we don't think you have a good case and we think you should cop out.' If you don't feel that way, it's up to you."
> *We* let *them* make the decision. (*011*)

> I always leave it up to the defendant. I lay it out for him what the risks are, and if he asks me I'll tell him what his chances of winning are. But just like I can't play God and say if he's guilty or not, I can't play God and tell a guy "You go to trial," or "You don't go to trial." (*006*)

> I always tell them, "it's no skin off my nose whether you go to trial or not. I'll do the best job I can if you want to go to trial; I'll negotiate the best deal I can if you don't want to go to trial." (*012*)

But, public defenders admitted, reasoning with a client does not always produce the desired result. One lawyer, now a supervisor, admitted that occasionally he would resort to a little "bullying."[6] What did he mean by that? "I would come in, and I would say things like, 'You know, you are a damn fool if you don't take this deal, because this is the

---

5. As a result of his nationwide survey of defense lawyers, Professor Albert W. Alschuler of the University of Chicago Law School noted that, in some measure, how the problem of the "innocent" defendant was handled helped to distinguish the strategies of public from private defense attorneys: "With only a few exceptions, public defenders refused to enter guilty pleas when their clients claimed to be innocent. Private defense attorneys, by contrast, were almost evenly divided between those who followed the same rule and those who maintained that 'guilt or innocence has nothing to do with it'" (1975, 1283).

6. It should be noted that public defenders say that, when the occasion demands, they will work just as hard to convince a client with a good case that he ought to go to trial:

> Some will say, "I'm guilty, and I'm going to plead." And if I think they have a good case, I'll say to them, "Look, I think we can win this; you have a good case."
> It takes something out of you when you have a case you think you can win and you want to try, but the guy pleads.
> The *worst* situation, though, is when you have a young kid with no record who can't stand it any more, being locked up and raped and beaten in jail, and they offer him a way out and he takes it—probation, or time served, or something. And you can't get him to trial fast enough; it's living hell for him in there (*012*).

best you are going to get. If you go on trial, in my opinion, you are going to be found guilty and you are going to get more time.' And then people would say—not often, but occasionally, the person would say—'I don't care; I didn't do it, and I want a trial!' And I would say, 'Okay, okay. If *that's* your attitude, let's go to trial!' "

If public defenders resist taking loser cases to trial because it will hurt the client, they resist too because it will be painful for the lawyer. One of the worst things about being a public defender, said one former assistant, was "not the realization that most of your clients were in fact guilty" but the fact that "there was very little you could do to get the system to give them a not guilty" (*036*) or that, as another said, "your clients never had any real obvious defense and you [the attorney] were just stuck" (*060*).

Ask any public defender "What was your worst case?" and you may or may not hear about some horrible crime; you may or may not hear about the case that lasted the longest or took the most preparation. Chances are, however, you will hear about a case that was a loser. Understanding the nature of a loser case is crucial, for embedded in the concept—and in the distinctions that lawyers make between losers and other sorts of cases—is the clue to what makes public defenders tick.

> The worst case is where the state has an overwhelming amount of evidence and there is nothing you can do with it. . . . It's a case where you are just overwhelmed by the state's evidence. It's a case where you get beat up in court. And that is just *no fun. (009)*

> You are so relieved when a guy pleads out on a case that you know you can't win and you are going to get your head beaten on, and the jury is probably going to throw rocks at you when you make the closing argument. *(011)*

> My worst case was a very hopeless case, a rape and armed robbery, and the persons were captured by the police and they were contending that they were the wrong guys.

> Q: Why was that your worst case? You've defended people accused of *murder* before.
> R: The fact that the individuals were given reasonable offers and they should have copped pleas, because there wasn't a chance of their being acquitted. And they were going through the ordeal because they opted for a jury trial. It was just a very painful process; it was just an *absurd* situation. (*014*)

> Q: Was it a particularly awful crime?

R: No. Well, he just beat up his girlfriend; he didn't kill her or anything. The evidence was just overwhelming against him. He should have pleaded, and he wouldn't. He made me go to trial.

The opposite of a loser case is not necessarily a winner. It is a fun case, which in turn must be distinguished from a boring case.

I don't like armed robberies because they are boring. There are only one or two issues—either the guy did it or he didn't—and that doesn't make for very interesting work.

The case I am trying with _____ right now is a murder that is really a lot of fun.

Listen to me! "A murder is a lot of fun." How can I say that? [Laugh] It's a murder of a baby, and here I am with my two little kids and you would think that I would feel terrible about that, wouldn't you?

But it's an interesting case because the facts are such that they [the state] don't really have much evidence in the case—a lot of other people could have done it. It's all circumstantial evidence. That's fun. It's something for me to get excited about and get into, whereas a lot of cases—there are just no issues and that makes them boring. (008)

I don't know if I have a favorite kind of case, there are some that are a lot more fun to do—if you just think of it in those terms. I may sound horrible, but, just because of the circumstances, usually murder cases are kind of fun.

Usually what kills you in a case is somebody is on the witness stand pointing a finger at your client, saying "that guy robbed me with his gun." Whereas in a murder case you don't have a victim.

Q: What you mean is that you don't have a victim who can come to testify in court, right?

R: Right, he's not there in court. And all the evidence—well, oftentimes you have a totally circumstantial case which gives you a lot to do.

And rape cases. I hate to say it, but there's a lot to play with in a rape case: identification, consent, much more so than in your average armed robbery. You never, for example, you never have the issue of consent in armed robbery. (009)

It is shocking to hear the lawyers talk about their favorite cases, and they are not unmindful of this. But the point is important: a favorite case is the opposite of a loser—a loser is not a loser just because it is a case that will be lost. A case is a loser when it leaves the lawyer nothing to do for the client.

The lawyers are possessed by the very human desire, as they put it, not to make "assholes" of themselves or be perceived as "jerks" in court.

The jury may not really throw rocks at them but, what is worse (or so the lawyers think), will think that they are naive or stupid for "falling for what the defendant told them."[7] A case is fun to the degree that it allows the lawyers to act in the way in which they think that lawyers ought to act; a case is interesting when it gives them an opportunity to "comport yourself in a professional manner, to be an advocate for your client without looking *ridiculous* in the process, when you can get across to the jury that there is, at least, a *respectable* difference of opinion here" (*014*).

Loser cases put the lawyer-as-a-professional at a terrible disadvantage:

I had one case where the, one of the defendants shot the leg off a ten-year-old girl with a shotgun. You know, that's kind of rough.

What are you supposed to say in defense of that? But because the state wasn't offering us anything decent in the plea bargain and we offered some pretrial motions that we could only preserve by going to trial, we had to go to trial.

The worst case is one where you just don't have anything. And you know you are just going to go out there and lose, and there is *nothing* you can do.

Like, they will have two counts and one will be for aggravated battery and one will be for robbery and [the state] will toss the agg. batt., drop it down to plain battery, if you plead. But if you don't, and if you go to trial, you get a finding of agg. batt.

Well, I had to go to trial on this case because the kid swears up and down that he didn't do it. But I haven't got *anything!* They've got two eyeball witnesses, and all I have is the kid saying, "But I didn't do it!" *And what am I going to do with that?*

And it's a sure loser, but I am going to trial because the kid won't admit.

The lawyers feel that, with a loser case, it is hard—if not impossible—to look respectable. With a loser case it is often difficult to look as if you are doing *anything*.

---

7. Despite the lawyers' insistence that they do not want to know, they are careful to learn enough so they will not look silly in court. That is one of the first lessons that public defenders learn. Ronald Himel, a former public defender, in 1971 assured a reporter from *Newsweek* that one just cannot afford to believe everything one hears: "My first case out of law school, the guy told me he walked around the corner and found the TV set. So I put that on [in court]. The judge pushed his glasses down his nose, hunched up and said, 'Fifty-two years I have been walking the streets and alleys of Chicago and I have never, ever found a TV set.' Then he got me in his chambers and said, 'Are you f- - - - - - crazy?' I said, 'That's what he told me.' The judge said, 'And you believed that s- - -? You're goofier than he is!'" (8 March 1971, 29).

Losing

In his look at the legal profession, sociologist Talcott Parsons (1954) commented that adherence to procedure (i.e., doing everything that can be done when it ought to be done and as it ought to be done) protects lawyers from being devastated when they lose: "The fact that the case can be tried by a standard procedure relieves [the attorney] of some pressure of commitment to the case of his client. He can feel that, if he does his best then having assured his client's case of a fair trial, he is relieved of the responsibility for an unfavorable verdict" (1954, 380).

One of the attorneys with whom I spoke seemed to confirm Parsons's hypothesis, at least with respect to loser cases: "There is a certain consolation of going to trial with a loser case. If I lose, what the hell. I gave it my best shot. If I lose, *it was a loser.* If I win, it's amazing."

Most of the attorneys, however, were not so sanguine and could not detach themselves from the outcomes of their cases so easily. Even losing a loser case, most of them said, is incredibly hard on the attorney.

It's hard, you know? You can tell someone the facts of the case, and they say, "What did you expect? It was a loser." But that doesn't make me feel any better when I lose a loser. I want to win.

Ah, idealistically I've talked about why I'm a public defender, about how I want to keep the state on the straight and narrow. And I *could* go home and say, "Well, I forced the state to prove their case beyond a reasonable doubt," but, ah, I still, that isn't what I *really* feel when I lose. What I *really* feel is just that I lost this case and I wanted to win this case. (*006*)

The attorneys are not much comforted by the fact that the client was guilty—or probably guilty, anyway.

Q: When you feel bad about losing a case, doesn't it help to know that the client was probably guilty anyway?
R: Yea [pause], maybe. But in the middle of the trial, it's you, you know? You are trying to make them believe what you are trying to sell them, and, if you don't win, it means that they don't believe *you.* That's probably one of the reasons that it doesn't help.
There was a case, not too long ago, that I really came to believe that they had no evidence on my man, and I fought very hard for him. We lost, and I felt very bad about that.

Afterward, he just fell apart, started screaming at me back in the lockup. We had this big fight. And I yelled at him: "You know, I really put myself on the line too, and I did everything I could for you, and what are you doing yelling at me? Cause I really believed, and I worked hard."

159

And then I misspoke myself, because I said, "And I really believed
that you didn't do this."

And he said, "Would it make you feel any better if I told you that I *did*
do it?" [Laugh].

Q: How did you answer him?

R: [Laugh] I said, "I don't want to know; don't tell me!" I still don't
want to know, and that's how it is. (*008*)

Most telling is how these lawyers talk about doing trial work. They
do not say, "I'm doing a trial now"; they do not ask, "Are you doing a
trial this week?" They say, "*I'm* on trial"; they ask, "Are *you* on trial?"

Lawyers hate to lose because, although reason tells them a case is a
loser, sentiment says that justice favors not the stronger case but the
better lawyer. What makes losing any case, even a loser, so bad is their
belief that, in the hands of a *good* attorney, there is really no such thing as
a dead-bang loser case. One attorney told me: "Fewer and fewer of my
cases are losers. . . . Because I am a better and better lawyer" (*008*).

Most of the attorneys seemed to feel the same way:

One of the maxims I've learned is that the evidence is always better than
the way it looks on paper. There is always some goof-up of a witness,
something that comes up in the trial, so that you always have something to
work with. Invariably that is so. (*014*)

By the time I walk into the courtroom, even if rationally I sat down when I
first heard the case and said "Well, there is no way I can win," by the time I
walk into the courtroom I will figure out some way to argue to the judge
or the jury that I think I can convince them. By that time, I believe I can
win the case. (*011*)

You start out thinking "I can't win this, no one can win this." Then you
start to get a glimmer, a way out of it being a loser case. Then you think
that, if only you can make the jury understand things the way you understand things, they will go along with you and give you a not guilty. Part of
you knows—or at least that is what you tell yourself later—part of you
knows you *can't* win, that you aren't going to win, but that gets lost in the
part of you that wants so much to win this case for your guy—and to win
this case for you.

Of course, you have to be good to take advantage of those goof-
ups, those things that invariably come your way in the trial. Because of
the suspicion that there is always something, when it cannot be found or
when it does not work, the lawyer is apt to feel at fault. Even when they

know that their client was factually guilty, public defenders are likely to feel, "I let my client down."

> The most stressful time is on a difficult case and you realize that, well, some *other* lawyer could win this, why the hell can't I? I will do everything I can, but there will still be something I miss. And yet, maybe nobody in the courtroom, not even my client, knows about it. But it can destroy our case. Then, when you lose, you feel the weight of your client's sentence on your shoulders. When my client gets sentenced, part of me is going with him. *(001)*

> You go home and you have those "ah, shit! God damn, why didn't I? If I only would have, if I only would have spent ten more minutes, if I only would have asked him this, if I would have gone out and asked, or done more investigations. . . . Your mistakes? Your mistakes go to jail. *(004)*

The stress of being on trial and the pain of losing are compounded on those rare occasions when the lawyer believes the defendant is innocent. For this reason, although the lawyers will say, "I don't care if he's guilty or innocent," their claim to neutrality is often a lie. When they say, "I don't care if my client is guilty," what they usually mean is, "I *prefer* my clients to be guilty."

> Most defense attorneys would rather not have a client they think is innocent, because it's just irrelevant. Because it's your job to fight the state's case no matter what. You *hate* to lose, and you are worried about losing just because it's your job to win. And if you think he's innocent, you worry more. And that is just aggravation, which is really irrelevant to your job. *(002)*

None of the current public defenders with whom I spoke said they preferred innocent clients, and all but two said they actually preferred representing defendants whom they believed were guilty.[8] Many of the

---

8. Consensus was not as high among former public defenders. When asked whether they agreed with the statement "Contrary to what you might expect, I preferred cases where I thought my client was guilty to cases where I believed my client was innocent," almost a third (32 percent) refused to answer, saying that it was irrelevant. Among those who did answer, about half (49 percent) agreed that they preferred guilty clients. When I compared the answers of those who had worked in felony courts with the answers of those who had not, there was a significant difference. Among those who only worked in misdemeanor, juvenile, or appeals divisions, only 21 percent agreed that they preferred guilty clients. Among those who had worked in a felony courtroom, 71 percent said that, as public defense lawyers, they preferred guilty clients.

attorneys did not want to talk about such cases, even hypothetically. Most of them just said something like, "In my own gut I know I have a harder time defending people I know are innocent than people I suspect are guilty—the pressure to win is so much greater then" (*012*), or "it is just harder to defend an innocent person because there is so much pressure" (*011*). Although no public defender said as much, given what they did say, I suspect that what makes defending an innocent client so stressful is the fact that if one should fail to win an acquittal, it would be difficult to avoid the conclusion that it was the lawyer's fault (although in theory, this may not be true). In such cases, the weight of the client's sentence really hangs on the defender. One lawyer told me how he protected himself from the possibility of that kind of "incredible stress." He explained that he "tried not to think about having innocent clients [pause], but it's academic since they are all guilty anyway" (*007*).

Coping with Losing

Losing is one of the costs of being an attorney; losing a lot (I was told) is one of the costs of being a public defender:

> You must try to convince the judge or the jury that what you are saying must be followed. But as a public defender, you get the realization that no matter how hard you do this, no matter how well you do this, you are probably not going to get it across. Or, even if you do, the judge or the jury is going to say no. You cannot be afraid to lose, because mostly it's a lost cause. You cannot have a personality where you must win or it's going to screw you. (*004*)

> Sometimes it's just that you get rotten case after rotten case. It drives you crazy. What it does is it makes you think you can't win. (*001*)

> When you lose a few in a row, you question yourself. And then it becomes real hard to go back into court and try again. (*006*)

Public defenders do not like to lose—but said that one must just learn to accept it. Nevertheless, watching them try their cases and listening to them talk about their cases made it clear to me that the attorneys do not just accept losing. In many instances, the attorneys seemed to try to outwit defeat.

However it looks to the spectator—or, for that matter, to the defendant—public defenders can show you how a trial is not a zero-sum situation. Even when the lawyer does not win freedom for his or her client, *something* may have been won: "I don't feel defeatist. There is a lot you can do, even if you lose—like mitigate a person's involvement or partly win by getting a guilty on one charge and not on another" (*003*).

Even when there is no way to mitigate the client's guilt or to partly win, there is such a thing as an almost win. Those count too—at least they are counted by the attorneys, especially if the case had seemed to be open and shut. There is a certain measure of satisfaction that can be drawn, for example, from keeping the jury out longer than could have been expected.

> It was a terrible case, a terrible case. It was a brutal, cold-blooded slaying of a ma-and-pa grocer. They had a witness, a flipper. The guy who drove the car flipped against them both. They found the guns in my guy's house; they had a dead-bang loser case against them.
>
> We tried to discredit the flipper and minimize the effect of the gun being found, saying that they couldn't absolutely prove that it was the same gun that had been used.
>
> We lost. We kept the jury out for about ten hours or so, and that was something. But we ended up losing.

> We did a jury trial a few weeks ago—the case was a rape, a 14-year-old. Both my partner and I felt he would be found guilty and that he probably did it. But we tried that case *so* hard, then we lost it.
>
> But we kept the jury out almost three hours. And we thought it was going to be like a 15-minute guilty verdict.

Moreover, the lawyers are helped some by their ability to distinguish a loss from a defeat. Even when they lose, public defenders search for evidence that they did a better job, that they "out-tried" the state's attorneys. Out-trying one's adversaries can mean anything from simply acting more professional to forcing your opponent to commit reversible error. Sometimes it just means making him or her look silly in court.

During long or tough cases the level of exchange between defense and prosecuting attorneys can destroy all ideals that one might have about noble adversaries. Attorneys (as they themselves admit) will sometimes bait each other, trying to force their opponents to do something regrettable. The following are snatches of dialogue from a death-penalty case. All these exchanges took place on the record (I have, however, changed the lawyers' names). Mr. Buford and Mr. Petrone speak for the prosecution; attorneys Carney, Stone, and Richert appeared for the defense:

[Time One]
Richert: [To the court] During Mr. Carney's remarks, Mr. Buford came

to me personally and pointed to Mr. Stone and said, "Do you realize
your partner looks like Lenin?" I would appreciate if the prosecutor
would avoid interfering with my participation in proceedings such as
these.

The Court: Which prosecutor? Who is he talking about? Who looks like
Lenin?

[Later that day]

Carney: [To Buford] Oh, put your foot down [off the table]. Act like an
attorney. What is wrong with you?

Buford: Come on.

Carney: Take your foot off the table!

Buford: You don't tell me what to do!

Carney: It insults me as an attorney.

Buford: I may do that, but you don't tell me what to do!

The Court: We will take a recess.

[Time Two]

Petrone: Let's go. We have been wasting seven months for it.

Stone: That's unprofessional.

Petrone: That's as unprofessional as you, Mr. Stone.

Stone: Wasn't it enough that we showed you how to pick a jury?

Petrone: You showed us how to pick a jury? You pleaded him right into
the electric chair!

[Time Three]

Buford [in chambers]: I am at this time requesting that we go out in the
court and requesting that—I just did—that we go on the record, because once again, I am not going to put up with any more of this state's
attorney baiting or this other *bullshit* that's gone on here in chambers.

Carney: *That's on the record!*

Buford: Right; exactly. That has gone on here for eight weeks. I request
that we go out in open court. Let the record reflect [pause]. [To judge]
Look at Mr. Carney!

Carney: And I am looking at Mr. Buford, Judge. And I have never heard
that word said in a court of law in eight years, Judge, by a state's attorney or any defense lawyer, and I am *really* shocked!

Buford: Look at these faces that they are making. I am asking that you
hold them in direct contempt!

The Court: All right, but I just wanted to know what witnesses are you
calling?

The defense lost the case. They had hoped to "win" by getting a
life sentence, but their client was sentenced to death. To any observer, it
was a total loss. After listening to testimony for several weeks, the jury
took less than an hour and only one vote to make the decision unanimous. Still, the attorneys (Mr. Carney, in particular) appeared to derive
a great deal of satisfaction from their belief that they had not been "de-
feated," that they had caused their opponents (Mr. Buford, in particular)

to "lose it" several times during the case. The night before the case ended, Mr. Carney recalled what for him had been a major highlight of the case. "Lisa, you know what Buford said to me that first day? He said, 'Carney, I heard you were a choker; I *collect* chokers, Carney.' When Buford said 'bullshit' in chambers, I leaned over and whispered to him: 'C-H-O-K-E.' " After the end of the last day in court, after hearing that their client would be sentenced to death, at a dinner that could more properly be called a wake, a deeply depressed Carney repeated several times: "We sure got that bastard Buford; we sure beat their asses, didn't we?" "Yes," he was assured again and again, "we *sure* did."

In retrospect the attorneys seemed a bit childish, their bickering like juvenile acting-out. Yet when one is trying to salvage something that is a lost cause, anyway, every little bit seems to help.

It should be noted too that the above exchanges are unusual, a result of the fact that, in the attorneys' minds, baiting the state's attorneys could not make things any worse for their client than it was inevitably going to be—and might, if they could push the prosecutor far enough, win him a mistrial. Normally (see chap. 5), the attorneys are mindful of the fact that acting out will probably hurt one's client. Even in this case, the lawyers (the defense lawyers, anyway) never got totally out of control. It should be noted that while all of these exchanges (and others like them) took place on the record, they took place out of the hearing of the jury.

But even if the public defenders do not usually feel free to really mix it up with the prosecutor in court, there is still an important kind of anticipatory satisfaction that emerges from knowing that oftentimes the "only reason the state wins is because the facts are on their side" (010). The satisfaction comes from knowing that *someday* most of those prosecutors are going to leave the state's attorney's office, and many of them are going to turn their hands to criminal defense work. That day, believe many public defenders, will be the day when these prosecutors will get what is coming to them. Public defenders sometimes sound almost smug when they talk about what is in store for prosecutors: "One of the ways I deal with [losing], with when I have to look over at the state's attorneys as they gleefully congratulate each other on their records of victory, when I know I have out-tried them on a case, well, you just say, 'chalk it up.' They are going to leave the office some day; they are going to find out that they are not such hot shit. That's a *big* satisfaction, a very big satisfaction" (012).

Perhaps the most important way in which they cope with losing is knowing that they do not always lose. When I asked one attorney "How do you keep going when you lose?" he said: "Always remembering that there is a flip side of that—you feel great when you win. There is no feeling like it. And *that* wouldn't feel as good if it weren't so hard to win" *(002)*. In fact, the lawyers seem to go into each trial with great expectations of winning. The knowledge that the next case may be the one you win seems to keep them going.

Coping with Winning

> I do not apologize for (or feel guilty about) helping to let a murderer go free—even though I realize that someday one of my clients may go out and kill again. Since nothing like that has ever happened, I cannot know for sure how I would react. I know that I would feel terrible for the victim. But I hope that I would not regret what I had done—any more than a surgeon should regret saving the life of a patient who recovers and later kills an innocent victim. (Dershowitz 1983, xiv)

Doctors lose patients; lawyers lose cases. Failure is something with which every professional must cope. But implicit in the question, How can you defend those people? is the idea that public defenders ought to have trouble coping with winning.

The possibility of getting a guilty person off is not a specter that haunts public defenders, at least not to the extent that you would notice it. In misdemeanor and juvenile courts, the majority of defendants represented by public defenders are relatively innocent and/or harmless criminals accused of relatively innocent or harmless crimes. The lawyers are protected by the fact that they rarely win cases for clients who are horrible criminals; winning an acquittal for a burglar or even an armed robber is, for a public defender, hardly cause for intense introspective examinations of one's morality or personal guilt. It is not that they have lost all sense of proportion but that they have gained a new one—by the time that they get to felony courtrooms, the lawyers are, most of them, con-

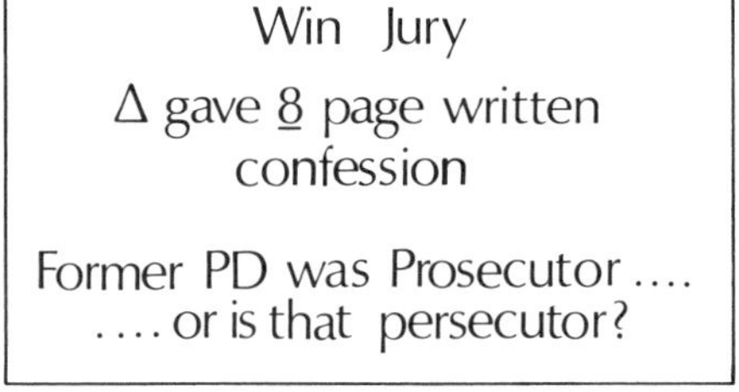

> O'Malley & Fletcher
> Win Jury
> Δ gave <u>8</u> page written
> confession
>
> Former PD was Prosecutor ....
> .... or is that persecutor?

FIGURE 12. Sign posted in public defender's office on November 30, 1982.

vinced that what they see happen to their clients in the jails or in the courts is as bad as or worse than most of what happens to victims out on the streets. There is, moreover, often a sense that the injustices perpetrated by the system are worse because they are committed by people who really ought to know better.

However rarely it occurs, the possibility of winning big someday and then having your client kill again exists in the future of every defense lawyer. It is not something that they seem to talk about very often. It is difficult to talk about it perhaps because there is so much emphasis on the importance of the defendant's right to a lawyer who will do everything possible to win a case. Moreover, in the tough, heroic world of the trial lawyer, it is perhaps difficult to conceive of feeling bad about winning.

A few years ago, an episode of the television show "Hill Street Blues" featured the story of a public defender who got a murderer freed on a "technicality." Some time later, the client murdered again. This time, the victim was a friend of the public defender, who, unable to deal with the guilt, quit the office.

At the time, many public defenders were avid fans of this television show, in large part (I thought) because the writers had created a very competent, tough, and sympathetic role for a public defender on the show. A few days after this particular episode aired, a group of lawyers in the office discussed the story-line and decided that it was unrealistic. I later asked one of them why. "Because the lawyer quit. That's just not the way it's done. You just move into the next case. As a lawyer you are very removed from the reality of it." Reflecting on his answer for a moment, I said, "I just can't believe that." "It's true," he assured me. I pushed him: "What would you do if it happened to you? What if you got a N.G. on a killer and he came around and killed again?" After a few moments he admitted that he "probably would move into another branch of law."

Most of the lawyers with whom I spoke said, as does Dershowitz, that it had not happened to them—and that while they hoped that it would not happen, they did not think that it would bother them. But one added: "As I say that, I am mindful of one public defender named _____ _____, I think one of the reasons he left was that he managed to get a guy acquitted on a murder and the guy went out and committed another murder. That really got to him. And I watched him suffer with that, and I wondered if I would suffer like that, and I came to no conclusion" (*014*).

A few of the lawyers admitted that they had come close to winning cases that, deep down inside themselves, they had not wanted to win: "I've never felt bad about winning a case. The last jury trial I did I almost won, and I *was* worried about that. It really bothered me. But all of it has

to do with the relationship you have with your client. He was a real
asshole and hard to deal with, and he was a mean son of a bitch" (*002*).

Often it seemed that one of the things that helps the lawyer not to
feel too bad about winning is one of the things that makes it so hard to
lose—that is, their relationship with the client. Most of the lawyers said
that usually, especially when they go to trial, they end up liking their
clients. In most cases, the lawyers spoke with some affection about their
"guys."

> There is in any human being a soul you can reach. [Pause] Now I use
> language like this hesitantly, you know, people usually look at you like
> you're crazy when you talk like this. But if you are willing to take the risk
> and open up your heart and reach into their hearts, you will reach it.
>
> You need to do that for yourself. You need to do that too because if
> you are going to try the case for either a judge or a jury . . . you have to
> make that person human. They are not some black or brown face—or
> white face, for that matter. They are someone. And that is what costs.
> 'Cause everytime you do that you are giving something of yourself away.
> You get something sure, but you give away a lot. (*003*)

> [At first] I was a little leery. You wonder, "Can I talk to a guy like this?"
> And you find out it's real easy [laugh], you find out that they are real
> people, just like you. Well [laugh], maybe not *just* like you, but real people.
> And you come to like most of your clients [laugh]. That surprised me, still
> does. (*009*)

> A lot of criminals I have gotten to like. There are some real nice human
> beings even if they are in real serious trouble. (*019*)

> [Recalling his first murder case] It was funny—I liked the shooter. He was
> a real nice guy. (*001*)

The danger, of course, is in getting too involved with your client,
getting to like him or her too much. That is when you lose your sense of
proportion. As one lawyer told me, you "must always remember that he
is a defendant, and you must treat him as a defendant."

Two of the lawyers with whom I spoke had experienced what one
called the "defense lawyer's nightmare." One would not talk about it;
one would:

> Once on a case with _____, he came up with a brilliant idea about collat-
> eral evidence, and I wrote a brilliant brief. It persuaded the judge to dismiss
> the indictment—just unheard of.
>
> And three months later he killed three other people. He participated in

a gang killing—didn't actually do the killing, but he was definitely part of it. That, of course, is the defense lawyer's nightmare.

There are people who can—for example, my partner—who can say, "that's not my concern," but that is bullshit. That is why he is losing his hair and I'm not. You feel bad. You *have* to feel bad.

However, the constitutional proposition was correct, and it made some important law in Illinois; and I would do it again. But I would not represent [that client] again. Because we could not wholeheartedly represent him zealously, we were let off representing him.

"How can you live with that?" I asked. "You either leave, stay and repress it, or you stay and cope. Sure you feel bad, but you deal with it by knowing that hopefully you are doing enough good to make you feel good about what you are doing."

At the time, that did not seem like much of an answer—but perhaps it is the only one.

Concluding Remarks: Public Defenders and Their Society

Justifying the public defender's rebellion against society is, in fact, a strict adherence to important social values. They believe that it is right to defend "those people" because of the principle that everyone is innocent until proved otherwise and so everyone is entitled to a defense. More important, they also believe that it is right to defend even the guilty because their clients *need* someone to defend them against police, prosecutorial, and judicial abuse. Because of what they see happen in the system every day, public defenders would be the last to claim that defense lawyers are unnecessary luxuries for defendants (guilty or innocent) in our criminal courts.

Beyond these rationales, public defenders are motivated by the desire to legitimize themselves as professionals, to act as professionals, and, as final proof of their right to professional status and respect, to win. Their desire to win makes them look very closely at each client's case: Where has the state failed to make its case? Did the state make an error? Did the police mess up the arrest? Public defenders want to find those cases, because those are the kinds of cases that make them look good. The closer they look, the more they find, and this, in turn, reinforces their view that their work is essential.

In an important sense, then, there is a synergistic relationship between the public defenders' egoistic and altruistic concerns, their desire to win, and their view that they are needed. It is that synergy that no doubt accounts for the combative tone of most of their remarks. In theory this could spiral into a process that is out of all proportion to reality. In truth, the lawyers—especially when they are on trial—do seem to get carried away with what they do. But what prevents them from losing all touch with reality is, I think, the fact that they are not totally enclosed in the cognitive ghetto of public defending. Each is still a member of a society that suspects the morality of what they do; this attachment to society is shown in a process that some public defenders call "honking." By honking each other, public defenders remind one another how the rest of their society regards their work:

> There is a term that I didn't know until I came to this office, a thing called honking. And that is needling or giving someone a hard time, ostensibly in a friendly manner—but it can be very pointed, very barbed. It goes on a great deal. People will get honked for their pretentiousness, for their actual performance on trial.
>
> And people will get honked *mercilessly* for things over which they have *absolutely no control*—the quality of the client, the heinousness of the act with which the person is charged. And people get honked for trying to defend people who really have hopeless legal positions. (*014*)

Conclusion: The Perils
of Obscurity

A popular distrust of governmental authority is one of this country's most enduring characteristics, and, in a sense, the public defender is simply a contemporary expression, the same "Crown-defying nonsense" that was early on codified in the Bill of Rights to the Constitution. Ironically, the poor reputation of the public defender's office—its lack of legitimacy as a professional organization—is in great part a product of this same tradition of distrust. Underlying most popular and many scholarly assessments of public defending is a very simple logic: public defenders cannot act as "real" defense attorneys because they owe their jobs to a system that will not allow them to really defend their clients. In light of the failure of many empirical studies to find evidence that clients of public defenders fare any worse than defendants who are represented by private counsel, stubborn adherence to this logic is testimony to the continuing strength of our distrust of the state.

My research sought a new logic, and in this work a model has been presented that, I suggest, better fits empirical findings about the quality of the public defender's work and helps also to explain the persistence of the more subjective accounts of how public defenders cannot defend

171

their clients. The public defender's office was created and is maintained, I have argued, because it is a critical asset in the court's negotiations of legitimacy with the broader society. Whatever public defenders contribute to the economy and orderliness of the criminal justice system must be seen as secondary to their value to the courts as the courts try to maintain the impression that the rights of individuals charged with crimes are being protected. It is from this aspect of the public defender's role, I argued, that lawyers who do public defense work find an unexpected source of power as they interact with the judges who are their nominal employers. This power of the public defender is analogous to that of the private attorney. The Supreme Court has ruled, for example, that

> the primary office performed by appointed counsel parallels the office of privately retained counsel. Although it is true that appointed counsel serves pursuant to statutory authorization and in furtherance of the federal interest in insuring effective representation of criminal defendants, his duty is not to the public at large, except in that general way. His principal responsibility is to serve the undivided interests of his client. Indeed, an indispensable element of the effective performance of his responsibilities is the ability to act independently of the Government and to oppose it in adversary litigation. (*Ferri v Ackerman*, 444 U.S. 193 [1979]; see also, *Polk County v Dotson*, 454 U.S. 312 [1981])

In many respects, the relationship of a public defender and a judge is like that of an auditor and a corporate executive officer. Although the CEO employs the auditor, that does not mean that the auditor who produces a negative report can simply be dismissed. When judges try to discipline public defenders who won't "go along," they become vulnerable to suits from outsiders (such as those experienced by Boyle, as described in chapter 5), or to humiliating orders from higher courts to follow the law properly (as mentioned in chapter 6).

The lack of structure and policy of the public defender's office also contributes to the lawyers' autonomy. That no one tells a public defender "what to do" means that the lawyers have only very loose ties to supervisors who might, for various reasons, wish to curtail their zealousness.

On the other hand, though the lawyers' autonomy vis-à-vis judges and supervisors helps to ensure that the mission of the public defender is not subverted by systematic institutional corruption, it does nothing to guarantee that individual public defenders will take proper advantage of their freedom to defend their clients properly. I have suggested that the success of the public defender's office—and its value as a resource to the court's negotiations of legitimacy—ultimately depends on the individual lawyer's desire to do a good job. The individual lawyers that I studied seemed to be strongly motivated to do their best—if not only because of their concern for their clients, then because of their desire to prove themselves competent lawyers, to prove the validity of their claims to "real" professionalism. Here too the lack of office structure and policy has a positive function: beginning lawyers are attracted by the freedom that they find in the public defender's office, the freedom to act as they believe that "real lawyers" act. Ironically, it may be also true that the very presence of the stigma of ineptitude acts as a motivating force, inasmuch as many lawyers seemed to be fighting hard in an attempt to beat that stigma.

The Importance of Legitimacy

Early social thinkers saw organizations as closed systems. Although the source of organizational structures and their methods of operating were understood primarily in terms of prevailing social values at the time that the organization was founded (see, e.g., Weber 1946, 204–209), once established, most believed that organizations calcified, became "hostile" and "remote" from life (Simmel 1976, 223), and embodied "insuperable obstacles" to change (Spencer 1971, 191). Today most sociologists see organizations as open systems and believe that much is to be learned from examining the ongoing negotiations that are carried out between organizations and their environments (March and Olsen 1979, 18; Pfeffer and Salancik 1978; Selznick 1952; Thompson 1967). This change in perspective has led many to an acceptance of Parsons's (1956) hypothesis that one of the more important things at stake in organization-society negotiations is "organizational legitimacy."

Just as legitimacy justifies the leader's command of compliant obedience in a power relationship, legitimacy justifies the organization's right to exist in the eyes of its peer and superordinate system—or its right to "continue to import, transform and export energy, material or information" (Maurer 1971, 361). Organizational legitimacy is a social—not an objective—thing; its nature is evaluative and subjective. Simply put, legitimacy reflects a social assessment of both what an organization accomplishes and how it accomplishes whatever it does: legitimacy is an evaluation of both an organization's means and ends (Perrow 1970).

The extreme point of view has it that legitimacy is, for the organization, a survival prerequisite: "The rule is: those who wield power must establish the right to do so. This is not a pious wish, or a peculiarly democratic canon, but a general political necessity. Every ruling group that presumes to gather prerogatives for itself, or to inflict deprivations on others, must identify itself with a principle acceptable to the community as justifications for the exercise of power. Such doctrinal tenets are known as principles of legitimacy" (Selznick 1952, 242).

The present view of legitimacy, on the other hand, is tempered by the difficulty of denying that illegitimate institutions survive and even thrive in society. Yet these "bastard institutions," as Hughes (1971) calls them, only survive at great cost and remain vulnerable in ways that legitimate institutions do not. Indeed, the processes that illegitimate institutions initiate (e.g., laundering funds, building legitimate fronts, etc.) (Gage 1972) suggest that legitimacy and the protection that it affords is sought by even the most profitable or successful illegitimate organizations.

The public defender's office seems to be a special case, for it neither has nor seeks social legitimacy as a legal institution. The reason for this, as I have argued, is that the public defender's situation is complicated by the contradictions inherent in its role: in order to carry out its role as court legitimizer, the office must provide competent representation for its clients. At the same time, because it is the defense attorney's job to pinpoint the mistakes of others (police, prosecutors, and even judges), competent defense attorneys pose a threat to the legitimacy of any criminal justice system that is less than infallible. In view of the complexity of its institutional role, the public defender's office's survival seems to hinge on its ability to remain obscure. It does its work—but does not trumpet its successes.

Each individual public defense lawyer's desire to achieve recognition as a real professional makes him or her an unwitting accomplice in the public defender's search for obscurity. The lawyers' conception of their role as lawyers is very much that of lone professionals: Public defenders do not act or speak collectively, for to do so would undermine their claims to being professionals. The lawyers' lack of collective presence probably contributes much to the public defender's office's ability to remain in the shadows; but it contributes as well to the lawyers' own lack of legitimacy, to their status as bastard lawyers.

But as much as it tries to hide and as much as its incumbents try to ignore the fact, the public defender's office is an organization. And however much obscurity protects it, the office's lack of legitimacy makes it potentially vulnerable. For example, should there be a shift toward social concern for the rights of poor people charged with crimes, because of its lack of legitimacy the office may become a scapegoat. To some extent, this is what occurred during the late 1960s and early 1970s when so many social scientists discovered the public defender and helped to cement the stigma of ineptitude. But the survival of the public defender is perhaps more threatened by its lack of policy and structure—or what might be called its *internal* obscurity.

Although most studies of organizational legitimacy have tended to follow Parsons's (1956) lead in treating legitimacy as a product of interactions between the highest or "institutional" levels of organizations and their external constituencies (see, e.g., Thompson 1967, 10–12), a broader view of legitimacy, one that includes the individuals who work within the organization, may be appropriate. Parsons himself was alert to the organization's need to justify itself in the eyes of its incumbents, for individuals who work within an organization are also members of the organization's superordinate system. This fact constrains the organization's behavior: "The essential point is that the conduct of affairs of an organization must in general conform with the norms of 'good conduct' as recognized and institutionalized in society. The most general principle is that no one may legitimately contract to violate these norms, nor may authority be used to coerce people into their violation" (1956, 65).

Membership in the superordinate system provides resources for the worker that may go unnoticed or be taken for granted. But when evaluating the quality of the relationship that exists between an employer and an employee, the benefits that accrue to a worker by virtue of his or her membership in the wider society ought not to be regarded as insignificant. Although the nature of such benefits may vary across time and societies, an approximation of their value can perhaps be had by comparison of the condition of the illegal alien worker with that of the legal worker. Organizations that fail to take into account the implications of workers' membership in the superordinate system and (as many sociologists apparently do) consider legitimacy only as something that is negotiated between their institutional level and their external constituencies may be unpleasantly surprised by the results. Organizations that seek legitimacy, for example, by hiding their illegitimate aspects remain vulnerable to social, legal, or economic sanctions brought down on the organization by whistle-blowing insiders (see, e.g., Ewing 1983).

As noted in chapters 6 and 7, many of the assistant public defenders enjoy the freedom provided them by the public defender's office's lack of official policy and loose supervision. Many share, however, a general sense of unease about the lack of structure. To some extent, the attorneys themselves have compensated by building up special units. Still, many public defense lawyers wonder, Is this any way to run an organization?

Sociologists Meyer and Rowan, among others, have noted that organizations increasingly have had to adopt "environmentally legitimated elements of structure" in order to protect against threats. For example, "The rise of professionalized economics makes it useful for organizations to incorporate groups of economists and econometric analyses. Though no one may read, understand, or believe them, econometric analyses help legitimate the organization's plans in the eyes of investors, customers (as with Defense Department contractors), and internal participants. Such analyses can also provide rational accountings after failures occur: managers whose plans have failed can demonstrate to investors, stockholders, and superiors that procedures were prudent and that decisions were made by rational means" (1981, 540).

Meyer and Rowan argue that without these elements of structure, "organizations are more vulnerable to claims that they are negligent, irrational, or unnecessary. Claims of this kind, whether made by internal participants, external constituents, or the government, can cause organizations to incur real costs" (*ibid.*).

Recent events involving the public defender's office support Meyer and Rowan's contention. In late 1983, a group of six assistant public defenders filed a class action suit in federal court. The lawyers charged in their suit that they had been "improperly denied equal treatment in promotions, salary, and job assignments based on race or national origin by the Cook County Public Defender's Office." At the same time, these lawyers filed a complaint with the Illinois Department of Human Rights, making similar charges against the public defender, the chief judge, and members of the county board of commissioners. Particulars included allegations that "minority assistant Public Defenders are started at lower pay than others; are not given their choice of assignments as are whites who have less seniority; are dissuaded from employment by the Office; are passed over for supervisory positions in the Office; are not employed at percentages commensurate with available minority lawyers or County population" (*132*).

As I have noted, none of the assistant public defenders with whom I spoke had any idea how decisions about hiring, transfers, promotions, and salary increases are made. As far as I could determine, there are no policies—racially biased or otherwise—governing these matters. What the public defender may find out, however, is that having no policies is as bad as having bad policies, for society expects organizations to have policies. The public defender has no easy defense against charges that its activities are biased against minorities, because it has no official policies to which it may refer in order to refute these charges.

Potentially more damaging, however, is another legal action, a suit instituted by a former client of the public defender's office, who charges that she had been incompetently represented by a lawyer from the juvenile division. In 1977, this young woman took the advice of her public defender and pleaded guilty to a charge of assault. She maintains that she was told that if she so pleaded, she would be given probation. Instead, she was sentenced to the Department of Corrections by the judge. Her mother called another lawyer who, after much effort, succeeded in getting her case heard by the Federal Court of Appeals. They agreed that her case had been poorly handled and granted her relief. In their written opinion the judges roundly criticized the public defender who had defended her, saying that he was incompetent and unconcerned. According to my informants in the public defender's office, the suit alleges negligence on the part of both the assistant public defender who handled the case and the office in which he worked. As one supervisor in the office reported, the suit has "turned into a wholesale investigation of the office . . . they are examining all of our procedures, especially our training and supervisory policies." Because of the public defender's lack of written policies, this action may well be difficult to defend against, for again the public defender has no policies to which it may refer in order to show that, in defending this young woman, it followed prudent procedures and made rational decisions. In fact, I have heard that one of the attorneys who is defending the public defender in this case has been stymied by the lack of office procedure; one public defender related to me the lawyer's frustration on finding that certain types of records did not exist: "He said, 'Well, where are the memos? What do you *mean* you don't write memos on your cases? How can you not write memos?'"

Whatever the outcome of these suits, they constitute a threat to the public defender's office's obscurity—and hence to its survival. In recognition of this, some changes are being made in the office. For example, several lawyers have reported that "training procedures are being beefed up in the office." This sort of remedial action may not be enough. Because of its importance to the court's image of legitimacy, other organizations are getting involved. Recently the Cook County Judicial Advisory Council began an investigation into the public defender's office. The executive director of the council is most concerned, he said, about the lack of training and supervision that occurs in the office and intimated that because of the attention that is being focused on the public defender—and especially because of the possibility that more attention will come to be focused on the office—some form of damage control for the courts is in the offing. One very well-placed source suggested to me, for example, that "we may be talking about a new public defender." Whether or not such dramatic damage control proves necessary most likely depends on how far out of the shadows these suits force the public defender's office to come.

As noted in chapter 6, most of the lawyers with whom I spoke agreed that some changes need to be made in the public defender's office. Decisions about what sorts of changes are appropriate will be tough to make. There is no gainsaying the fact that the freedom that seems to protect the lawyers from an institutional undermining of the defense of their clients is no protection against an individual lawyer who refuses to do—or cannot do—his or her job properly. Stated more simply, the freedom that gives the lawyers an opportunity to do their best also provides the lawyers with the opportunity to do their worst. Hence, it would seem that additional structure might well be in order. Certainly one can suggest that beefing up training and other sorts of resources for these lawyers might be done without any great injury to the lawyers' ability to maintain their presumption of competency. At the same time, whether or not the imposition of additional structure would not simply make the office vulnerable to more insidious sorts of corruption is something that will need to be carefully considered.

Postscript

On December 11, 1986, James J. Doherty stepped down from his position as head of the Cook County Public Defender's Office. The *Chicago Tribune's* account of this noted that, "Doherty's ouster comes as a special commission is preparing to issue a final report on its study of the office" (13 December 1986).

Two months later, the Special Commission on the Administration of Justice in Cook County, which had been established by Chief Judge Harry G. Comerford of the Circuit Court, issued its report. According to the *Chicago Lawyer Magazine,* the commission's key recommendation was that the public defender's office "be given more independence from the Circuit Court." The commission also recommended that "the salaries for PDs be substantially increased to bring them more in line with those in comparable areas." Finally, the commission reported that "the old Democratic Machine patronage system was waning in the PD's office but that it was being replaced with a more ad hoc kind of patronage involving relatives and friends of judges." The commission recommended, then, that "a clear policy for hiring, firing, and promotions be established."

Having noted the problems uncovered by the commission's investigation as well as the two recent lawsuits against the office, the *Chicago Lawyer Magazine* commented: "Under the circumstances, perhaps it is lucky that the problems are not worse. Despite the personnel practices, most knowledgeable observers, including members of the special commission and the defense bar, say the vast majority of assistants in the office are dedicated lawyers who do the best that could reasonably be expected" (*Chicago Lawyer Magazine,* March 1987).

___ Cases Cited _____

Ake v. Oklahoma—U.S.—105 S. Ct. 1087, 84 L. Ed. 2d 53 (1985)

Argersinger v. Hamilin 407 U.S. 25 (1972).

Betts v. Brady 316 U.S. 455 (1942).

Brown v. Board of Education of Topeka 349 U.S. 294 (1955).

Chicago Milwaukee & St. Paul Railroad Company v. Minnesota 134 U.S. 418 (1890).

Coffin v. United States 156 U.S. 432 (1895).

Coleman v. Alabama 399 U.S. 1 (1970).

Davis v. United States 160 U.S. 469 (1895).

Douglas v. California 372 U.S. 353 (1963).

Escobedo v. Illinois 378 U.S. 478 (1964).

Ferri v. Ackerman 444 U.S. 193 (1979).

Gardner v. Florida 430 U.S. 349 (1977).

Gault, In re 387 U.S. 1 (1967).

Gideon v. Wainwright 372 U.S. 335 (1963).

Johnson v. Zerbst 304 U.S. 458 (1938).

Joint Anti-Fascist Refugee Committee v. McGrath 341 U.S. 123 (1951).

Lisenba v. California 314 U.S. 219 (1941).

Mapp v. Ohio 367 U.S. 643 (1961).

Miranda v. Arizona 384 U.S. 436 (1966).

Palko v. Connecticut 302 U.S. 319 (1937).
Polk County v. Dotson 454 U.S. 312 (1981).
Powell v. Alabama 287 U.S. 45 (1932).
Quicksal v. Michigan 339 U.S. 660 (1950).
Rochin v. California 342 U.S. 165 (1952).
United States v. Wade 388 U.S. 218 (1967).
Weeks v. United States 232 U.S. 383 (1914).
Winship, In re 397 U.S. 358 (1970).
Witherspoon v. Illinois 391 U.S. 510 (1968).
Wolf v. Colorado 338 U.S. 25 (1949).

__ Bibliography

Albert-Goldberg, N., and M. J. Hartman. 1983. Indigent defense systems: Characteristics, alternatives, and relative benefits. In *The Defense Counsel,* edited by W. F. McDonald, 67–102. Beverly Hills, California: Sage.

Alschuler, A. W. 1972. Courtroom misconduct by prosecutors and trial judges. *Texas Law Review* 50:629.

———. 1975. The defense attorney's role in plea bargaining. *Yale Law Journal* 84:1179–1313.

Arado, C. C. 1935. The public defender. *Chicago Bar Association Record* 16:173–174.

Arnold, T. 1937. *Folklore of capitalism.* New Haven, Connecticut: Yale University Press.

Arthur Young & Company. 1975. *Seattle-King County Public Defender Association Evaluation Project: Final report.* Sacramento, California: Author.

Bachrach, B. C. 1930. The public defender. *Chicago Bar Association Record* 14:10–11.

Baker, N. F. 1934. The public defender's work in Cook County. *Journal of Criminal Law and Criminology* 25:5–9.

Barber, B. 1983. *The logic and limits of trust.* New Brunswick, New Jersey: Rutgers University Press.

Battle, J. D. 1971. In search of the adversary system—the cooperative practices of private criminal defense attorneys. *University of Texas Law Review* 50:60.

————. 1973. Comparison of public defenders' and private attorneys' relationships with the prosecution in the city of Denver. *Denver Law Journal* 50:101–136.

Beany, W. M. 1955. *Right to counsel.* Westport, Connecticut: Greenwood.

Bear, J. 1939. Legal aid service to injured workmen. *The Annals of the American Academy of Political and Social Science* 205:50–56.

Beck, J. M. 1930. *May it please the court.* New York: Macmillan.

Becker, H. S. 1977. *Sociological work.* Chicago: Aldine.

Berger, P. L., and T. Luckmann. 1967. *The social construction of reality.* New York: Anchor.

Bierstedt, R. 1976. An analysis of social power. In *Sociological theory: A book of readings,* edited by L. A. Coser and Bernard Rosenberg, 136–147. New York: Macmillan.

Blau, P. M. 1964. *Exchange and power in social life.* New York: Wiley.

Bloom, M. T. 1950. Justice on the cuff. *Colliers,* November 18, 26–27.

Blumberg, A. S. 1967. The practice of law as a confidence game: Organizational cooptation of a profession. *Law and Society Review* 1:15–39.

————. 1979. *Criminal justice: Issues and ironies.* New York: New Viewpoints.

Bosk, C. L. 1979. *Forgive and remember: Managing medical failure.* Chicago: University of Chicago Press.

Brown, E. L. 1938. *Lawyers and the promotion of justice.* New York: Russell Sage Foundation.

————. 1939. Legal aid and the promotion of justice. *The Annals of the American Academy of Political and Social Science* 205:1–8.

Bruce, A. A. (1929) 1979. Introduction to the survey of organized crime. In *Organized crime in Chicago: part III of the Illinois crime survey,* edited by J. Landesco, 1–7. Chicago: University of Chicago Press.

Bucher, R., and A. Strauss. 1961. Professions in process. *American Journal of Sociology* 66:325–334.

Burgess, E. W. (1929) 1979. Summary and recommendations. In *Organized crime in Chicago, part III of the Illinois crime survey,* edited by J. Landesco, 277–286. Chicago: University of Chicago Press.

Callahan, R. E. 1964. *Education and the cult of efficiency: A study of the social forces that have shaped the administration of the public schools.* Chicago: University of Chicago Press.

Casper, J. D. 1978. *Criminal courts: The defendant's perspective.* Englewood Cliffs, New Jersey: Prentice-Hall.

Chandler, H. P. 1933. What the bar does today. *American Law School Review* 7:26–29.

Chapin, B. 1983. *Criminal justice in colonial America, 1606–1660.* Athens, Georgia: University of Georgia Press.

Chicago Bar Association (CBA). 1924. Comment. *Chicago Bar Association Record* 7:3.

_____. 1926. Committee on defense of indigent prisoners. *Chicago Bar Association Record* 13:96–99.

Cleaver, E. 1968. Interview. *Playboy Magazine,* December, 89–108, 238.

Cohen, M. 1982. Her caseload is murder. *American Lawyer,* November, 87–88.

Collins, R. 1975. *Conflict sociology: Toward an explanatory science.* New York: Academic Press.

_____. 1979. *The credential society: An historical sociology of education and stratification.* New York: Academic Press.

Cook County Court Watching Project, Inc. 1984. *Citizens look at their courts.* Chicago: Cook County Court Watching Project, Inc.

Dahl, R. 1961. *Who governs?* New Haven, Connecticut: Yale University Press.

_____. 1964. *Modern political analysis.* Englewood Cliffs, New Jersey: Prentice-Hall.

Dahlin, D. C. 1974. Toward a theory of the public defender's place in the legal system. *South Dakota Law Review* 19:87–120.

Dershowitz, A. M. 1983. *The best defense.* New York: Vintage.

Dimock, E. J. 1956. The public defender: A step towards a police state? *American Bar Association Journal* 42:219–221.

Doherty, J. J. 1966. Bullpen ethics of a plea of guilty. *National Legal Aid and Defender Association Briefcase* 24:123–132.

_____. 1971. Out on the street. *National Legal Aid and Defender Association Briefcase* 29:90–94.

Dorsen, N., and L. Friedman. 1973. *Disorder in the court.* New York: Pantheon.

Downie, L., Jr. 1971. *Justice denied: The case for reform of the court.* New York: Penguin.

Durkheim, E. 1974. *Sociology and philosophy.* New York: Free Press.

Dworkin, R. 1977. *Taking rights seriously.* Cambridge, Massachusetts: Harvard University Press.

Eisenstein, J., and H. Jacob. 1977. *Felony justice: An organizational analysis of criminal courts.* Boston: Little, Brown.

Ewing, D. W. 1983. *"Do it my way or you're fired": Employee rights and the changing role of management.* New York: Wiley.

Feeley, M. M. 1979. *The process is the punishment: Handling cases in a lower criminal court.* New York: Russell Sage Foundation.

Ferreira, A. J. 1968. Family myth and homeostasis. In *The Family,* edited by N. W. Bell and C. F. Vogel, 541–550. New York: Free Press.

Finnegan, P. J. 1936. The public defender of Cook County. *Journal of Criminal Law and Criminology* 26:709–718.

Fishkin, J. S. 1982. *The limits of obligation.* New Haven, Connecticut: Yale University Press.

Freedman, M. H. 1975. *Lawyers' ethics in an adversary system.* Indianapolis: Bobbs-Merrill.

Friedman, L. M. 1973. *A history of American law.* New York: Simon & Schuster.

_____. 1975. *The legal system: A social science perspective.* New York: Russell Sage Foundation.

Friedson, E. 1975. *Doctoring together: A study of professional social control.* Chicago: University of Chicago Press.

_____. 1986. *Professional powers.* Chicago: University of Chicago Press.

Friedson, E., and B. Rhea. 1972. Processes of control in a company of equals. In *Medical men and their work,* edited by E. Friedson and J. Lorber, 185–199. Chicago: Aldine-Atherton.

Fuchs-Epstein, C. 1983. *Women in law.* New York: Anchor-Doubleday.

Gage, N. 1972. *Mafia, USA.* Chicago: Playboy.

Galanter, M. 1974. Why the haves come out ahead: Speculations on the limits of legal change. *Law and Society Review* 9:95–106.

_____. 1975. Afterword: Explaining litigation. *Law and Society Review* 9:347–368.

Galloway, P. 1977. A winner for losers. *Midwest Magazine,* 5 June, 8.

Gariepy, M. R. 1939. Legal aid as part of a community program. *The Annals of the American Academy of Political and Social Science* 205:72–78.

Goldman, M. C. 1917. *The public defender: A necessary factor in the administration of justice.* New York: G. P. Putnam's Sons.

_____. 1939. Public defenders in criminal cases. *The Annals of the American Academy of Political and Social Science* 205:16–23.

Goldman, R., and D. Holt. 1971. How justice works: The People v. Donald Payne. *Newsweek,* 8 March, 20–37.

Goss, M. E. W. (1959) 1980. *Physicians in bureaucracy: A case study of professional pressures on organizational roles.* New York: Arno.

Gouldner, A. W. 1954. *Patterns of industrial bureaucracy.* Glencoe, Illinois: Free Press of Glencoe.

Greene, B. 1982. Lawyer closes the book on criminal defense. *Chicago Tribune,* 3 November, sec. 4.

Haber, S. 1964. *Efficiency and uplift.* Chicago: University of Chicago Press.

Haller, M. H. 1970. Urban crime and criminal justice: The Chicago case. *Journal of American History* 57:619–635.

_____. 1979. Introduction. In *Organized crime in Chicago, part III of the Illinois crime survey,* edited by J. Landesco, vii–xviii. Chicago: University of Chicago Press.

Handler, J. D. 1939. Social agencies and legal aid theory. *The Annals of the American Academy of Political and Social Science* 205:219–233.

Harrington, C. J., and G. W. Getty. 1956. The public defender: A progressive step toward justice. *American Bar Association Journal* 42:1139–1142.

Hazard, G. 1978. *Ethics in the practice of law.* New Haven, Connecticut: Yale University Press.

Heinz, J. P., and E. O. Laumann. 1982. *Chicago lawyers: The social structure of the bar.* New York: Russell Sage Foundation, American Bar Foundation.

Herman, R., E. Singel, and J. Boston. 1977. *Counsel for the poor.* Lexington, Massachusetts: Lexington.

Heumann, M. 1978. *Plea bargaining.* Chicago: University of Chicago Press.

Heydebrand, W. V., and J. J. Noell. 1973. Task structure and innovation in professional organizations. In *Comparative organizations,* edited by W. V. Heydebrand, 294–322. Englewood Cliffs, New Jersey: Prentice-Hall.

Hobbes, T. (1651) 1962. *Leviathan.* New York: Collier.

Homans, G. C. 1950. *The human group.* New York: Harcourt, Brace & World.

Hughes, C. E. 1971. *The sociological eye.* Chicago: Aldine.

Hunter, J. D. 1939. Social agencies and legal aid theory. *The Annals of the American Academy of Political and Social Science* 205:129–133.

Jackson, B. 1983. *Law and disorder: Criminal justice in America.* Urbana: University of Illinois Press.

Jacob, H. 1980. *Crime and justice in urban America.* Englewood Cliffs, New Jersey: Prentice-Hall.

————. 1983. Presidential address: Trial courts in the United States: The travails of exploration. *Law and Society Review* 17:407–424.

Janowitz, M. 1978. *The last half century.* Chicago: University of Chicago Press.

Jones, E. E., and Nisbett, R. E. 1971. The actor and the observer. In *Attribution,* edited by E. E. Jones, D. E. Kanouse, H. H. Kelley, R. E. Nisbett, S. Valins, and B. Weiner. Morristown, New Jersey: General Learning Press.

Kahn, M. H., and D. D. Kahn. 1977. Specialization in criminal law. *Law and Contemporary Problems* 41:252–292.

Kalvin, H., and Zeisel, H. 1966. *The American jury.* Boston: Little, Brown and Co.

Kantor, R. M. 1972. *Commitment and community.* Cambridge, Massachusetts: Harvard University Press.

Kamisar, Y. 1965. When the cops were not handcuffed. *New York Times Magazine,* 7 November, 34–35, 102–110.

Katz, J. 1982. *Poor peoples' lawyers in transition.* New Brunswick, New Jersey: Rutger's University Press.

Kelley, H. H., and J. W. Thibaut. 1978. *Interpersonal relations.* New York: Wiley.

Kelly, T. J. 1968. *Public defender manual and trial procedure.* Chicago: Cook County Public Defender's Office.

Kets de Vries, M. F. R., and D. Miller. 1984. *The neurotic organization.* San Francisco: Jossey-Bass.

Kobler, J. 1971. *Capone: The life and world of Al Capone.* Greenwich, Connecticut: Fawcett.

Kogan, H. 1974. *The first century: The Chicago Bar Association, 1874–1974.* Chicago: Rand McNally.

Kornhauser, W. 1962. *Scientists in industry: Conflict and accommodation.* Berkeley: University of California Press.

Kunen, J. S. 1983. *How can you defend those people?* New York: Random House.

Kurland, P. B. 1970. *Politics, the Constitution, and the Warren Court.* Chicago: University of Chicago Press.

Landesco, J. (1929) 1979. *Organized crime in Chicago, part III of the Illinois crime survey.* Chicago: University of Chicago Press.

Larson, M. S. 1977. *The rise of professionalism: A sociological analysis.* Berkeley: University of California Press.

Lepawsky, A. 1932. *The judicial system of metropolitan Chicago.* Chicago: University of Chicago Press.

Leuchtenberg, W. E. 1958. *The perils of prosperity, 1914–42.* Chicago: University of Chicago Press.

Levin, M. A. 1977. *Urban politics and the criminal courts.* Chicago: University of Chicago Press.

Lewis, A. 1964. *Gideon's trumpet.* New York: Vintage.

Lipset, S. 1963. *Political Man.* Garden City, New York: Doubleday.

Literary Digest. 1935. Public defenders, 27 July, 29.

Lubove, R. 1965. *Professional altruist: The emergence of social work as a profession.* Cambridge, Massachusetts: Harvard University Press.

Lydon, S. T. 1973. The public defender as an adversary: The Alameda County public defender revisted. In *Alameda County Public Defender, Forty-sixth Annual Report.* Oakland, California: Alameda County Public Defender.

Mann, K. 1985. *Defending white-collar crime: A portrait of attorneys at work.* New Haven, Connecticut: Yale University Press.

March, J. G., and J. P. Olsen. 1979. *Ambiguity and choice in organizations.* Bergen: Universitetsforlaget.

March, J. G., and H. A. Simon. 1958. *Organizations.* New York: John Wiley & Sons.

Marke, J. J. 1977. *Vignettes of legal history, 2nd series.* Hackensack, New Jersey: Fred B. Rothman.

Marquis, A. N. 1936. *Who's who in Chicago.* Chicago: A. N. Marquis Publishing Co.

Maurer, J. G., ed. 1971. *Readings in organization theory: Open systems approaches.* New York: Random House.

Maynard, D. 1984. *Inside plea bargaining: The language of negotiation.* New York: Plenum.

Meyer, J. W., and B. Rowan. 1981. Institutionalized organizations: Formal structure as myth and ceremony. In *The sociology of organizations,* edited by O. Grunsky, and G. A. Miller, 530–554. New York: Free Press.

Meyers, L. 1977. Dial them for murder. *Chicago Reader,* 1 July, 19–21.

Miller, G. A. 1967. Professionals in bureaucracy: Alienation among industrial scientists and engineers. *American Sociological Review* 32:755–767.

Mishkin, C. 1933. The public defender. *Chicago Bar Association Record* 14:98–111.

Moore, L. E. 1973. *The jury—tool of kings, palladium of liberty.* Cincinnati: Anderson.

Morgan, R. E. 1984. *Disabling America: The "rights industry" in our time.* New York: Basic Books.

Nardulli, R. F. 1978. *The courtroom elite: An organizational perspective on criminal justice.* Cambridge, Massachusetts: Ballinger.

National Advisory Commission on Criminal Justice Standards and Goals. 1974. *Report.* Washington, D.C.: Government Printing Office.

Neely, R. 1981. *How courts govern America.* New Haven, Connecticut: Yale University Press.

Nelson, W. E. 1975. *The Americanization of the common law: The impact of legal change on Massachusetts society, 1760–1830.* Cambridge, Massachusetts: Harvard University Press.

Ness, E., with O. Fraley. 1969. *The untouchables.* New York: Award.

Neubauer, D. W. 1974. *Criminal justice in middle America.* Morristown, New Jersey: General Learning Press.

Norris, C., and S. Washington. 1979. *The last of the Scottsboro boys: An autobiography.* New York: G. P. Putnam's Sons.

Oaks, D. H., and W. Lehman. 1968. *A criminal justice system and the indigent: A study of Chicago and Cook County.* Chicago: University of Chicago Press.

O'Connor, L. 1975. *Clout: Mayor Daley and his city.* New York: Avon.

Packer, H. L. 1964. Two models of the criminal process. *University of Pennsylvania Law Review* 113:1–68.

Parker, B. D. 1982. The Hinckley trial: Another point of view. *The University of Chicago Law School Record* 28:2–6.

Parsons, T. 1947. Introduction. In *Max Weber, the theory of social and economic organizations,* edited by T. Parsons, 1–86. New York: Oxford University Press.

———. 1954. A sociologist looks at the legal profession. In *Essays in sociological theory,* 370–385. New York: Free Press.

———. 1956. Suggestions for a sociological approach to the theory of organizations. *Administrative Science Quarterly* 1:63–85.

Perrow, C. 1970. *Organizational analysis.* Belmont, California: Brooks/Cole.

———. 1979. *Complex organizations: A critical essay.* Glenview, Illinois: Scott, Foresman.

Perry, M. J. 1982. *The Constitution, the courts and human rights.* New Haven, Connecticut: Yale University Press.

Pfeffer, J., and G. R. Salancik. 1978. *The external control of organizations: A resource dependence perspective.* New York: Harper & Row.

Platt, A. M. 1969. *The child savers.* Chicago: University of Chicago Press.

Platt, A. M., and R. Pollock. 1974. Channeling lawyers: The careers of public defenders. *Issues in Criminology* 9:1–31.

Posner, R. A. 1981. *The economics of justice.* Cambridge, Massachusetts: Harvard University Press.

Pound, R. (1930) 1975. *Criminal justice in America.* New York: Da Capo.

Rakove, M. 1975. *Don't make no waves. . . . Don't back no losers: An insider's analysis of the Daley machine.* Bloomington: Indiana University Press.

Reitz, L. 1960. Federal habeas corpus postconviction remedy for state prisoners. *University of Pennsylvania Law Review* 108:461–480.

Rembar, C. 1980. *The law of the land.* New York: Simon & Schuster.

Reuschemeyer, D. 1973. *Lawyers and their society.* Cambridge, Massachusetts: Harvard University Press.

Robin, G. D. 1984. *Introduction to the criminal justice system.* New York: Harper & Row.

Rogge, O. J. 1959. *Why men confess.* New York: Da Capo.

Royko, M. 1971. *Boss: Richard J. Daley of Chicago.* New York: Dutton.

Schaefer, M. V. 1956. Federalism and state criminal procedure. *Harvard Law Review* 70:1–26.

Schorer, M. 1959. The necessity of myth. In *Myth and mythmaking,* edited by H. A. Murray, 354–357. Boston: Beacon.

Scott, J. C. 1972. *Comparative political corruption*. Englewood Cliffs, New Jersey: Prentice-Hall.

Scott, R. 1965. Reactions to supervision in a heteronomous professional organization. *Administrative Science Quarterly* 10:65–81.

Selznick, R. 1952. *The organizational weapon*. New York: McGraw-Hill.

Silberman, C. E. 1978. *Criminal violence, criminal justice*. New York: Random House.

Silverstein, L. 1965. *Defense of the poor in criminal cases in American state trial courts*. Chicago: American Bar Association.

Simmel, G. 1976. The conflict of modern culture. In *Georg Simmel: Sociologist and European*, edited by P. Lawrence, 223–242. New York: Harper & Row.

Singer, S., and E. Lynch. 1983. Indigent defense systems: Characteristics and costs. In *The defense counsel*, edited by W. F. McDonald, 103–125.

Skolnick, J. 1967: Social control in the adversary system. *Journal of Conflict Resolution* 11:52–72.

Smith, G. 1915. Making the law work both ways. *The Independent*, 18 October, 94–95.

Smith, H. L. 1958. Contingencies of professional differentiation. *American Journal of Sociology* 63:410–414.

Spear, A. H. 1967. *Black Chicago: The making of a ghetto, 1890–1920*. Chicago: University of Chicago Press.

Speek, P. A. 1916. The need for a socialized jurisprudence. *American Journal of Sociology* 22:503–518.

Spencer, H. 1971. *Principles of sociology*. Hamden, Connecticut: Archon.

Spencer, J. 1984. No glamour, no money: Public defenders still seek justice for all. *Chicago Tribune*, 8 January, sec. 2.

Stewart, J. B. 1982a. Third and fourth year associates rate their firms, part one. *American Lawyer*, March, 37–46.

————. 1982b. Third and fourth year associates rate their firms, part three. *American Lawyer*, May, 38–45.

Stewart, J. D. 1983. *The partners: Inside America's most powerful law firms*. New York: Simon & Schuster.

Stewart, W. S. 1936. A criticism of the public defender system. *John Marshall Law Quarterly* 3:245–291.

Stinchcombe, A. L. 1968. *Constructing social theories*. New York: Harcourt.

Sudnow, D. 1965. Normal crimes: Sociological features of the penal code in the public defender's office. *Social Problems* 12:255–277.

Thibaut, J. W., and H. H. Kelley. 1959. *The social psychology of groups*. New York: Wiley.

Thibaut, J. W., and L. Walker. 1975. *Procedural justice: A psychological analysis*. Hillsdale, New Jersey: Lawrence Erlbaum.

Thompson, J. D. 1967. *Organizations in action*. New York: McGraw-Hill.

Turner, R. H., and L. M. Killian. 1972. *Collective behavior*. Englewood Cliffs, New Jersey: Prentice-Hall.

Turner, V. 1969. *The ritual process: Structure and anti-structure*. Chicago: Aldine.

U.S. Department of Justice, Bureau of Justice Statistics. 1984. *A national survey of criminal defense systems*. Washington, D.C.: Government Printing Office.

Utz, P. J. 1978. *Settling the facts: Discretion and negotiation in criminal court*. Lexington, Massachusetts: Lexington.

Walker, S. 1980. *Popular justice: A history of American criminal justice*. New York: Oxford University Press.

Warren, R. K., ed. 1969. Criminal justice *in extremis:* Administration of justice during the 1968 Chicago disorder. *The University of Chicago Law Review* 36:455–613.

Weber, M. 1946. Bureaucracy. In *From Max Weber, essays in sociology*. edited by H. H. Gerth, and C. W. Mills, 196–244. New York: Oxford University Press.

_____. 1978. *Economy and society*. Berkeley: University of California Press.

Weibe, R. 1967. *The search for order*. New York: Hill & Wang.

Weick, K. 1979. *The social psychology of organizing*. Reading, Massachusetts: Addison-Wesley.

Weinberg, A., ed. 1957. *Attorney for the damned*. New York: Touchstone/Simon & Schuster.

Wheeler, G. R., and C. L. Wheeler. 1980. Reflections on legal representation of the economically disadvantaged: Beyond assembly line justice. *Crime and Delinquency* 26:319–332.

Wice, P. B. 1983. Private criminal defense: Reassessing an endangered species. In *The defense counsel,* edited by W. F. McDonald, 39–64. Beverly Hills, California: Sage.

Wigmore, J. H. 1931. The public defender in our large cities. *Illinois Law Review* 25:687–689.

Wishman, S. 1981. *Confessions of a criminal lawyer*. New York: Penguin.

Wood, A. L. 1967. *Criminal lawyer*. New Haven, Connecticut: College & University Press.

Zemans, F. K., and V. C. Rosenblum. 1981. *The making of a public profession*. Chicago: American Bar Foundation.

Author Index

191

Subject Index